International Socialism 115

Summer 2007

Contributors

Chris Bambery is the editor of *Socialist Worker*

Ian Birchall is author of *Sartre Against Stalinism*

Robin Blackburn is author of *The Overthrow of Colonial Slavery 1776-1848* and is a member of *New Left Review*'s editorial committee

Antoine Boulangé is an activist in the Ligue Communiste Révolutionnaire

Alex Callinicos is author of *An Anti-capitalist Manifesto* and *The Resources of Critique*

Katherine Connelly is a student at Queen Mary, University of London

Iain Ferguson is a member of Solidarity and the SWP in Scotland

Mike Gonzalez is author of *Che Guevara and the Cuban Revolution*

Andy Jones is a member of the SWP in south London

Nikos Loudos is a postgraduate student at Panteion University in Athens and writes for the Greek weekly paper *Workers' Solidarity*

Naz Massoumi is a leading member of Campaign Iran

John Molyneux is author of *Marxism and the Party* and *Rembrandt and Revolution*

Kim Moody is author of *US Labor in Trouble and Transition: The Failure of Reform from Above, the Promise of Revival from Below*

John Newsinger is author of *The Blood Never Dried: A People's History of the British Empire*

Chris Nineham is on the steering committee of Stop the War Coalition and has been active in the international anti-capitalist movement since 2001

Paul O'Brien is author of *Shelley and Revolutionary Ireland*

Ken Olende is a journalist on *Socialist Worker*

Matt Perry is a history lecturer at Newcastle University and author of *Marxism and History*, *Jarrow Crusade* and *Prisoners of Want*

Aditya Sarkar is a research student from Delhi, currently studying at Soas

Viren Swarmi is a psychologist at the University of Liverpool and author of *The Missing Arms of Vénus de Milo*

Jim Wolfreys is co-author of *The Politics of Racism in France*

Britain after Blair

Is Gordon Brown going to run into an unexpected obstacle in his first weeks in office—a sudden revival of class struggle after the low ebb since the firefighters' strike of four years ago? It seems very possible as we go to press.

Certainly anyone who imagines that disillusion with New Labour is leading to a massive swing to the right should carefully examine the results of May's elections for the Scottish Parliament, the Welsh Assembly and most local authorities outside London. Labour's share of the vote was only 27 percent across Britain, and in Wales it was lowest in any election since 1918. As in 1931, the late 1960s and the late 1970s, the experience of Labour in office has led to mass disillusion. But there is one great change from these previous periods. Disillusionment has not automatically benefited the Tory right. In Scotland and Wales the nationalists gained seats. What enabled them to do so was not their nationalism but their identification with what the Scottish National Party leader Alex Salmond calls a "social democratic" agenda, some way to the left of New Labour—complete with outright opposition to the Iraq War.

It is true that in southern England the Tories gained at the expense of Labour (and the Liberal Democrats). But their leader David Cameron feels he can only get votes by ditching much of the old Tory agenda of tax cuts for the rich, promotion of private health care, near-overt racism and even support for grammar schools. There is, of course, no real conversion involved here (every so often the Tories let slip their ruling class instincts), but there is recognition that there is no electoral advantage to be gained from a rabid neoliberal message. After all, the sections of the petty bourgeoisie (in its old and new versions) who have traditionally formed the mass base of the party are as dependent on the NHS and state schools as are the mass of manual workers. Even more so are those sections of white collar workers (teachers, nurses) who traditionally voted Tory but voted Labour for the first time ten years ago. The popular 1990s backlash against unadulterated Thatcherism is still having its impact on Thatcher's own party.

Gordon Brown takes over against a background of massive disillusion with New Labour among people who once enthused over Tony Blair. Yet, as John Newsinger shows in his article later in this journal, he was even more important in laying down New Labour's agenda than was Blair.

This does not rule out the possibility of him enjoying some sort of honeymoon of increased electroral popularity. In 1990-2 John Major was able to restore the Tories' fortunes sufficiently from their low point at Thatcher's overthrow to win the 1992 election—although to do so he had to ditch the poll tax, while Brown shows no signs of immediately ditching Blair's equivalent unpopular policy, the war. The word "Iraq" may not be inscribed on Brown's heart as it is on Blair's, but he has financed the bombing and the killing, and we should not let anyone forget it.

He also faces problems on the home front in a way that New Labour has usually been able to avoid over the past decade. Despite all his boasts about his performance as Chancellor, luck rather than judgement explains the relative stability of the economy over recent years, as we show in our briefing piece on Brown's economic record. Now, as the Bank of England suddenly fears inflation and raises interest rates, Brown's response is to announce a wage limit for the public sector of 2 percent—at a time when the retail price index is around 4.5 percent and average household income already declining slightly. This amounts to an attempt by the government to cut the living standards of millions of employed workers—something threatened in the Thatcher-Major years but never actually implemented.

The main public sector union leaders fear getting caught in a vice. Most have in the past tried to distance themselves from the unpopularity of Brown by claiming he would be different to Blair when it comes to listening to their members' complaints. But now it is Brown is who is leading the attack on wages. There are loud protests even from those who will do their utmost to stop the protests turning into action.

There has already been action by the civil servants' PCS union, whose leader Mark Serwotka is one of the few to have faith in neither Blair nor Brown. The PCS has held two national one-day strikes and is now calling on other unions to unite to form a joint challenge to government policy. The postal workers' CWU has overwhelmingly voted for industrial action. Meanwhile, some other union leaders, like those of the teachers' NUT and the public sector workers' Unison, are talking about united action even if they are doing little to prepare for it as yet. The non-TUC affiliated Royal College of Nurses and the Royal College of Midwives are considering action for the first time in their histories.

The test for the left over the summer will hinge upon the ability of its activists to intervene in this situation. There needs to be a response that combines politics and traditional forms of trade union action. Most public sector workers lack the confidence to go beyond one-day strikes or selective action if it is a question of fighting alone. Such stoppages can be inspiring the first time they occur, but the failure to hurt the employer often leads to cynicism when they are repeated as the only tactic without escalation. Typically they are solid but uninspiring, with little sense of them leading anywhere. This is where fighting for unity across the public sector in political opposition to the government's schemes becomes important. Unity in action between different sections can provide a cutting edge to the strikes and create the sort of forward momentum that can win.

Finally, on the political front the efforts of the left inside the Labour Party and the unions to "reclaim Labour" have come to a dead end. The left in the Labour Party was not able even to test its strength in the leadership election—blocked by the refusal of sufficient MPs to support a candidate to oppose Brown. In the deputy leadership election, some of the five pro-occupation, pro-Brown candidates have made nice noises. But they could hardly do otherwise, given the general anti-Blair mood and their need to pick up union votes which might otherwise go to Jon Cruddas. He is the only candidate sufficiently "left of centre" to call for the withdrawal of troops from Iraq (Harriet Harman's admission that she was mistaken in voting for the war is combined with continued insistence that the troops must stay).

Yet the May elections showed there are substantial numbers of people ready to vote for candidates to the left of labour. Here the three successes of Respect, in councils seats in Preston, Bolsover and Birmingham, are significant. Not because they put Respect in anything like same league yet as the major parties, or even the nationalists in Scotland and Wales, but because they show that where the effort is put in it is possible to win people to a serious left alternative. And those who claimed Respect's previous successes in Newham and Tower Hamlets were simply the result of a "Muslim vote" (as if the major parties did not also angle for Muslim votes in such areas) should understand that in Preston and especially in the former mining area of Bolsover its victories depended on workers who are not Muslim turning out in considerable numbers to back it.

The importance of Respect's successes is that many people with inclinations to the left are still voting Liberal or Labour for fear of casting a vote that is "wasted" in a "first past the post" election. Respect is beginning, however modestly, to show that it is possible to break with Labour and win.

Next year sees one of the few elections in England to contain an element of proportional representation—the London mayoral and assembly elections. Respect has an above evens chance of making a big impact and winning seats. Those who have so far put their faith in reclaiming Labour should now consider the alternative. And established activists in industry should see that posing a political alternative to New Labour—especially in relation to the wars in Iraq and Afghanistan—is the easiest way to attract younger people not worn down by the long years of often demoralising defensive struggles.

The French Thatcher?

"Sarkozy, Brown, Merkel. Neoliberalism has its people in power in the main European countries and is free to proceed full speed ahead as it wishes." That, in effect, is what the optimistic capitalist commentators are saying, and this view finds its mirror image among pessimists on the left. Sarkozy, they say, is now fully equipped to replicated what Margaret Thatcher did in Britain—to launch a full blooded assault on the last bastions of resistance to the neoliberal agenda. And all sorts of "theories" about what has happened to the working class and the wider movements are being formulated to explain in advance why he will succeed.

But things are not so simple. What Sarkozy wants to do and what he succeeds in doing are two different things. France has seen recurrent upsurges of resistance over the past 12 years. The most recent, just 14 months ago, left Sarkozy himself floundering. And, as Antoine Boulangé and Jim Wolfreys explain later in this journal, there is every possibility of that happening again.

Four or five people in a hundred changing how they mark their ballot papers does not in itself transform society overnight. At most it alters the level of confidence among those who will fight the issues out on other terrains.

The Thatcher example, which is repeated over and over again, forgets some basic facts about her government. She did not simply wave a wand and see resistance disappear. She did win in the end—but only at the cost of seeing a miners' strike, which she provoked in the expectation it would last just a few weeks, drag on for 12 months, at considerable cost to British capitalism (sterling fell to its lowest value ever—of one dollar to the pound). She herself was in despair on more than one occasion, and through much of the strike a majority of her cabinet would have settled on terms favourable to the miners if she had given them the chance. Her eventual victory resulted from a mixture of luck (a relatively mild winter which left coal stocks at the power stations intact), of important union leaders fearing a miners' victory as much as a victory by the Tories (as coal boss McGregor explained in his memoirs), and of the weakness of the left forces trying to build real, active solidarity with the strikers.

It was, as one her naval commanders said of her Falkland-Malvinas War, "a close run thing". And the wounds the government suffered in that struggle opened up schisms that led to her eventual fall as some of her closest allies turned against her—first Michael Heseltine, then Geoffrey Howe and finally Nigel Lawson.

If Sarkozy really wants to emulate Thatcher he will have to take the same risks she took—and with no certainty of success. The outcome will depend, in part, on how the French left, and those who influence their mood outside France, react. There is a great deal of despondency over the election result. The danger is that, as often happened in the Thatcher years in Britain, it will become a self-fulfilling prophesy. Bar room talk of "semi-fascism" and academic discourses about "authoritarian populism" encouraged sections of the left to abandon the field of battle, with even as eminent a historian as Eric Hobsbawm telling us there was no possibility of defeating the poll tax by mass struggle.

The situation in France today is not comparable to that in Britain in 1984, when the record was already one of seven or eight years of defeats. Not all of France's movements of the past dozen years have been successful. But there have been notable victories, and the forces that fought back are still intact. The point is to see the attack which is going to come and to prepare to fight it.

It is worth recalling that just four years ago the axis which was meant to push through a frontal attack on any resistance across Europe was that of Blair, Berlusconi and Aznar. Now all three have gone, unable to make the major breakthrough about which they were so confident. It is also worth recalling the expectation just two years ago that Merkel was the answer to European capitalism's prayers. She is still with us, but no longer the toast of the neoliberal hardliners, as she runs a weak government faced with wage claims from workers wanting to take advantage of a limited economic upturn to restore their earnings.

To rephrase an old saying—don't moan, organise.

Greece: waves from the student struggle

Nikos Loudos

The right wing government in Greece is likely to call an early general election this autumn following a year of resistance by workers and students. A wave of student struggle began in May 2006 and continued through to April 2007, forming the focus for a wider workers' movement which has blunted the government's neoliberal offensive.

Costas Karamanlis's New Democracy government was elected in May 2004 and represented the great hope of Greek capitalists eager to axe workers' rights, especially in the state sector; privatise sections of the economy; cut health and education expenditure; and, in particular, attack pension rights. Governments formed by the social democratic Pasok party from 1996 to 2004 had opened way for these attacks, with party leader Costas Simitis managing to draw Pasok's cadres and leading trade unionists behind a Blairite agenda of "modernisation".

Two general strikes in 2001 derailed Pasok's attacks, and New Democracy came to power promoting a "centre-right" profile. It even claimed to be on the left of Pasok over certain policies, distancing itself from the most hated government of recent decades—the Thatcherite Mitsotakis government, which collapsed after a wave of strikes in 1993. Nevertheless it set out to complete the assault begun by Pasok. One of New Democracy's greatest assets was the new Pasok leader, George Papandreou, who was committed to neoliberalism but also able to win the support of previously marginalised cadres of "old Pasok". Papandreou echoed the new government's rhetoric regarding the need to put aside old divisions of left and right, and replace "politics" with "management". He also defended closer US-Greek relations, clearing the way for Karamanlis's Bush-friendly foreign policy.

For the first two years after its election the New Democracy government kept the pace of change slow. Eventually it chose education as the key battleground, betting on the dominance of the right wing DAP student front, and the weakness and divisions in the student movement. Education minister Marietta Giannakou presented a bill that aimed to privatise large sections of higher education.

The resistance to this bill was unprecedented. The universities staff union Posdep was the first to take action against it in March 2006, and at this point a small number of student unions went into occupation in solidarity. This proved the leaven for a wider movement. By May over 60,000 students were involved in gatherings to debate and decide on action. Mass demonstrations were held in Athens every fortnight. On 25 May, after one of the national demonstrations in Athens, a university hall was packed by students who formed a national body to coordinate the occupations. They agreed to go for non-stop occupations in all universities and colleges. At another hall nearby Posdep decided on an all-out strike beginning on 1 June and called for greater coordination with the students.

The student movement was led by the far left and the anti-capitalist movement—reformist groups such as the Communist youth organisation were opposed to the occupations. The movement also had to overcome a tradition within the student left of treating teachers as "class enemies".

These, and many other obstacles, were swept aside by the May-June 2006 movement. After many years students, seen in Greece as examples of a growing "social conservatism", were fighting, and the growing demonstrations were becoming a focus for every worker opposed to neoliberalism. The unions called a successful one-day general strike in solidarity with the students. Bank employees, hospital workers, doctors and others mingled with demonstrating students. There was a large contingent of primary school teachers, who had just voted to stage a five-day strike when the schools returned from the summer break, with an aggressive demand for 1,400 euros a month as an entry salary. The motion passed at their conference cited the students' struggle as an example to be followed.

Mainstream newspapers noted that the government was haunted by the "ghost of France"—a reference to the victory of the French students' movement against the CPE labour law attacking young workers. Fearing that the student struggle could fuel a far wider workers' revolt, the government pulled back and promised further discussion on the bill.

The primary school teachers' strike had an even more unexpected climax. It began on 18 September, and even the most militant participants were sure that the strike, led by what many considered the most passive education union, would last just five days. In fact it lasted six weeks. The first week's strike was 90 percent solid, and strike committees were formed in order to organise the strike from below. They began winning support from neighbourhoods and from secondary education teachers. Weekly demonstrations in Athens and around Greece drew together thousands of teachers and their supporters, especially students and civil servants who also staged three 24-hour strikes.

By mid-October another movement emerged, this time among secondary schools students. Students at over 1,000 secondary schools occupied. They were fighting against a law by the same education minister, Giannakou, which sought to limit the number of students gaining entry to college.

The political turmoil brought about an unexpected result. Article 16 of the Greek constitution specifies that universities must be owned and financed by the state, not by private individuals. An amendment to this article was due to be voted on in October 2006. Pasok's leadership had promised to join New Democracy in voting in favour of an amendment to allow university privatisation. Pasok's votes were crucial because constitutional amendments require support from 180 out of the 300 MPs. In the face of the revolt by students and teachers, Pasok leader Papandreou brokered a deal to postpone the vote until January 2007. The result of this move was to allow the struggle to continue for several months.

The impact of the primary school teachers' strike was immense, but the outcome was not a happy one. The government offered a bonus of just 105 euros a month. This reflected weaknesses in the movement. First, the secondary teachers' union never wholeheartedly joined the strike by primary teachers, merely staging two 48-hour strikes as a show of "symbolic support". The Greek equivalent of the TUC called only a single four-hour strike.

Second, the university students staged only a handful of occupations in support of the teachers, mainly in universities with active groups of Greek Socialist Workers Party members. The common sense, even among many radical left students, was that the students should rest after the May-June 2006 struggle and prepare for the time when Giannakou's bill would come back.

Third, inside the primary school teachers' movement the strike committees never managed to coordinate on a sufficient level to take the initiative in leading the dispute. This left the strikers helpless when they were faced with two major political challenges. There was a coordinated right wing attack on the school occupations, with charges of criminality, rape and drug abuse directed against school students. The occupations started to retreat, with the Communist Party, which has the largest organised base among the school students, calling for an end to the movement. Then there were municipal elections on 15 and 22 October 2006. The absence of left alternative slates of candidates able to express the ongoing struggle made it easy for New Democracy to claim victory, despite a strong showing by the radical left. The strike leadership, which was tied to Pasok, used the election results to argue that there was no political mood for a continuation of the strike.

After the teachers' strike was called off the momentum shifted back into the universities in the run-up to the crucial vote on the constitutional amendment. Some universities occupied before Christmas and, in the couple of weeks that followed, over 300 universities and colleges followed suit. Posdep, the universities staff union, resumed its all-out strike.

The government sought to apply a "strategy of tension". Riot police began attacking demonstrations, with the ministers using the anarchists' actions to blackmail students, saying they were "either with us or with the 'black block' terrorists". But by this time the pressure on the Communist youth movement to join the struggle was overwhelming, and now it, Pasok and the radical left voted together in the universities. On 2 February Papandreou announced in parliament that Pasok was withdrawing its support for the constitutional amendment. This was a triumph for the movement, a second victory, bigger than that of June 2006.

An internal current in Pasok played a role in this U-turn. This was the first occasion on which an organised force inside Pasok challenged a right wing policy of the leadership by getting involved in the movement. For the first time since the years following the fall of the Greek junta in the 1970s, militants of the left, students, trade unionists and members of Pasok came together in neighbourhood and workplace committees—numbering about 1,000 across Greece—to organise a common battle. The divisions and confusion on the left have not been overcome, but the committees began to give a sense of the dynamics of common struggle.

What really ended slavery?

Robin Blackburn, author of The Overthrow of Colonial Slavery 1776-1848, spoke to International Socialism on the bicentenary of the abolition of the transatlantic slave trade

What was your reaction to the official commemoration of the banning of the slave trade, and what do you think was left out of this?

When looking at the coverage of this commemoration, on the BBC and elsewhere, I was instantly reminded of the comment by Eric Williams, the great Trinidadian historian and nationalist leader, in an essay on the British historians and abolition. He said how incredible it was that they conveyed the view that Britain had only constructed the largest and most profitable slave system in the Americas in order to have the satisfaction of suppressing it.

One notes, for example, the coverage by Melvyn Bragg, ennobled by Tony Blair as a sort of outrider of New Labour. He has a programme, *In Our Time*, on Radio 4. It can be quite good because you have a number of people in the studio who are scholars who've really studied the topic. For some reason the question of abolition and Wilberforce is a sort of sacred heart of British nationalist mythology and it couldn't be subjected to this normal critical process. Instead of having a normal studio discussion with people who really knew about the subject, Lord Bragg ventured out and interviewed the great and the good. There was, I think, one interview with a West Indian historian, but Bragg didn't go to the West Indies or Africa. His star contributors were William Hague, the former leader of the Conservative

Party, and John Prescott, the then deputy prime minister. Neither man was at all knowledgeable, but both were anxious to contribute to the national mythology in which Britain is portrayed as the abolitionist par excellence.

Wilberforce did not in fact lead emancipation, although he played a role in the campaign to end the Atlantic slave trade, which was successful in 1807. However, there is a continuing confusion here: slavery went on for more than 30 years. What the coverage failed to convey was the full shape and scale of the forces that did contribute to the suppression of the slave trade. There was no discussion of the Haitian Revolution, no discussion of the various black abolitionists. So my first feeling is that it was a very shallow commemoration, one that did not want to engage with the fact that anti-slavery developed as a significant force, had the guidance of some black abolitionists and African former slaves, and represented an upwelling of class consciousness.

What were the key forces involved in this process?

This was the first big issue that mobilised hundreds of thousands of people. In a city such as Manchester, a newly industrialised urban centre, you found almost every adult person subscribed to the petition to abolish the slave trade. This was a broad and important movement.

Of course, it must also be put in its wider Atlantic context. That is the context of the American Revolution that first created a deep sense of unease, the demand that democratic reforms were needed in the 1780s. The Americans were fighting for English liberties against the Hanoverian oligarchy. In response, a wing of the oligarchy began to feel that it had to reform—reform the way the empire worked in India and suppress the Atlantic slave trade, which it saw as weakening the empire rather than strengthening it.

As well as this current within the ruling class, the Quakers played an important role, and later the Baptists and the Methodists—the Methodist leader John Wesley wrote on slavery in 1774, criticising the institution and calling on slave owners to give up their slaves. These represented religious currents that developed in the wake of the industrialisation of society, during which many people were uprooted and sought to re-establish their identity and sought self-help in difficult circumstances. There was definitely a rivalry between the evangelical Baptists and Methodists on the one hand and those who were inspired by radical democratic ideas on the other. The outstanding figure among the latter was Tom Paine, who published an attack on the slave trade in the early 1770s, and who inspired the emancipation law in Pennsylvania in 1780 and the 1777 Vermont constitution, when Vermont broke away from the colonial assembly in New York. The latter was the first occasion on which slavery was outlawed in a territory.

Both the radical democrats and the evangelicals found that this was a cause they had to support. Sometimes they were reluctant, but there was a hatred of the oligarchy and its privileges, and of what William Cobbett later called "old corruption" and the denial of political rights to those who were not members of the Church of England. For example, you couldn't be an MP unless you were willing to swear a Church of England oath. So quite wide layers were drawn into political life at a time of imperial crisis. The middle classes and the rising bourgeoisie, the manufacturers and merchants in the industrialising regions, were beginning to demand a voice, and this offered openings to radical artisans and workers in the new factories. The great agitation around slavery was one of the first times there was a broad, popular canvassing of an issue. Women were widely involved in this agitation. It should be said that large numbers of women at this time were domestic servants—there were millions in the houses of the upper and middle classes—who faced abuse. The anti-slavery issue had great appeal for these layers, and they were also quite likely to have been drawn into the new evangelical religious movements.

The whole issue was made more dramatic still with the outbreak of the French Revolution, which initially encouraged the anti-slavery movement. Thomas Clarkson, who played a big role in organising the anti-slavery movement in the country as a whole, went over to France and supported the revolution. This greatly worried Wilberforce, who tried to caution him. However, after about 1792 and certainly by 1793, when Britain and France were at war, things changed. There was a general anti-Jacobin panic and radicals were greatly persecuted, even people such as Joseph Priestley were threatened, and many had to go into exile in the United States. The whole first phase of the anti-slavery movement was really brought to a close by the 1790s and it looked as if the great campaign had been completely blocked.

But then, once again, you have to put this into the context of Atlantic history, not just the history of individual nations beloved of nationalist mythology. In August 1791 a slave rebellion broke out in Saint Domingue, a French colony in the Caribbean and the richest slave colony in the Americas. Initially this involved 30,000 to 40,000 slaves, mainly in the northern plain, and as it spread it fused together with Jacobin demands. "Black Jacobins" emerge along with independent rebel groups in the hills. War was, by this time, raging between Britain and France. The British tried to seize French islands and tried to occupy Saint Domingue, but the slave rebels fought back. Eventually the French republic won over Toussaint L'Ouverture, one of the black generals, and he became lieutenant governor and then governor of French revolutionary Saint Domingue. He inflicted a historic defeat on the British who were forced to withdraw in 1798.

Unfortunately, by this time, things were not going so well in France itself. This period saw the emergence of restorationist currents and the rise of Napoleon Bonaparte, who was eventually persuaded, partly by the British and American governments and partly by French colonialists, to take the disastrous step of trying to restore slavery. This led to further military struggle between the black rebels in Saint Domingue and Napoleon, who sent a huge army under his brother in law General Leclerc. Leclerc died and the French expedition was defeated, and in 1804 the republic of Haiti was declared.

I don't think there is any doubt that this was a huge event for the whole Atlantic world. It was not just an event in French history, but also in British and American history, and it gave a shot in the arm to the whole idea that the slave trade should be suppressed—not necessarily purely on idealistic grounds, but also on prudential grounds. One pamphlet by Lord Brougham in 1804 said it was crazy to import new African captives into such an unstable situation as the Caribbean. This was throwing fuel on the flames, he said, and it would be better to stop the Atlantic slave trade. This pamphlet was distributed to all MPs. By 1806-7 there was some recovery of the petitioning campaign, and in the election the abolitionists called for people to support only candidates committed to ending the Atlantic slave trade.

The slave trade was abolished in a context in which Britain was locked in battle against Napoleon, and Napoleon had defeated most of Britain's allies on the continent. It was an enormously difficult moment for the British ruling class, as difficult as 1940. The Hanoverian monarchy was obliged to enrol nearly a million soldiers and sailors, and had to give them something to fight for. The abolitionist cause had resonance among those excluded by the Hanoverian oligarchy. In this moment of great difficulty they offered a concession, which was above all symbolic. They were not prepared to abolish the basic structure of the oligarchy—that was a future battle—but they were prepared to symbolically deal a blow to slavery. The suppression of the British slave trade was not as important as the Haitian Revolution, and it was in large part a consequence of that revolution, but certainly it should be registered as a success, one that was forced on the British parliament and royal family, who had been great supporters of the slave trade.

It did represent an advance in the consciousness of millions in Britain and other parts of the Atlantic zone, but in the end it was an act of the British parliament, and these were hardhearted men, these Hanoverian oligarchs. They were deeply corrupt, and quite willing to see a trade in pauper apprentices, child labour which took place on a horrendous scale. But they needed to come up with a cause that would elevate the struggle against Napoleon. There is not some intrinsic virtue of British culture, as I think Simon Sharma is suggesting when he talks of "British freedom". Indeed Britain's abolitionist crusade was to animate the 19th century imperial Pax Britannica and to justify colonialism and the carve-up of Africa in the 1880s—supposedly this was all done with the aim of suppressing the slave trade! In fairness it should be said that some radical abolitionists, especially the pacifists, rejected this attempt to steal and distort their cause.

There is a background to all this of changing economic interests—slavery had been central to the first big expansion of wealth in Britain, but this began to change. Adam Smith turned against slavery and empire, reflecting a wider change in the bourgeoisie.
Slavery was extremely important to Britain. Although Britain borrowed some techniques from Portugal and Spain, the British and Dutch were the main players. They completely revolutionised slave production on the plantations, making them far more productive. All of this was due to the fact that Britain and the Netherlands were already undergoing a transition to capitalism, with its origins as much in the countryside as in the towns. This transition meant there was a rise in wage labour, and farmers who owed rent to landlords and who had to hire lawyers, and so on. You had an economy where money was in great demand and of growing significance. The demand for plantation products—above all tobacco and sugar in the 17th century—was a critical development.

The Spanish Americas, before 1650, imported something like 300,000 captive Africans, the Portuguese about the same number. The British, over the next century and a half, imported something like ten times that number of slaves. Capitalism was responsible for enlarging the internal market in ways that greatly stimulated plantation production. This created a critical labour shortage in the plantations. At first the labour force included white indentured servants, but soon the demand rose above levels that this could meet, and it was at this point that the slave trade was resorted to.

It is true that political economists such as Adam Smith said that the best way to develop an economy was on the basis of wage labour, not slavery: slave labour was not as productive as the labour of the free worker, and so on. But most capitalists and not a few economists believed that, as things actually were, slavery was necessary to the expansion of trade. After 1807 Britain greatly enlarged its trade with Brazil, Cuba and the United States. That trade, which was by this time especially in cotton, was important to the industrial growth of Britain, and the commodities were still produced by slave labour.

When the British ruling class thought they could capture Saint Domingue (Haiti) they were strongly in favour of slavery. Pitt the Younger dropped all his support for anti-slavery when this was on the cards. They only returned to the question later.

It's fascinating that Pitt changed his tune. He had encouraged Wilberforce to take up the issue of the slave trade. But once Britain was at war with France, Pitt became quite committed to a strategy of taking over the French islands, with the full collaboration with resident French planters and merchants. Most of these planters and merchants were inclined to monarchy and opposed to the French republic, especially when it issued the Jacobin decree of emancipation in 1794. A huge British army of about 90,000 soldiers was despatched. The loss of this great army, its defeat at Saint Domingue and heavy losses in eastern Caribbean, helped create the new context for 1807 and the abolition bill. It also draws our attention to the huge importance of exchanges with the slave zone.

Eric Williams, in *Capitalism and Slavery*, drew attention to the way British capitalists and merchants were linked to the "triangular trade"—trade with Africa, trade with the plantations and the trade in plantation goods, with the West Indies as a market as well as a source of coveted goods such as sugar and cotton. You get a whole nexus which helps explain both the British willingness to try to seize the French islands and their refusal in 1807 to do what the Jacobins had done, and issue a proclamation to abolish slavery itself. They maintained slavery for more than another generation.

The actual abolition of slavery didn't take place until the 1830s. In your book you show how this took place against a background of revolts in Europe and further slave rebellions.

The act was passed in 1833, and it came into force between 1834 and 1838. The slaves were not entirely freed: there was supposed to be an eight-year apprenticeship. One has to register that the more enlightened wing of the oligarchy, which had favoured the end of the slave trade, believed that this would improve the condition of slaves. In fact conditions got worse as prices of commodities went down and planters put slaves to work even more intensively.

After the rebellion in Haiti there was a string of rebellions of the new type—fully emancipationist. Of course there were still African memories and themes that played an important role here, but they were combined with aspirations that grew out of the conditions of the slaves themselves. Partly it was simply a demand for freedom. Often they claimed that the king had secretly passed a law emancipating them and that the colonial elite was hiding this information. You had the "free paper come" movement, you had an uprising in Barbados in 1815, in Demerara, Guyana, in 1823.

These involved thousands of slave rebels, sometimes demanding freedom and sometimes three free days in a week—changing the terms of slavery before questioning it entirely. Then from December 1831 until February 1832 there was a great uprising in Jamaica, sometimes called the Baptist War. In these cases, in Demerara and Jamaica, Baptist and Methodist missionaries seem to have proselytised among the slaves and seem to have given the black deacons some space to work out their own ideas, which added to the coordination and independent thinking among the slaves.

There was a rising crescendo of revolt, which inclined the planters towards compromise, and in particularly "compensated emancipation". Slaveholding began to seem very unsafe. There was also the growth of a new movement in Britain itself. The Hanoverian oligarchy, "old corruption", was still firmly in place and the numbers it sought to exclude, exploit and oppress were very great—in Ireland as well as England. It faced the new working class, radical artisans and the middle classes. Then there was the rural revolt of Captain Swing in 1832 in rural England, which was very similar in many ways to the slave uprisings of the Caribbean and which was harshly put down. An interesting feature of this period was how the oligarchy became extremely repressive. When it put down the slave rebellion in Demerara 250 slaves were killed outright.

The anti-slavery movement in Britain radicalised. Women played an important part in this radicalisation. The anti-slavery society was re-established in 1823, but called itself the Society for the Gradual Emancipation of the Slaves. The Birmingham Ladies Negroes Friends Society in 1825 published a pamphlet by Elizabeth Hayrick in which she said that she hoped that none of the ladies' anti-slavery organisations would have the word "gradual" in their name.

News was also coming from South America that Simon Bolivar was issuing decrees against slavery, and in 1829 Mexico became the first Spanish American country to completely abolish slavery, the work of a president partly of African descent. There was the French Revolution of 1830. There was a feeling that the Hanoverian oligarchy in Britain was on its last legs. The narrow-minded middle class hoped to extend the vote, only to a narrow spectrum of property holders, and sought to dignify the reformed parliament with the 1833 act, which set the terms for the abolition of slavery.

This act did, however, massively compensate the slave owners, giving just a little less than £20 million, a huge sum in those days, and giving them, in theory, another eight years of service from their former slaves at nominal wage rates. Interestingly, at this point the battle moved back to the West Indies where in 1837-8 there were great protest actions and strikes for better wages. The final act of emancipation was in 1838, when the British parliament, realising that law and order had broken down in the West Indies, entirely suppressed the claims of the planters over their former slaves.

It is really important to see the whole cause of emancipation as the consequence of class struggle, both in the plantations and in the metropolitan zone, of the great distaste for slavery among common people, even those with some racist ideas in England or France who nonetheless hated the slave owners.

What was the cultural source of the black revolt?

It's important to see that African revolt played an important part, and historians increasingly accept that it did, even in the recent weak and misguided commemoration. I'm a great fan of C L R James's work *The Black Jacobins*, and in a way the title of that book is trying to alert us to the fact that there is a new and surprising mixture going on—elements of Jacobinism questioning property and privilege, amalgamated with something new and different. Since James published his great book historians have been able to examine the African contribution to slave resistance.

James uses, as epigraphs to some of the chapters, chants of the slaves. This stands in for the fact that African themes were important. Sixty percent of the slaves were African born. The slavery of the new world was something vastly more intense, oppressive and racialised than slavery had been in Africa, the old world or ancient Rome. Africans played a significant role in the upsurges. There was a point when Toussaint L'Ouverture tried to do a deal with Napoleon, and at that point the resistance to Napoleon was maintained by the grassroots leaders. This resistance was far more consistent than the great leaders of the revolt. Many of the grassroots leaders were Africans and they were doing something of importance to the whole world—making the first slave revolt in modern history and helping give rise to the notion of freedom in the modern sense. There was something coming in from African ideas, and even from native American ideas—the name Haiti is actually native American—and something coming from the radicalised class struggle of the French Revolution and in Britain.

There have been attempts to share the responsibility for slavery with African ruling elites and Arab traders who participated in the slave trade. What was specific about the British role?

Slavery was always objectionable and oppressive, but there was something peculiarly oppressive and intense about slavery in the New World. The slavery of the African kings had something in common with that of the New World—the idea that someone could be bought and sold—but the fate of the former slave in Africa or the Middle East was not to become a plantation worker. The women might become recognised concubines and eventually wives. The men, in Africa or Egypt, might become soldiers; some might even eventually become rulers. In the ancient world in Europe slavery encompassed the enslavement of Greek tutors or the civil servants of the Roman empire. So slavery was quite a diverse and by no means intensely racialised institution. Slaves in ancient Rome were from a wide variety of backgrounds and were not for the most part black Africans. In Africa slavery was a fate most likely to befall the stranger, but it was not a permanent institution in the sense that after a generation or two descendants might aspire to manumission. In the New World the racialised nature of slavery meant the great majority of the descendants of slaves were also condemned to bondage.

So this line of thought does not soften the nature of this great historical tragedy, the enslavement of 12 million taken in captives, and maybe as many again killed in slave raiding wars. The slave trade with the Middle East was, year by year, much smaller than the Atlantic slave trade, even if it went on much longer. The Atlantic slave trade took off at a modest rate in the 1520s, but it really became intense from 1650. From 1700 to 1850 you had tens or hundreds of thousands a year—it was intensely concentrated in time and its impact was therefore very great.

It also encouraged a predatory involution of society in Africa, putting modern weaponry and industrialised goods in the hands of the slave raiders. You had the rise of some kingdoms dedicated to slave raiding. You had some kingdoms that also tried to withdraw from the trade. There was a Jihadi movement in West Africa around 1776 (which we think of as the year of the American Revolution), which historians think represented an attempt to restrain the slave trade. The Jihadis would not enslave fellow Muslims, although they might enslave people they saw as infidels. It was not a purely abolitionist movement, but it certainly had some anti-imperial meaning.

How did slavery help lead to a system of racist ideology and how much purchase did it have in Europe?

There were some forms of ethnic particularism, which we might view as the source of racism, even at the time the slave plantations were being set up. There was a lot of harsh work to be done and European workers coming out to the plantations could find convenient a system of white skin privilege which exempted them from this toil. But this didn't make these workers like the plantation owners any more, and the whites tended to get out of the Caribbean plantations. The systems, once they were up and running, did encourage a hardening of racism. What had been a form of aversive racism, hating people not like ourselves, became a sort of dominating racism, which was mobilised to keep down a particular population. That's what the planters encouraged, and they were able to enlist a fear among poor whites of slave revolt.

As for people back in Britain and France, I find it difficult to say how much racism there was. They were not being asked to vote on whether slave plantations should exist—the elites were making the key decisions. I'm sure people had prejudices against Papists, the Irish, the Spanish and probably against Africans too. But in the rough and tumble of life aboard ships and in port towns you also had real friendships formed between whites and those of African origin. If you read Equiano's narrative you'll find some racial rebuffs, but these tended to be in the slave zone itself, and much less so in England, where he eventually married an English woman and where he became a popular speaker up and down the country.

We shouldn't project back the racism of the high colonial era of the 1880s on the England of the 1780s or even the early 1800s. The first steps of the anti-slavery movement were the freedom lawsuits like the Somerset freedom suit in the 1770s brought before Lord Mansfield, or in the American ports, which usually relied on a white free person helping to champion a courageous slave, or perhaps someone who had been wrongfully enslaved. This does show, not modern standards of multiculturalism, but a willingness to resist racialised stereotypes.

What books would you recommend?

The most recent book on the British abolition movement is Adam Hothschild's *Bury the Chains*. This is a pretty good book. It doesn't scrutinise the motives of the Hanoverian ruling class, but it does try to put abolition in a wider context of the French and American revolutions. There is David Brian Davis's *Slavery in the Age of Revolution*. This is a tremendous book of the 1970s by the leading American historian of slavery. He tried to understand why even some of the oligarchy adopted anti-slavery, reflected in huge votes in parliament. He argued this was a reflection of how the wage system was justified and universalised, and the cause of anti-slavery was about establishing a hegemony of bourgeoisie society. My only quarrel with him would be that black resistance is not foregrounded. Seymour Drescher, who I've quarrelled with in the past because he doesn't give its due to the Haitian Revolution, reveals the depth of abolitionism as a movement in newly industrialising areas in a series of books and essays.

Nandigram and the deformations of the Indian left

Aditya Sarkar

On 14 March this year, the state government of West Bengal, headed by the Communist Party of India (Marxist), sent several thousand police troops into the rural district of Nandigram in East Midnapur, the scene of a three-month movement by peasants against the establishment of a Special Economic Zone on their land.

Over 19,000 acres of peasant land in its various forms—cropped land, homestead, schools, mosques and temples—were to be turned over the Indonesian-based Salim group for chemical and pharmaceutical units, shipbuilding and real estate.[1] Peasant resistance ushered in the new year as villagers began digging up and barricading roads, blocking the entry of police, and the state and party apparatus, into their land. A series of clashes between party cadres and villagers culminated in the decision of the chief minister, Buddhadeb Bhattacharya, to send in the police on 14 March. Whether the Left Front government that rules West Bengal actually orchestrated the massacre of villagers—official estimates say it left 14 dead, the unofficial count ran into hundreds—or not, it certainly stood by and watched while policemen and CPI(M) cadres, some disguised as police, ran amok among the villagers, in an orgy of killing, torture and rape. Since March Nandigram has witnessed

1: Mohammed Salim, the businessman to whom the land was to be turned over, helped bankroll Suharto's genocide of Indonesian Communists. The Communist-led government of West Bengal is eager to do business with him. If ever proof was needed of the irony of the current conjuncture of the Indian left, or of the way capital swallows up and transcends ideological animosities in its expansionary drives, it is here.

further confrontations between the party and peasants, the fraying of the livelihoods and networks that held the local economy together, and the slow strangulation of protest by the state government.

Nandigram exposed the horrific possibilities at the heart of the Bengal left's embrace of global, neoliberal capital, but it was not unprecedented. It was foreshadowed at Singur, one of the most fertile and prosperous tracts of agricultural land in the state and in the country. Here the West Bengal government had turned over a thousand acres of cultivated land to the Tatas, India's biggest industrial house, for the establishment of a motor factory—a takeover that entailed the loss of over 20,000 livelihoods. A movement with its roots in the villages of Singur sparked off solidarity campaigns in Calcutta, attempts by the chief opposition party, the Trinamul Congress, to climb on board the bandwagon, initiatives by far-left Naxalite groupings, and protests across the country by left leaning cultural activists and intellectuals disgusted by the prolonged deformations of a party and government many of them had once identified with. It brought to the forefront of national politics the issue of Special Economic Zones (SEZs), with their conjoined logics of mass displacement, the right of companies to administer their territory largely independently of state law, the abrogation of constitutionally guaranteed labour rights and the violation of environmental standards. These themes were repeated and amplified during and after the mayhem at Nandigram, and the battle continues.

The paradox of an apparently left wing administration embracing the most brutal and intrusive contemporary regime of global capitalist expansion threw into relief the antagonism between India's chosen path of economic development and the livelihoods and aspirations of the majority of its citizens. This tension was not in itself new. SEZs are the flashpoint, but land can be grabbed for many purposes—real estate hubs, factories, townships. Land grabs have been the source of major confrontations setting local communities against big business and the state in Jharkhand, Orissa, Punjab, Maharashtra, Gurgaon, Gujarat and various other places.

The most important sites of resistance to state sponsored corporate invasions are the land and people affected by them. At Kalinganagar in Orissa, where a bauxite plant is planned, fierce resistance continues despite the charming decision of the national government to install anti-personnel landmines against the incursions of resisting tribals. At Jagatsinghpur, also in Orissa, the South Korean steel company Posco has been allotted land for an SEZ, and here the local resistance has taken the form of kidnappings of company officials, who are unharmed, in order to induce the government to take account of the demands of those affected by the project. In

Jharkhand dozens of SEZ projects hang in the balance, unable to get off the ground because of fierce mobilisations against them. At Singur villagers still regularly breach the wall separating them from the Tata factory site, despite the heavy presence of punitive state mechanisms. At Haripur, not far from Nandigram, the central government had planned a nuclear power plant. Local inhabitants have blockaded their villages and set up something akin to an autonomous zone.

In each case powerful companies and a mammoth state apparatus have negotiated agreements on massive land grabs, but in each case actual construction work has been indefinitely stalled by the strength of local mobilisations. In this sense, the expansion of neoliberal capitalism in India has finally hit a genuine roadblock, and confronts, in its own way, as intense a crisis as the populations affected by its projects do. The state and the companies involved have at present only two options. To back off entirely, jeopardizing investor confidence, the kickbacks from these agreements for ministers and bureaucrats, and the future of the strategy of unmandated land acquisition. Or they can violently repress resistance, producing instant crises, as at Nandigram, where the CPI(M) has been forced to suspend, for the moment, the planned SEZ.

In a way, the clear "no" to current economic policy in India parallels the resistance to recent attempts to impose free trade agreements on Latin America, though perhaps without the same depth of ideological ferment. In both cases, the dominant trajectory of capitalist growth has run up against the obstacle of utter, uncompromising popular refusal, and the cosy myth of a consensus around a particular model of economic growth—apparently "value-neutral" but actually deeply ideologically constituted—has been shattered. Nationally and globally, this is a crucial moment in the history of capital.

The new battle lines beginning to take shape in India cross and blur the antagonisms of official party politics. The major political formations in India seem increasingly united over the legitimacy both of the currently hegemonic national economic policy and the use of state repression to enforce it. In West Bengal the organised left is at the helm of the SEZ drive. In Maharashtra the Congress party is in charge of implementing comparably brutal drives. In Orissa a coalition of the Biju Janata Dal and the BJP, India's major right wing formation, have been administering a similar assault upon tribal communities with the aid of the army. In Gujarat and Jharkhand the state BJP administrations are the initiators and executors of this drive.

In each of these cases the takeover of land that sustains thousands of people and its transfer to companies that are accountable only to their shareholders is presented as a fait accompli—something the state has the right to do, regardless of the wishes not only of local populations, but also of their democratically elected local representative bodies. This is the heart of the new consensus. The divisions between left, right, and centre, real and bitter as they are in other arenas of national politics, have virtually ceased to matter.

The opposition to this does not run along the lines of party politics either. The CPI(M)'s propaganda machines have been working overtime to convince us that the resistance to the Nandigram and Singur land grabs were machinations of the Trinamul Congress, on the one hand, and the revolutionary left wing Naxalites, on the other. Nothing could be further from the truth. The uprisings stemmed from the extremely rational desire of local agrarian populations to hold on to their land, and the resistance cut across party lines, in Nandigram consisting overwhelmingly of people who had been supporters or even members of the CPI(M).

The real battle being fought here, then, is not principally between rival ideologies—though we can usually assign "left wing" and "right wing" labels to the objective positions taken up in this struggle. It is, rather, a direct confrontation between democracy and capital, which are increasingly incommensurate with one another. If democratic accountability were taken seriously by those who govern, corporate land acquisition could not be conceived of as an inevitable outcome, since it entails the disruption of mammoth numbers of lives and livelihoods. Pushing it through necessarily involves the curtailment of democratic procedures and entitlements. But the use of coercion to push such an agenda through invites further and increasingly militant forms of resistance, and the impasse, far from being resolved, grows. Things fall apart, the centre cannot hold.

Losing the Left

For most people in West Bengal the spectacle of the organised left's recourse to bloody massacre and authoritarian repression is nothing new. The CPI(M) in this state wins election after election, partly on the strength of land reforms it undertook in the 1980s (and is now abandoning), but also on the strength of sustained ballot rigging and intimidation. It cushions corrupt and venal bureaucracies, a trade union culture stripped of its once legendary vitality by utter subservience to party dictates, a politics of patronage and nepotism at all levels, and, across vast parts of the countryside, local networks of party authority that function as armed fiefdoms. Lakshman Seth, the CPI(M) MP from Tamluk, the constituency in which Nandigram is located, and in many ways the architect of the 14 March massacre, is only one of many cases in point.

While many on the left internationally celebrate the CPI(M)'s achievement of 30 years of unbroken Left Front power as an example of democratically mandated Communist success, the state level administration subverts democracy at every point, and is in the process of reinventing itself as a party driven by corporate interests and the aspirations of the upper middle class. Indicators of this are the enormous leeway given to real estate speculation,[2] the abysmal state of primary education and health services, and the eagerness with which the government has embraced global capital. A poster at a recent demonstration against the massacre gave us an effective, if hysterical, evaluation of the West Bengal government: "CPI(M) = Capitalist Party of India (Murderer)".

This is an evaluation that many on the far left in India would extend to the organised left as a whole. They would point out that there is a long history of violence, intimidation, and bullying here—that the official Communist movement in India has both blood and compromise on its hands. They would point out, unassailably, that the party has never repudiated Stalinism—indeed, its annual conferences still contain accolades to the Soviet Union that make it sound as if 1956 never happened. They would point out that the Left Front government in West Bengal was party to the massacre of Bangladeshi settlers in the Sunderbans in 1979, and also that Jyoti Basu, its chief minister for more than two decades, superintended the brutal eviction of hawkers ("Operation Sunshine") from the pavements of Calcutta in 1994 to make the city look pretty for the British prime minister John Major's visit. They would point to the organised left's assaults upon revolutionary Naxalite and Maoist groups in West Bengal, and perhaps also claim that these latter formations represent the only true, authentic face of left wing politics in India.

For its part, the CPI(M) nationally has done more than its fair share of work in giving weight to these accusations. The central party leadership lied through its teeth while citing figures of consensual land acquisition in Singur and Nandigram. It has consistently refused to issue a condemnation of the West Bengal state unit's repression of popular protest, or to acknowledge the resistance to the SEZ as anything but a conjuration of its

2: Real estate is at the heart of the new model of development in various parts of India. The township of New Rajarhat in Calcutta, a recently constructed urban space that was built upon the displacement of an agrarian community, is a testament to the physical excision of poor and underprivileged communities for the establishment of luxury apartments, malls and enclaves of leisure, residence and work for the upper middle classes. This logic permeates urban planning in most of India's major metropolitan cities, most visibly in Bombay, and in Gurgaon near Delhi.

political rivals. And it has, unforgivably, done absolutely nothing to restrain the excesses and brutalities of party cadres in Nandigram, which continue as a matter of course today. Such an approach is due in large part to the party's utter dependence on its units in West Bengal and Kerala, the only major states where it is powerful, for its clout in national politics. But whatever the reasons, the approach constitutes a break, perhaps irrevocable, with radical and progressive politics, and more generally with anti-capitalism.

These failures and betrayals are fatal at this conjuncture in Indian politics. Social movements across the country, most of which share left wing values and perspectives, have organised bravely against big dams, corporate takeovers of land, the exploitation of labouring people, the ecological consequences of industrial capitalism, and the continuing erosion and marginalisation of the livelihoods of millions as a result of national economic policies. Until Nandigram happened, it was possible for the left to share a common platform with these movements, for instance during the World Social Forum and its offshoot, the Indian Social Forum. After Nandigram, it is difficult to see where this shared space is.

The organised left, it is true, has taken up significant issues in parliament—for instance, in its protests against airline privatisation and pension reform. Bitterly and ironically, this left provided a public space for arguments against the course of national economic policy, and in particular—here the ironies grow hideous—the establishment of SEZs.

Countless party loyalists have been shaken to the core by the events in West Bengal and there are major struggles within the CPI(M). In Kerala, the Communist chief minister, V S Achyutanandan, follows a policy trajectory radically at odds with his counterpart in West Bengal (though there have been significant moves within the state party unit to oust him and move rightwards). But the dogma of party line, the compulsions of loyalty towards comrades (however erring) and the need not to break rank hold back these tensions, and refuse them meaningful public space.

Officially the CPI(M) is opposed to the current economic policy of the Indian national government, and the track it has been on for over a decade. Equally officially the CPI(M) nationally endorses the policies and chosen trajectory of its West Bengal unit. These are irreconcilable positions. Perhaps these are dialectical contradictions that will be miraculously transcended. But if we are reduced to praying for magic to save the organised Indian left from itself, we must at least acknowledge how grim things are. The left has apparently deserted the battleground at a time when the struggles against global capitalism in India are more urgent and relevant than they have ever been.

After Nandigram the CPI(M) has lost any claim upon the trust of movements and mobilisations that actually do the work of resisting the invasions of capital. But it would be a serious mistake to see this, as many on the far left do, as something inevitably written into the script of the organised left decades ago, or to see these betrayals as anything but tragic. The official left in India, for all its Stalinism, its compromises and blunders, was historically at the forefront of massive mobilisations of workers and peasants, and nowhere more powerfully than in West Bengal, where generations of Communists worked tirelessly for the rights of workers, sharecroppers and poor peasants, and against brutal social inequalities. Its power, both in West Bengal and Kerala, was founded on its responsiveness to agrarian discontent, its ability to mobilise politically around it, and its responsibility in leading land and labour struggles. It led one of the largest labour movements in history, in Bombay (now Mumbai); it organised incredibly important peasant movements in Bengal and Telengana in the 1940s and 1950s; it put India's most progressive land reforms in place in the states it governed. If this left has been lost then mourning, rather than celebration or vindication, is the response most appropriate to left minded people.

More may have been lost, however, than a legacy and a memory of historic struggles, which were fought by other—and better—men and women, in other times. There is, after all, an active, though far from powerful, official left outside its regional centres of accumulated power. Organisations of women, teachers, students, workers, and social activists affiliated to or allied with the CPI(M) have been working in Delhi and across North India, in large parts of the south, in Maharashtra and in various other parts of the country, against the kinds of policies that drive the poor and the marginalised to the wall and embed social injustice within the governing political ethic. As a left wing student who grew up in Delhi, I have always seen the official left, in meetings, in campaigns and on demonstrations, as a space one could turn to for succour, comfort and political solidarity, despite the frustrations and differences one may have had with the official line of the party. The mobilisations against the Hindu right at the time of BJP rule would have been unthinkable without the presence—indeed, the protective umbrella—of the organised left. I believe this is also the relationship that many of India's most serious social movements have had with the left: a relationship of simultaneous irritation and gratitude, disappointment and solidarity. At any rate, a shared space used to exist. After Nandigram it is difficult to see where that shared space is any more. The political paths of a party that calls itself left wing and movements that follow some of the best values of the left increasingly diverge. Medha

Patkar, India's most important social activist and arguably the leader of the global movement against big dams, was the most prominent public face of the protests around Nandigram. This is symptomatic of the necessary but deeply tragic constellation of oppositions and fissures within progressive circles after the massacre.

The tensions of resistance

The organised left's greatest failure comes at a time when the battle against neoliberal capitalism in India is intensely alive and vocal. The loss throws into sharp relief the choices and pitfalls facing an emergent resistance. This resistance takes various forms.

First, and most importantly, there are the movements launched from the grassroots. The corporate takeover of basic human and natural resources produces, at each step, more or less complete refusal on the part of the local communities who stand to lose. Political parties and outfits may or may not join in the resistance. But even where they do not, the threat experienced by communities from the state and capital produces, inevitably, its own strategies of mobilisation and organisation, and its own debates. The immediate, automatic act of refusal has been clarified in many cases into structures of resistance, through the formation of committees, the election of representatives, and the planning of short term and long term strategies.

Such structural solidifications of resistance, however, need to be situated in their immediate social contexts, which often enough have the shape of deeply divided and hierarchical local community relations, fissured by class, caste and gender. Does the partial unity that resistance necessarily engenders disturb older, deep rooted patterns of local injustice and exploitation? The answer is still open and unresolved. The incredibly vocal and militant participation of Nandigram's women in the resistance points in one direction, but the persistence of certain caste divisions and the reluctance of some of the lowest groups in the caste hierarchies to join the movement in Singur points in another. There is no automatic logic that weds the opposition to big capital to a "progressive" political consciousness that calls all sources of injustice and hierarchy into question. But equally, there is no guarantee, in a time of uprising and the need to create a consensus around resistance, that the existing social orders will maintain their stability and not undergo a process of internal churning. Time alone will answer this question.

Second, there has been an efflorescence of largely uncoordinated citizens' initiatives, loosely seen in terms of "civil society", since Singur and Nandigram. The sudden outburst of protest in Calcutta in the wake of the West Bengal government's land acquisition policies exemplifies this.

Calcutta was a city that for decades had seen virtually no serious progressive oppositional politics, with the staleness of both the ruling administration and the official opposition (the Trinamul Congress) producing a crippling sense of cynicism and jadedness. It woke up to a frenzy of mobilisation and activism that testified both to the residual strength of Bengali nationalism and a deeply entrenched left wing structure of feeling, a sympathy for the unprivileged that, ironically, the organised left had in earlier times done much to produce and disseminate.

Students' associations organised protest and relief campaigns, medical teams visited Nandigram and galvanised a sense of active disgust among doctors and nurses, who took to the streets in large numbers, and associations of lawyers, journalists and artists also joined in the campaigns of solidarity with the resistance. Similar initiatives were set in motion in Delhi, and the symbolic effect of protests in the capital city, as always, in excess of their immediate practical value, helped force the issue of land grabs into national media headlines.

These citizens' mobilisations are enormously important, for, while the real battle continues to be fought in villages, tribal belts and localities, publicly visible manifestations of solidarity in high profile metropolitan spaces help sustain the mood of opposition and demonstrate the mythical nature of the neoliberal policy "consensus". It remains to be seen, however, whether they will be able to reproduce the resilience of committed activism, through coordination and organisation, over a sustained period of time.

Third, there are the social movements that have been campaigning for social justice and ecological sustainability. Many of these—the campaign against the Narmada dam, the fishworkers' movement in Madurai, various organisations working for the rights of Dalits, women's groups and associations set up to fight for unorganised labour—are clustered under the umbrella of the National Alliance of People's Movements (NAPM), which held a month-long protest sit-in in central Delhi shortly after Nandigram. These groups vary immensely in size and importance, but demonstrate the range and plurality of progressive initiatives in India. Most of them have no direct links with any political parties, though some of them are on good terms with movements of the far left and others have worked closely with state administrations where these have been responsive. There is a continuum between them and some of the more progressive NGOs: the lines often blur, but the tensions between social-welfarist drives and more radical, political forms of mobilisation are felt at various levels.

It is too early to say whether these largely single issue groups can produce a plausible challenge to the agenda of the Indian state and big business, and coalesce around a coherent political platform that seriously disturbs the governing consensus.

Finally, there is the revolutionary far left, in its various factions and forms. To many, the Naxalites and Maoists represent the authentic vanguard of popular resistance, as the only politically organised and ideologically coherent movements that are genuinely committed simultaneously to fighting against big capital and mounting a radical offensive against the state. But this is far too roseate a picture.

The far left in India is a patchwork of deeply divided organisations, all loosely committed to the legitimacy of armed resistance to the state, but some more open to the question of parliamentary participation than others. One of the most disturbing features of their history has been their unwillingness to rethink the need for armed revolutionary violence of the most savage sort. The decision to keep the option of armed resistance open is in a sense understandable in the context of prolonged state repression of an order of savagery that far exceeds their own. In Nandigram the counter-violence of villagers against the CPI(M) was clearly produced by a sense that it was either kill or be killed. In such a situation it is not easy to stand back and pre-judge "Naxal" strategies of resistance. It is possible, however, to ask whether such violence, which breeds its own vicious, cyclical logic, can actually be politically productive. In various parts of India—Bihar, Chhattisgarh, and Andhra Pradesh, for instance—the cycle of state repression, exploitation by big landholders and revolutionary violence has bred situations where we are often left with little more than the machinations, brutality and terror wreaked by rival mafias. This is not the only form of "resistance" practised by far left outfits, but it would be fair to say that it has been a dominant trajectory ever since the tragic foundational episode of Naxalbari (in Begal in the late 1960s), where revolutionary left wing idealism soon gave way to internecine warfare and bloodshed.

Those who celebrate the revolutionary drive of the Maoists and Naxalites against the corruption and degeneration of the organised left tend to forget something very important. For the longest period of its existence this organised left occupied the very ground that the "far" left does today: it took up issues of deprivation and injustice at levels where none of the mainstream political formations had anything to say, and it drew its legitimacy from that. It was always crippled by its internal authoritarianism, by the blind dogmas of party line, and by its slavishness to the shifts and turns of Soviet policy. But the revolutionary left today, for all its principled opposition to capital, is usually equally authoritarian in its internal structures (equally committed to what is calls "democratic centralism"), equally defined by party line and as blindly worshipful of Mao as Communists used to be of Stalin.

It is difficult to see a progressive and genuinely democratic left wing politics emerging from such locations, though the real and often heroic resistance offered to capital and the state by many far left groupings should not be underestimated. It is also true that the "far left" is a complex animal, not only divided into a range of legitimate or underground parties split over tactics, strategies and ideology, but also spread across other spaces—civil and democratic rights campaigns, citizens' mobilisations against state terror, independent radical trade unions, and social movements of various kinds, where one can usually find both conservative and revolutionary factions. One has to hope for internal transformations, or for the emergence within the far left of strands that valorise not only revolutionary zeal and consistency, but also work towards achieving cross-regional, democratic mandates for their politics. This would, however, mean eschewing both the violent excesses and the righteous vanguardism that permeates so much of their politics today.

The question of democratic mandate defines most sharply the dilemmas confronting the resistance to corporate capital in India today. The state, for all practical purposes, is accountable only to itself. The "legitimate" political parties, from left to right, are rapidly coming to share a neoliberal consensus with no foundations in popular consent and are accountable, increasingly, only to top-down structures of leadership. The various movements and mobilisations that have risen to resist them are accountable mainly to their adherents, and unable so far to formulate a coherent politics open to wider democratic debate. If this is true of the Naxalites, it is also true of the far less ethically problematic rainbow coalition of social movements. These movements usually organise around limited issues and have trouble widening their horizons into a politics that can command generalised consent and establish a real hegemony.

It is here that the loss of the organised left pinches most sharply. It means the loss of a space, however limited, of constitutionally protected and "legitimate" political opposition. This is the impasse progressive resistance finds itself in today. There is no democratically accountable location within the "legitimate" political spectrum from which attacks upon the embrace of state and capital, with its disastrous consequences for the whole country, can be mounted. At the same time, the discontent with the chosen path of national development has never been more sharply pronounced and more visible than it is today, and this has produced a rich harvest of oppositional mobilisations, engaged in the search for a definite political space in which to anchor themselves.

It is a situation where one finds oneself feeling that something has to give. India is crying out for a real democratic left, stripped of old dogmas and able to face up to its role with responsibility, accountability and humility. For that, however, significantly new forms of political radicalism and left wing practice are needed that break from the dead past and the stifling present. Perhaps the clamour of democratic protest in the wake of Nandigram signals a new beginning, a signal towards new directions. Perhaps global capital and the powers of the state simply remain too strong, too resilient, to allow a dent to be made. It is a moment of political impasse that we live through at present, even as tensions mount and boil and break to the surface of our times.

Gordon Brown: from reformism to neoliberalism

John Newsinger

"The distribution of income in Britain has now become so unequal that it is beginning to resemble a Third World country", wrote Gordon Brown in his 1989 indictment of Thatcherism, *Where There Is Greed*. He complained that since 1979 "an extraordinary transfer of resources, from poor to rich, has taken place". Indeed, so great had the level of inequality become that it was "difficult to argue that there remains even a common interest between the top 1 percent to whom Mrs Thatcher has given so much, and the rest of the nation". And, of course, inequality was even more glaring with regard to the distribution of wealth. According to Brown, the richest 10 percent of the population owned more than 50 percent of the wealth, while the bottom 50 percent of the population owned only 7 percent. Even more outrageous, under Thatcher "the wealth of the top 1 percent, who now own 17 percent, had more than doubled".[1] Remember, this was written in 1989 and the situation was to get considerably worse in the run-up to Labour's 1997 election victory.

Now that he has been chancellor of the exchequer for ten years in a New Labour government with a large majority, what has Brown done to remedy the injustices and inequalities of the Thatcher years? Not only has he done nothing to reverse "the extraordinary transfer of resources from

1: Brown, 1989, pp119, 121.

the poor to the rich" that so outraged him in 1989; under New Labour the situation has continued to get worse. When New Labour came to power in 1997 the proportion of the country's wealth in the hands of the richest 1 percent had reached 20 percent. By 2004, with Brown as chancellor, it had increased to 24 percent.[2] According to one commentator, the 600,000 individuals who make up the richest 1 percent were, on average, £737,000 richer than they had been under the Conservatives.[3] More recently, according to the Institute for Fiscal Studies, 2005-6 saw both relative and absolute poverty increase. The institute reported that income inequality today is "higher than Labour inherited by a statistically significant amount".[4] Brown is still trumpeted as the Labour Party's most successful chancellor ever.

In *Where There Is Greed* Brown not only condemned increasing inequality under Thatcher, but also savaged the Conservative policy of privatisation. He was particularly critical of the dramatic increases in pay that the top executives of the privatised utilities awarded themselves. He also censured the erosion of civil liberties under the Conservatives, complaining that "information on individuals is now compiled and held on an unprecedented scale" and that "the right of assembly and the right to protest have been curtailed in ways that were not contemplated under any other post-war Conservative administration". New Labour have, of course, far surpassed the Tories in their assault on civil liberties—with Brown's full support. But back in 1989 he even complained of the government allowing "the Murdoch empire" to take over the *Times*.

What was Brown's answer to all this? "Socialism has always been about more than equality," Brown insisted, very deliberately distancing himself from the Labour right. Indeed, he warned that hard-won political and social rights were always in danger while they "existed side by side with huge concentrations of private unaccountable power". The way forward was to forge "a strong economic democracy". This was his vision of socialism.[5]

How did Gordon Brown, the champion of "a strong economic democracy", become the champion of privatisation, of the market, of the interests of the super-rich, of globalisation, of the whole neoliberal agenda? The Brown who in 1989 warned of the danger posed by "huge

2: Self and Zealey, 2007, pp70-71.
3: Carvel, 2004.
4: Institute for Fiscal Studies, 2007.
5: Brown, 1989, pp10, 176-178.

concentrations of private unaccountable power" went on to embrace them, court them and govern in their interests. And this was openly celebrated: in March 2006, for example, Brown proudly announced the establishment of an International Business Advisory Council to help ensure that British economic policy remained in the best interests of global capital. Its members included Lee Scott, president and chief executive officer (CEO) of Wal-Mart; Lord Browne, chief executive of BP; Jean Pierre Garnier, CEO of GlaxoSmithKline; Bill Gates, chairman of Microsoft; Robert Rubin, chairman of Citigroup; Ratan Tata, chairman of the Tata Group; Sir John Rose, CEO of Rolls Royce; Sir Terry Leahy, CEO of Tesco; and Meg Whitman, CEO of eBay.[6] Needless to say, these people are not friends of the labour movement, either in Britain or abroad; they are its enemies, extreme examples of those whose huge wealth Brown had once considered made it difficult to believe that they still had any "common interest" with the rest of humanity.

Brown's courtship of Rupert Murdoch, conducted in competition with Tony Blair, has been even more grotesque. This competition between the prime minister and chancellor led Murdoch to complain in a recent interview that whenever he visited Britain he always had to "have tea" with both men "or they are very suspicious that you are lining up with the other one". For Murdoch, the test for Brown as prime minister will be "how much would he let the private sector get involved in health and education".[7] This courtship of the reactionary, union-busting, tax-dodging Murdoch, something unprecedented in Labour Party history, tells us everything we need to know about the politics of New Labour.

This article will examine how Brown got to where he is today. It will chronicle and attempt to explain his remarkable trajectory from student radical to left Labour MP to becoming one of the principal architects of New Labour and, at last, to the enthusiastic embrace of neoliberalism.

Student radical

Brown was born in 1951, the son of a Presbyterian minister. He was brought up in a middle class household with a strong social conscience. In 1967 he arrived, aged 16 and with this social conscience still intact, as a student at Edinburgh University. Here Brown, along with thousands

6: HM Treasury, 2006.

7: Cassidy, 2006. Murdoch's ambassador to Britain, Irwin Stelzer, has gone on record to recommend that Brown appoint Ed Balls as chancellor, and that Balls's wife, Yvette Cooper, should also be given a cabinet post. The support of someone like Stelzer would once have destroyed the prospects of a Labour politician, but today it does not even raise eyebrows (see Stelzer, 2007).

of others, found himself part of a student revolt. Although he was certainly influenced by the radical ideas of the time, Brown never embraced the politics of direct action and in 1969 he joined the Labour Party. This did not involve any commitment to Harold Wilson's Labour government, but rather a belief that the Labour Party in Scotland could be transformed into a vehicle for radical change. Brown first came to prominence as a student politician in 1970 when the university principal, Michael Swann, categorically denied that the university had investments in any companies involved in apartheid South Africa. This was a lie of Blairite proportions. Brown received leaked documentary proof of this, and a special issue of the student newspaper was produced to expose the scandal. He went on to get a first class degree and began a PhD on the history of the Scottish Labour Party.

Brown continued to be involved in student politics and in 1972 campaigned on a "student power" platform for election as rector of the university. The rectorship was an office elected by students, usually contested by various notables and celebrities, and, once elected, the rector only ever played a nominal role. To the horror of the university authorities, Brown won an overwhelming victory, and immediately demanded that the university should support the campaign for increased grants. During his time as rector, he argued for working class representation on the university court, proposing that two vacancies be filled by the president of Edinburgh Trades Council and by the secretary of a tenants' association. In retrospect, Brown was to regret this protracted involvement in student politics, but to his credit he was actively involved in the Chile Solidarity Campaign, set up in response to the CIA-sponsored military coup that overthrew the government of Salvadore Allende on 11 September 1973 ("the other 9/11"), and supported the miners during the 1974 strike that brought down the Heath government.[8]

It was in this period of military coups, American defeat in Vietnam and governments brought down by industrial action that Brown edited *The Red Paper on Scotland*, a collection of articles published in 1975. It was a new leftish celebration of radical politics, which included contributions from Tom Nairn, John McGrath, John Foster, Robin Cook and others. Brown's own contribution condemned "the gross inequalities which disfigure Scottish life", and argued that the times cried out for "a new commitment to socialist ideals". He urged "a coherent strategy" of reforms designed "to cancel the logic of capitalism" and to lead "us out of

8: For Brown's career as a student radical see his semi-official biography: Routledge, Paul, 1998, pp 41-63.

one social order into another". This would involve "a phased extension of public control under workers' self-management and the prioritising of social needs by the communities themselves". He called for "a planned economy" and for "workers' power", identifying himself with "Scotland's socialist pioneers, Hardie, Smillie, Maxton, Maclean, Gallacher, Wheatley and others"—a pantheon that included both revolutionary and reformist socialists. What was needed was "a positive commitment to creating a socialist society".[9]

Brown's student activism denied him a teaching post at Edinburgh University. Instead he got a post at Glasgow College of Technology in 1976, and in 1980 gave up academic life to work as a producer at Scottish Television. Brown was elected onto the executive of the Scottish Labour Party in 1976 and eventually, in 1983, was elected Labour MP for Dunfermline East in the face of Thatcher's post-Falklands general election victory.

Labour MP

Brown became a Labour MP as the Thatcher government's assault on the labour movement was moving towards a climax with the Great Miners' Strike of 1984-5. He confronted this turning point in the class struggle as a left wing Labour MP, someone who was never to embrace Bennism, but who nevertheless continued to advocate a reformism that he believed would raise up the working class, confound the capitalist enemy and accomplish a peaceful transition to socialism. In 1983, together with Robin Cook, he published a powerful collection of articles on poverty and deprivation in Scotland entitled *Scotland: The Real Divide*. In his introduction Brown argued that the "first prerequisite for eradicating poverty is the redistribution of income and wealth from rich to poor". In what reads like an indictment of his later policies as chancellor, Brown insisted:

> Taxation should rise progressively with income. Programmes that merely redistribute poverty from families to single persons, from the old to the young, from the sick to the healthy, are not a solution. What is needed is

9: Brown, 1975, pp7, 9, 18,19. The book was actually printed by the Institute for Workers' Control and among the influences that Brown acknowledges were Institute publications, the *Socialist Register*, Antonio Gramsci and Edward Thompson. He even footnotes the publications of the International Marxist Group and of the International Socialists (the forerunner of the Socialist Workers Party). The front cover of the book is illustrated with a photograph of Upper Clyde Shipbuilders workers voting to occupy the shipyards, and the back with a photograph of Leith dockers on strike in 1913.

> a programme of reform that ends the current situation where the top 10 percent of the population own 80 percent of the wealth and 30 percent of the income, even after tax. As Tawney remarked, "What some people call a problem of poverty, others call the problem of riches."

Such views would later become anathema. At the time, however, he was adamant that "the goal would not simply be the minimalist one of equalising opportunities, a strategy akin to what Tawney described as 'the impertinent courtesy of an invitation to unwelcome guests in the certainty that circumstances would prevent them from accepting it'." So much for the cornerstone of New Labour's claim to be "progressive" today. Moreover, a crucial point of the package of reforms that Brown was advocating was that taxation of the rich should be increased—increased, that is, from the then top rate of 60 percent.[10]

The 1984-5 miners' strike was the most bitter and hard fought class struggle in Britain since before the Second World War. It was a decisive moment when the opportunity to defeat Thatcherism was lost and the labour movement went down to a historic defeat.[11] In Scotland, Brown gave the miners his full support throughout the battle, appearing on picket lines, donating a significant proportion of his salary and challenging the Thatcher government's decision to confiscate the benefits of striking miners' families. His commitment to the miners' cause earned him honorary membership of the Scottish Miners' Union. In the aftermath of the strike he published his biography of the Scottish leader of the Independent Labour Party (ILP), James Maxton, a labour of love that it had taken him 20 years to write. Maxton was one of the great spokesmen for reformist socialism in the period between the two world wars. He supported workers' struggles, savagely attacked the capitalist class and was a constant critic of the compromises and betrayals of the Labour Party leadership that were to culminate with Ramsay Macdonald's defection to the Conservatives in 1931. The collapse of the Labour government saw Maxton lead the ILP out of the Labour Party in 1932. He condemned the Labour Party as irredeemably compromised and no longer a vehicle for socialist change. Any sympathy with Maxton would be inconceivable for the Gordon Brown of today, but the Brown of the mid-1980s was different. He produced a sympathetic and scholarly account that celebrated a tradition of militant reformism, an account that was still fuelled by anger at the defeat of the miners.

10: Brown, 1983, pp20, 22.

11: Callinicos and Simons, 1985.

Some commentators have seen the book as marking a turning point for Brown: he celebrates Maxton's principled intransigence, but in the end rejects it because it can only lead to political impotence. This is to read Brown's subsequent trajectory into the book in a way that is not substantiated by the actual text. Certainly Brown acknowledges contemporary criticisms of Maxton's "purism", but he goes on to reject them. He insists, "Maxton's journey through the politics of the twenties and thirties must be viewed in context." Just at the moment when the Great Depression "cried out for a radical political response, the British Labour Party seemed immobilised, frozen by the enormity of the challenge". The great weight of his criticism is of the Labour Party, not of Maxton. There is, I would argue, no doubt that at this time Brown's loyalties still lay with some sort of militant reformism. The book ends with a strong endorsement of Maxton's socialist vision.[12]

We have already looked at Brown's 1989 book, *Where There Is Greed*, a book in which he continues to condemn Thatcher and all her works and argues for a left Keynesian reformism. What was to transform him into a champion of neoliberalism?

Architect of New Labour?

One of the problems with bourgeois political science as it is practised in British universities is that it focuses on the shadows cast by the class struggle rather than on the class struggle itself. From this point of view New Labour is regarded primarily as an electoral phenomenon, as a necessary step if the Labour Party was to secure the votes of the Thatcherite middle class and have any chance of taking power. The problem with this particular view of politics is that it ignores, indeed helps conceal, the way that power is actually exercised in capitalist societies, and in particular it renders the ruling class invisible. The reality is that New Labour was the product of class struggle or, more to the point, of defeat in the class struggle. The emergence of New Labour was predicated on the defeat of the miners' strike and of the print unions (by Rupert Murdoch) at Wapping. These defeats registered a historic shift in the balance of class forces in Britain, and New Labour was a product of that shift. Whereas previous Labour

12: Brown, 1986, p298. Brown's *Maxton* compares favourably, for example, with William Knox's academic study, *James Maxton* (Knox, 1987). In his biography of Brown, Tom Bower argues that "in his head" Brown "understood how Maxton had undermined his ambitions for a better society by refusing to compromise to obtain power" (Bower, 2004, p51). On the contrary, in his book, Brown recognises that compromise led to MacDonald joining the Conservatives to help save capitalism at the expense of the working class.

governments had served as mediators between the trade unions and the capitalist ruling class, in the aftermath of defeat this was no longer a viable role.[13] After Thatcher's victories the ruling class no longer needed a party to mediate with the trade unions. If the Labour Party was to get into government again it needed to make itself acceptable to the ruling class—it needed to embrace Thatcherism and transform itself into the party of business, the party of globalisation. This was to become Brown's objective in the 1990s.

Defeat in the 1992 general election is often seen as decisive in transforming Brown from a reformist socialist into a neoliberal. In reality, it only consolidated developments that were already under way. The task of making Labour acceptable to big business began under Neil Kinnock, continued under John Smith and was merely carried forward to completion by Brown and Blair. Whereas, for Blair, the embrace of neoliberalism involved no great personal struggle because he had no previous beliefs to dispose of, for Brown it involved a deliberate decision to change sides. The effort, one suspects, damaged his personality. Nevertheless, for Brown, the class struggle was over and the capitalist class had won, both domestically and globally. Once he had come to terms with this, he embraced the neoliberal agenda with all the fervour of the recently converted. While there is no evidence to show that Brown was ever an admirer of the Soviet Union, at the very least, the victory of the United States in the Cold War would have reinforced this conclusion. And it was to the United States that he turned for the model of the New Jerusalem that beckoned humanity. It began with an enthusiasm for Bill Clinton, but has since generalised into a belief that the United States is the global future.[14]

What seems clear, looking back, is that it was Brown and not Blair who was the principal architect of New Labour. Blair was more the salesman. Brown was by far the most substantial of those pushing the neoliberal agenda within the Labour leadership. George Galloway has provided an interesting assessment of the calibre of the two men:

> Brown was a political titan compared to Blair; as deep as Blair was shallow, as serious as Blair was slick. Brown versus Blair was like a contest between

---

13: The best study of the Labour Party remains *The Labour Party: A Marxist History* (Cliff and Gluckstein, 1988). A new edition would be extremely useful.

14: As one recent sympathetic account has argued, Brown's "allegiance and enthusiasm for the American way is as great as Blair's" (Hassan, 2004, p211).

Bertrand Russell and Bob Monkhouse (whose motto, incidentally, could easily be Blair's: "Once you learn how to fake the sincerity, the rest is easy").[15]

This makes Brown's culpability all the greater.

Nevertheless, when Labour leader John Smith died from a heart attack in May 1994, Brown found himself outmanoeuvred for the party leadership by Blair.[16] He regarded himself as having been betrayed by people he had trusted, something he has never forgotten or forgiven. His position was still remarkably strong, however. He extracted from Blair an agreement (the Granita agreement) that gave him control of economic and social policy in a future Labour government, together with the promise that Blair would hand the prime ministership over to him in the not too distant future. This unprecedented agreement was testimony to the extent to which Brown was the driving force behind New Labour.

As shadow chancellor, Brown played the decisive role in remaking the Labour Party as New Labour, "the party of business". In speech after speech to business leaders, he insisted that Labour had accepted the results of Thatcherism, embraced market forces, adapted itself to the supposed realities of globalisation, and cherished the entrepreneur above all others. He even tried to invent a business background for himself. In November 1996 Brown told the Confederation of British Industry conference that "business is in my blood". His mother had been a company director and "I was brought up in an atmosphere where I knew exactly what was happening as far as business was concerned". He was, indeed he had always been, one of them. The only problem is that it was not true. As his mother subsequently admitted, she would never have called herself "a business woman": she had only ever done some "light administrative duties" for "a small family firm" and had given up the job when she married, three years before young Gordon was even born.[17] While there have been Labour politicians who have tried to invent working class backgrounds for themselves before, Brown is the first to try and invent a capitalist background.

15: Galloway, 2003, p 141.

16: Brown coedited a volume of tributes to John Smith (Brown and Naughtie, 1994). Brown's own contribution includes extensive quotations from Smith's speeches, attacking John Major's Tory government for sleaze, every word of which could apply to New Labour today. He even quotes Smith's condemnation of "the too-close relationship that has developed between this government and the private sector" (p96). He understandably does not mention the fact that he was criticising Smith for not moving far enough to the right when he died.

17: Peston, 2005, pp23-24.

"Britain is made for globalisation"

Since becoming chancellor of the exchequer Brown has regularly boasted to business audiences, both at home and abroad, of how New Labour has made Britain "the most business friendly environment in Europe", although on this particular occasion he did go on to acknowledge that there was still a lot to learn "from the entrepreneurial and flexible labour markets of the American economy". Some of these speeches have been collected in his recently published *Speeches 1997-2006*. They provide a wealth of evidence of the way in which he has transformed himself from a reformist socialist into a full-blown neoliberal. In a speech to the Social Market Foundation in February 2002, Brown admitted that making Britain a paradise for business and the rich had involved "a break from a hundred years of Labour history". Indeed, he went on to warn that "we need to affirm a yet more radical break with Labour's past". Whereas, in the past, the left had seen markets as "leading to inequality, insecurity and injustice", now he could "assert with confidence that promoting the market economy helps us to achieve our goals of a stronger economy and a fairer society". He actually went on in the same speech to accuse the Conservatives of not being pro-market enough. It had been necessary to make "fundamental changes" to Labour Party policy, but he was now confident that Britain would "be a beacon for the world, where enterprise and fairness march forward together".

Brown was even prepared to pay tribute to the contribution made by Margaret Thatcher, no longer "the betrayer of Britain's future", but the country's saviour. In a speech made in July 2004, he was fulsome in his praise: "She recognised the need for Britain to reinvent itself and rediscover a new and vital self-confidence". She, he went on, "understood that we could gain strength from the glories of our past which could point the way to a glorious future". While Thatcher had made mistakes, nevertheless there had been many "advances, achievements and important changes". In this same speech, he recited some of "the real achievements" of Britain's glorious past, which included the country's "imperial mission" and the fact that Britain was once "centre to the world's largest empire—the global economy of the day".

What was needed, according to Brown, was not just the transformation of the Labour Party into "the party of business", but the transformation of British culture. In July 2001 he urged that "a truly entrepreneurial culture" should be created in Britain. He went on:

> We want every young person to hear about business and enterprise in schools; every college student to be made aware of the opportunities in business and

to start a business; every teacher to be able to communicate the virtues and potential of business and enterprise.

Socialism, for Brown (and he still used the word to trade union and Labour Party audiences), had become "the creation of a deeper and wider entrepreneurial culture where enterprise is truly open to all". One can imagine the outcry if any previous Labour government had ever suggested that schools should inculcate socialist values or trade union solidarity!

Brown returned to this theme later the following year (December 2002) in a speech to the Growing Business Awards. New Labour, he boasted, had "done a lot to make businessmen and women role models for young people" and to "make successful business leaders role models in every community". They were creating "a wider and deeper enterprise culture". In effect, British culture had to be "Americanised".

On 2 December 2005, addressing business leaders at the Advancing Enterprise Conference in London, Brown welcomed the event as "a concrete expression of our partnership". They had "a shared agenda" and New Labour could be relied on to "take it forward". He was, he told his audience, particularly looking forward to the session on "our educational priorities" that was being led by that great educationalist Terry Leahy, the chief executive officer of Tesco. Brown promised them that "if we work together then I believe we shall prove that Britain is made for globalisation and globalisation is made for Britain".[18]

The politics of spin

One point worth considering is how it is that Brown has still managed to appear to some people (admittedly a declining number) as being to the left of Blair. To a considerable extent this has been the result of "spin", reinforcing wishful thinking, although it also derives from a very deliberate effort, in which Brown has played an important part, to locate New Labour within the Labour Party tradition, arguing that it is a development of "Croslandism". Let us consider the question of "spin" first.

In 1998, in what one commentator described as a "frenzy of privatisation" that "bordered on the messianic", Brown proposed the privatisation of the Post Office.[19] This was opposed by the then secretary of state for trade and industry, Peter Mandelson, who instead proposed that it be retained in the public sector, but be given commercial "freedom". In this

---

18: For this and the other quoted speeches, see Stevenson, 2006, pp26, 34, 35, 37, 59, 63, 64, 124, 125, 127, 133, 146-147, 342, 370.

19: Jenkins, 2006, pp258-259.

particular battle Mandelson carried the day. Charlie Whelan, Brown's press officer, gave two alternative briefings, "one to right-leaning papers claiming that Mandelson had funked a desirable privatisation of the Post Office, and another to left-leaning papers and the trade unions, that Brown had 'saved' the Post Office from privatisation".[20]

Much the same story can be told with regard to the minimum wage. This is inevitably championed as one of the great achievements of New Labour by its supporters. Brown, however, only agreed to it because experience in the United States, where there has been a minimum wage since 1938, showed that it was not a serious inconvenience to business. Indeed in the United States the minimum wage has proven to be perfectly compatible with the sustained attack on working class living standards and workplace conditions that has been under way since the 1980s. All that had to be ensured was that the minimum wage was set low enough. In Britain, as Simon Jenkins observed, it was set so low "as to be almost invisible".[21] The man responsible for this was Gordon Brown.

When it was proposed that the minimum wage should be set at £3.70 an hour, Brown insisted that the most business could afford was £3.50. In the face of his intransigence, TUC general secretary John Monks, certainly no militant, intervened. Monks, according to Tom Bower, was "puzzled that Brown, posing as the champion of the working class and diligently attending the birthday parties of the movement's leaders, could suggest that the economy was unable to afford the increase". Monks warned Brown that if he did not drop his opposition he would make it public and thereby "put an end to Brown's bid to become the Labour Party's next leader". Brown retreated, but once again Charlie Whelan spun the story to his advantage. Stephen Byers, who had replaced Mandelson as secretary of state for trade and industry, had publicly advocated a rate of £3.60 an hour. Brown threw his weight behind this. Whelan now briefed journalists that Brown had always favoured £3.70, but had been forced "to compromise with Byers...and accept a £3.60 minimum wage". Brown did still insist, however, that the full rate should be payable, not from age 21 as the Low Pay Unit (LPU) urged, but from age 22. When George Bain of the LPU told him that only 8,000 young people were affected, Brown remained adamant, telling Bain, "I won't allow 21 year olds to be classed as adults".[22]

20: Macintyre, 2000, pp474-475.

21: Jenkins, 2006, p257.

22: Bower, 2004, pp 276, 294-295.

"Croslandism" and New Labour

While "spin" is the main factor in accounting for whatever remnants of a left reputation Brown still has, he has also been centrally involved in the effort to identify New Labour as a species of "Croslandism". This fascination with the intellectual standard-bearer of the right wing of the Labour Party in the 1950s and 1960s is rather sudden. In the "anthology of Socialism", *Values, Visions and Voices*, that Brown co-edited with Tony Wright in 1995, there are only four contributions from Crosland's writings out of nearly 200 selected extracts. Even that intellectual giant Neil Kinnock has five contributions![23] By early 1997, however, Brown had decided to lay claim to "Crosland's rich and lasting legacy to Labour". He was aware of the need to at least maintain the pretence that New Labour still had some connection with "Old Labour", even if it was with the Labour right. He fastened on "Croslandism" as the way to achieve this. In a speech that was later published in an edited volume, *Crosland and New Labour*, Brown emphasised the way that Crosland had placed "equality" at the centre of the Socialist project. This was what New Labour was all about, Brown argued: "everyone should have the chance to bridge the gap between what they are and what they have it in themselves to become". Brown tried to update Crosland's understanding of equality with a more modern New Labour definition: "employment opportunity for all", "continuing and lifelong educational opportunity", "genuine access to culture" and "a redistribution of power that offers people real control over the decisions that affect their lives".

The great advantage of this updating of the definition of equality is that it is perfectly compatible with "inequality". And, moreover, one of the

23: Brown and Wright, 1995. *Values, Visions and Voices* is an appalling book, where any hint of class struggle has been altogether exorcised. In its pages Sheila Rowbotham rubs shoulders with Ramsay Macdonald, George Orwell with Neil Kinnock, and William Morris with Hugh Gaitskell. There is, of course, nothing from Karl Marx or Frederick Engels, both of whom had quite a lot to say about Britain. Indeed the Marxist tradition is effectively suppressed. Still, despite every effort to make the collection as inoffensive as possible, some moments of embarrassment still creep in. There is an extract from an interview with Dennis Potter where he lambasts the *Sun* newspaper: "Just pick up a copy of the *Sun*. Is this Britain? Is this what we've done to ourselves? How can the people who work on that paper go home and face their families without a sense of shame" (pp149-150). This was, of course, before Blair and Brown had had to abase themselves before Rupert Murdoch, had both written for the *Sun* and had made it New Labour's favourite newspaper. Indeed, on 1 May 2007, May Day no less, Brown actually had an article in the *Sun* on "Blair's decade of achievement". Here he identified Blair's most memorable success as being "how we stood shoulder to shoulder with America" after 9/11. This was not written to reassure *Sun* readers of his continuing support for the United States, but to reassure Rupert Murdoch. Dennis Potter, of course, named the cancer that was to eventually kill him "Rupert Murdoch".

ways that power is to be redistributed is through the market! What Brown is about is substituting "equality of opportunity" for equality of wealth and income—that everyone should have an equal opportunity to become rich. This, of course, has a particular attraction for today's Parliamentary Labour Party. To be fair though, Brown does concede that "even in a global marketplace", it might still prove necessary to "address wealth and income inequalities". "I believe", he wrote, "that these inequalities can be justified only if they are in the interests of the least fortunate." This truly original contribution to socialist thought looks remarkably like the good old "trickle-down" effect championed by the Thatcherites. At the very least, it leaves him with considerable leeway. Indeed, judging from his performance as chancellor, he has yet to find any of the increasing levels of inequality in New Labour Britain that are not in the interests of "the least fortunate".[24]

More recently, in 2006, Brown contributed an introduction to a new edition of Anthony Crosland's *The Future of Socialism*. First published in 1956, this book was the intellectual mainstay of Labour's right wing, the bible of Gaitskellite revisionism. Now, 50 years later, Brown celebrated its publication as "a decisive moment in post-war Labour history" and praised its "freshness" and "relevance". What Crosland showed was that Socialism "was about the dignity of human beings and the equal right of each individual to realise their potential in a supportive community". Socialism was "opportunity for all". All of Brown's earlier campaigning for "the redistribution of income and wealth from rich to poor" was effectively repudiated.[25]

This supposed commitment to equality has become central to New Labour's claim to be a party of "the centre-left". They are absolutely passionate about it, so much so that, when it was proposed to include an explicit unambiguous commitment to equality in the Labour Party's new Clause IV in 1995, Peter Mandelson had it removed.[26] Nevertheless "equality" continues to be a tricky concept, encouraging all sorts of unhelpful ideas and attitudes. It has to be continually redefined so as to pose no threat to the rich and the super-rich. The most promising redefinition so far has been that provided by the Equalities Review, set up by Blair in 2005. A panel consisting of Trevor Phillips; Sir Robert Kerslake, the chief executive of Sheffield Council; and Dame Judith Mayhew Jonas, a top lawyer who was

24: Brown, 1999, pp36, 41, 43, 44.

25: Crosland, Anthony, 2006, pp vii, viii. Tony Blair had no interest whatsoever in any of this laying claim to a Labour heritage, indeed in 2004 he contributed a chapter to a collection entitled *Neo-Conservatism* (Stelzer, 2004). Other contributors included Margaret Thatcher, Condoleezza Rice and various luminaries of the US Republican right.

26: Macintyre, 2000, pp316-317.

made a dame for her services to the City, deliberated at great expense. They came up with something so spurious as to take the breath away:

> An equal society protects and promotes equal, real freedom and substantive opportunity to live in the ways people value and would choose so that everyone can flourish. An equal society recognises people's different needs, situations and goals and removes the barriers that limit what people can do and can be.[27]

This is New Labour at its most intellectually rigorous.

"Old Labour"

What would Anthony Crosland himself have made of all this? Crosland, after a brief flirtation with Stalinism at university, positioned himself on the right of the Labour Party in the early years of the Second World War. As early as 1941, while serving in the army, he had stated his intention to be "the modern Bernstein" who would defeat Marxist influence within the labour movement.[28] *The Future of Socialism* was his attempt at realising this ambition. What is crucial for our purposes is that Crosland's arguments were premised on a belief that capitalism had been defeated, tamed, fundamentally changed, and that all that remained for the left was the implementation of a programme of democratic reforms, including "democratic equality". New Labour is founded on the very opposite premise, on the belief that capitalism has triumphed and that the left has been defeated once and for all. There is nothing in Crosland's writings to suggest that he would have responded to this defeat in the way that Brown and New Labour have. From this point of view Roy Hattersley, a vocal opponent of New Labour, can be best seen as Crosland's heir. One obvious consequence of the difference in context is worth pointing out: New Labour is far to the right of anything that Crosland and the Labour right would ever have contemplated in the 1950s, 1960s and 1970s. Indeed, New Labour is to the right of the Conservatives in this period.

Interestingly, Crosland had a much more robust attitude to equality, or "democratic equality" as he called it, than anything evidenced by New Labour. While Brown has tried to redefine equality as a watered down equality of opportunity, Crosland explicitly ruled that out. Indeed, he described equality of opportunity as "the doctrine of Tory radicalism". What Crosland, a Labour right winger, called for were "measures...to

27: Equalities Review, 2007, p7.
28: Jeffreys, 1999, p16.

equalise the distribution of rewards and privileges so as to diminish the degree of class stratification, the injustice of large inequalities and the collective discontent".[29] This certainly did not amount to socialism, but nevertheless, it has nothing in common with New Labour.

In 1962 Crosland published another book, *The Conservative Enemy*. Here he was even more forthright than in the earlier volume. According to Crosland, inequality in Britain was "still greater than should be tolerated in a democracy" (it was less than today) and he complained of the rich receiving rewards "far higher than any civilised person should want or need" (they received considerably less than today). He urged that a future Labour government "must grapple with the maldistribution of property". He was particularly critical of the concentration of newspaper ownership which was a threat to "a healthy democracy" and was contemptuous of "the more depraved and poisonous of the capitalist press". This was, of course, long before the advent of Rupert Murdoch. In short, Crosland would not have recognised New Labour as Labour at all.[30]

Crosland talked more radically than he was ever prepared to act. Most famously, while secretary of state for education he had remarked: "If it's the last thing I do, I'm going to destroy every fucking grammar school in England".[31] In practice, he rejected the compulsory introduction of comprehensive schemes in favour of "persuasion", which is why there are still grammar schools today. Similarly, while he argued that the state should take over the public schools and democratise them, he never actually did anything about it when in office. He certainly never suggested that the public schools should be invited to take over state schools as New Labour does today. Nevertheless, during the International Monetary Fund (IMF) crisis that crippled James Callaghan's Labour government in 1976, Crosland was one of those arguing for rejection of the IMF's demand for cuts in government spending. What is the point of the government surviving, he complained, "if Labour measures can't be implemented". Callaghan's government, he went on, "is the most right wing Labour government we've had for years".[32] He had not, as they say, seen anything yet.

New Labour in power

Brown's wholehearted commitment to markets, globalisation and today's rampant capitalism was made absolutely clear to the whole world by the

29: Crosland, Anthony, 2006, pp173,191.
30: Crosland, Anthony, 1962, pp7, 28, 37, 211,212.
31: Crosland, Susan, 1982, p148.
32: Meredith, 2006, p245.

decision to make the Bank of England independent. He was showing the capitalist class, both at home and abroad, that he was their man and that New Labour was their government. As one sympathetic historian observed, "At a stroke much of the political economy of the Labour Party since 1945 was abandoned".[33] It is worth remembering that at least one of the reasons Clement Attlee's government had nationalised the bank had been because of its role in the 1931 financial crisis, which had brought down Ramsay MacDonald's government and seen him defect to the Conservatives. The bank had represented the interests of international finance, rather than the interests of the Labour government. This was never to be allowed to happen again, although the reality was that the bank always retained considerable independence. What Brown's action signalled was that New Labour would never find itself in conflict with international finance. Brown had out-Thatchered the Thatcherites. His "great political coup" successfully positioned New Labour to the right of the Conservatives.[34] Brown was committed to what can usefully be described as "globalisation in one country".[35] What followed was Brown's rush to privatise as he came out as "Thatcherism's most coveted St Paul". As Simon Jenkins observes:

> Brown tore up all he had said in opposition and hurled himself into a frenzy of privatisation, scouring the cupboard for things to sell. He faced down union opposition by seeking to dispose of air traffic control, the Royal Mint, the Commonwealth Development Corporation, and Tote on-course betting. The privatisation of the Post Office...was halted in 1998 only because its departmental sponsor was Brown's sworn enemy, Mandelson... Privatisation spread even to Whitehall. The Inland Revenue sold its entire estate to a property developer, John Ritblat, who transferred it, quite legally, to an off-shore tax haven... The Treasury even sold and then leased back its own headquarters in Parliament Square.

Brown's frenzy of privatisation has yet to run its course. His supposed opposition to privatisation in education and the NHS is largely a matter of spin and of the factionalism within the New Labour government. Brown has carried big business into areas of the public sector that the Thatcherites never dreamed of.

33: Brivati, 1999, p 245.

34: Keegan, 2004. Keegan emphasises the American influence on the decision, quoting Brown thanking Alan Greenspan, then chair of the US federal reserve, for the discussions on "how central bank independence would work for Britain" (p156).

35: The term is not original, but comes from Hirst and Thompson, 2000.

Jenkins goes on to write of Brown's privatisation of "public borrowing" through Private Finance Initiatives (PFI) and Public-Private Partnerships. As he points out:

> By July 2003 Brown was boasting of the completion of 450 PFI projects, including 34 hospitals, 239 schools, 34 fire and police stations, 12 prisons and 12 waste projects. The NHS had by 2005 borrowed some £6 billion for PFI schemes, with a further £11 billion in the pipeline. By the mid-2000s virtually all health investment was being financed by the private sector.[36]

What Brown had done was to find a way to make government spending attractive to and profitable for big business. The inevitable end result will be a public sector, if that is still the right term, that will be effectively in the hands of capital. The first charge on revenue will inevitably be payment of the debts incurred by PFI. In the NHS this makes the introduction of charges a certainty, and one can predict with considerable confidence an attempt by a Brown government to introduce such a scheme, limited to begin with, but preparing the way for later expansion.[37]

One other thing that Jenkins points out is New Labour's effective privatisation of civil service functions. Instead of turning to the civil service for advice, New Labour turns to private consultants. This is not a small matter. Whereas in 1995 £300 million was spent on consultants by the Conservative government, by 2003 the cost was £1.7 billion and by 2004 £2.5 billion. Indeed, from 1997 to 2006 New Labour's spending on consultants has been estimated at £70 billion.[38]

Why has the Labour Party allowed all this? Well, first of all, many party members, including lifelong members, have voted with their feet and resigned in disgust and despair. Those who remain inhabit a party that is radically different from the Labour Party in 1990, let alone 1964 or 1945. As Stephen Ingle has pointed out, the new intake of Labour MPs in 1997 "contained as many millionaires as it did manual workers". Indeed, he goes on to put New labour into some sort of historical perspective: "The New Labour government is less representative of organised Labour than was the

36: Jenkins, 2006, pp259-260, 272. His chapter on Brown is simply entitled "Gordon Brown, Thatcherite".

37: New Labour's foremost academic apologist, Anthony Giddens, calls precisely for "user-charging" in his advice to a Brown government: Giddens, 2007, pp83-84. He comforts fellow Blairites with the assurance that while "Brown's political philosophy is often said to be to the left of that of Tony Blair—meaning that he leans more towards the Old Left... his speeches and writings over the past few years reveal nothing of the kind" (p35).

38: Jenkins, 2006, p266.

Liberal Party of Campbell Bannerman and Asquith".[39] The Labour left has never been weaker, and it has been completely unable to seriously hinder, let alone stop, the drive to the right.

What of relations between Brown and Blair? Throughout Blair's period of office one of the most important features of his government has been the power exercised by the chancellor of the exchequer. To a considerable extent, Blair was effectively excluded from social and economic policy making, with Brown famously refusing to even discuss the budget with him. This unprecedented situation reflected the strength of Brown's position within New Labour, but, for all that, Brown has never felt strong enough to bring Blair down and at the same time ensure his own succession. Over the introduction of student "top-up fees", for example, Brown covertly encouraged backbench opposition, but in the end backed down. On Blair's part, there seems little doubt that if the Iraq War had been the triumph he expected it to be, then the overthrow of Saddam Hussein would have been swiftly followed by the overthrow of Gordon Brown. Far from strengthening Blair so as to enable him to remove Brown from the Treasury, the war mortally damaged him. It is the Iraq War that in the end has made it possible for Brown to take over from Blair.

It is important to recognise, however, that this bitter struggle within the government has not been over any fundamental policy differences, between a left and a right within New Labour. Brown and Blair's mutual hatred has been personal rather than political. The differences between them are more differences of style than of substance. Brown, for example, does not share Blair's relaxed attitude towards political corruption, something he evidenced as far back as the Ecclestone affair.[40]

But those who believe, against all the evidence, that Brown was not fully behind the invasion of Afghanistan and Iraq are deluding themselves. One recent New Labourite discussion of a Brown government's likely foreign policy argues that we should "expect small but symbolic statements" distancing themselves "from aspects of Bush's foreign

39: Ingle, 2000, p157.

40: Blair rode into office on a white charger, without anyone realising it had been given to him in return for a favour. The character of the man was demonstrated immediately by the Ecclestone scandal. In return for a £1 million donation to party funds and the promise of more, the government exempted Formula One motor racing from the ban on tobacco advertising. Darts and snooker were not exempted. This was one of the most blatant acts of political corruption in modern times, carried out by a man and a government elected on an anti-sleaze ticket. Blair defended himself by famously arguing that he was "a pretty straight sort of guy". Brown, to his horror, was caught out on Radio 4's *Today* programme, having to lie to cover up for Blair. See Rawnsley, 2001, pp97-98.

policy—Guantanamo, the practice of extraordinary rendition and US hostility towards the UN". Maybe. It goes on to argue that as far as a US attack on Iran is concerned, "it is almost inconceivable that a Brown government would support such action".[41] This is so much wishful thinking. It shows the extent to which people still have illusions in Brown. Indeed, it is inconceivable that a Brown government will not support the attack on Iran when it comes. New Labour and the Conservative opposition are both married to the United States, for better and increasingly for worse, and will support US actions, either overtly or, if it is too politically damaging, covertly. There is no comfort whatsoever to be taken from developments inside the Labour Party at the present time. Hope lies outside.

41: Mepham, 2006.

References

Bower, Tom, 2004, *Gordon Brown*, (HarperPerennial).

Brivati, Brian, 1999, "Gordon Brown" in Kevin Jefferys (ed), *Labour Forces: from Ernest Bevin to Gordon Brown* (IB Taurus).

Brown, Gordon, (ed) 1975, *The Red Paper On Scotland* (Edinburgh).

Brown, Gordon, 1983, "Introduction" to Gordon Brown and Robin Cook (eds), *Scotland: The Real Divide* (Mainstream).

Brown, Gordon, 1986, *Maxton: A Biography* (Mainstream).

Brown, Gordon, 1989, *Where There Is Greed: Margaret Thatcher and the Betrayal of Britain's Future* (Mainstream).

Brown, Gordon, 1999, "Equality—Then and Now", in Dick Leonard (ed), *Crosland and New Labour* (Macmillan).

Brown, Gordon, and James Naughtie (eds), 1994, *John Smith: Life and Soul of the Party* (Mainstream).

Brown, Gordon, and Tony Wright (eds), 1995, *Values, Visions and Voices* (Mainstream).

Callinicos, Alex, and Mike Simons, 1985, *The Great Strike* (Bookmarks).

Carvel, John, 2004, "Super-rich Have Doubled Their Money Under Labour", the *Guardian*, 8 December 2004, http://politics.guardian.co.uk/economics/story/0,11268,1368505,00.html

Cassidy, John, 2006, "Murdoch's Game", the *New Yorker*, 16 October 2006, www.newyorker.com/archive/2006/10/16/061016fa_fact1

Cliff, Tony, and Donny Gluckstein, 1988, *The Labour Party: A Marxist History* (Bookmarks).

Crosland, Anthony, 1962, *The Conservative Enemy* (Cape).

Crosland, Anthony, 2006, *The Future of Socialism* (Constable and Robinson).

Crosland, Susan, 1982, *Tony Crosland* (Jonathan Cape).

Equalities Review, 2007, *Fairness and Freedom: The Final Report of the Equalities Review*, available from: www.renewal.net/Documents/RNET/Research/Fairnessfreedomfinal.pdf

Galloway, George, 2003, *I'm Not The Only One* (Penguin).

Giddens, Anthony, 2007, *Over To You, Mr Brown: How Labour Can Win Again* (Polity).

Hassan, Gerry, 2004, "Labour's Journey from Socialism to Social Democracy: A Case Study of Gordon Brown's Political Thought", in Gerry Hassan (ed), *The Scottish Labour Party* (Edinburgh University Press).

Hirst, Paul, and Geoff Thompson, 2000, "Globalization in one Country: The Peculiarities of the British", in *Economy and Society*, volume 29, number 3 (August 2000).

HM Treasury, 2006, press release, 21 March 2006, www.hm-treasury.gov.uk/newsroom_and_speeches/press/2006/press_19_2006.cfm

Ingle, Stephen, 2000, *The British Party System* (Continuum).

Institute for Fiscal Studies, 2007, press release, 28 April 2007, www.ifs.org.uk/pr/hbai07_pr.pdf

Jeffreys, Kevin, 1999, *Anthony Crosland* (Politicos).

Jenkins, Simon, 2006, *Thatcher and Sons: A Revolution in Three Acts* (Allen Lane).

Keegan, William, 2004, *The Prudence of Mr Gordon Brown* (Wiley).

Knox, Willian, 1987, *James Maxton* (Manchester Univesity Press).

Macintyre, Donald, 2000, *Mandelson and the Making of New Labour* (HarperCollins).

Mepham, David, 2006, "Gordon's world", in *Prospect Magazine*, 124 (July 2006), www.prospect-magazine.co.uk/article_details.php?id=7535

Meredith, Stephen, 2006, "Mr Crosland's Nightmare: New Labour and Equality in Historical Perspective", in the *British Journal of Politics and International Relations*, volume 8, number 2 (May 2006).

Peston, Robert, 2005, *Brown's Britain* (Short Books).

Rawnsley, Andrew, 2001, *Servants of the People: The Inside Story of New Labour* (Penguin).

Routledge, Paul, 1998, *Gordon Brown* (Simon & Schuster).
Self, Abigail, and Linda Zealey (eds), 2007, *Social Trends 37* (Office for National Statistics), www.statistics.gov.uk/downloads/theme_social/Social_Trends37/Social_Trends_37.pdf
Stelzer, Irwin (ed), 2004, *Neo-Conservatism* (Altantic).
Stelzer, Irwin, 2007, "When Brown Moves To No 10, He Will Need His Closest Ally Next Door", the *Guardian*, 27 February 2007, www.guardian.co.uk/commentisfree/story/0,,2022216,00.html
Stevenson, Wilf (ed), 2006, *Gordon Brown: Speeches 1997-2006* (Bloomsbury).

Gordon Brown: the economic "record"

Chris Harman

As Tony Blair departed and Gordon Brown prepared to take over as prime minister one great myth was boomed out by New Labour's propaganda machine—that Brown had achieved a "miracle" for the British economy. He achieved no less than the "longest period of sustained economic growth for more than 200 years...the longest period of sustained growth since the beginning of the industrial revolution".[1] It was a myth that most mainstream commentators avoided puncturing, eager as they are to see the major continental economies follow in Britain footsteps and embracing measures of "labour market flexibility", "market testing", privatisation and "contracting out" in the public sector, and longer working hours.

Yet the claim itself is simply false.

The years 1948 to 1973 witnessed continual economic growth. The period was characterised by a "stop-go" pattern—but there was positive growth even in the "stop" phases. And the growth was faster than under New Labour. From 1949 to 1973, the UK economy grew at average rate of 3 percent per annum. It is true that growth averaged 3.2 percent a year in the first three years of New Labour, but after that it fell to an average of 2.4 percent a year for 2001 to 2006.[2]

The recent growth has not been sufficient to cover national expenditure. This is shown by what has happened to Britain's trade figures. In

1: Brown, 2004.

2: McMorrow and Roeger, 2007, p82.

March the UK imported £7 billion more in goods than it exported—a trade deficit of more than 6 percent of GDP. Under the conditions of modern capitalism a national economy can continue to operate on that basis for a time (particularly, as with the British economy, if it has higher interest rates than most of its competitors and attracts foreign money eager to benefit from these). But such luck cannot continue indefinitely.

In some ways more significant than total growth rates are those per hour worked. These give some indication of the possibilities that are open to people to enjoy better lives—although whether they do depends on what the growth consists of and how it is divided between classes. The rate of GNP growth per hour worked was lower from 1995 to 2004 than during the previous 45 years (figure 1).

Figure 1: Annual growth of GNP per hour worked[3]

1950-75	2.86%
1973-95	2.48%
1995-2004	2.20%

In 2004 the UK's GNP per hour worked was *lower* than in France, Germany, Denmark, Austria, Belgium, the Netherlands and Norway. As Nicholas Croft observed, the UK has "lower employment protection than elsewhere in Europe...less product market regulation than in its European peer group... However, it has a substantial productivity gap with the European leaders, and the rate of growth of UK labour productivity was only 2.20 percent per year 1995-2004—hardly tigerish".[4]

The slow level of productivity growth translates into an even lower growth in real disposable income—by only 1.3 percent a year over the past three years, and by just 0.8 percent last year. That was the lowest increase since the recession of 1982, and we are not currently in a recession. The figures for household income are even worse. This figure has been rising only 0.35 percent a year since 2001-2002, and is actually falling slightly this year.[5]

3: Croft, 2007, p70.
4: Croft, 2007, p72.
5: Giles, 2007.

The result has been an increasing tendency for people to cover their personal spending by reliance on debt (figure 2).

Figure 2: Total UK personal debt (£ billions)
Source: Bank of England

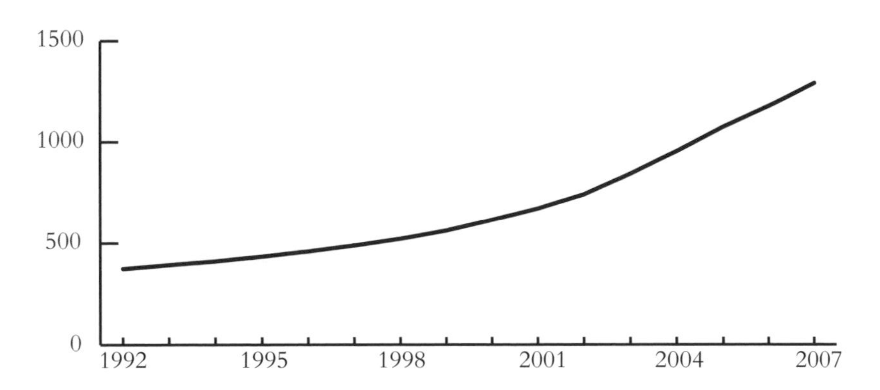

This is the background to Brown's attempt to hold public sector pay rises down to 2 percent or less, at a time when the Retail Price Index is over 4 percent.

But averages themselves to do not say what is happening to the mass of workers, since they include the incomes of the rich as well as the rest of the population. The disposable income figures, for instance, are boosted considerably by the huge bonuses paid to those on top salaries in the City and Canary Wharf.

One feature of New Labour which constitutes clear continuity with the Tory years is the high level of inequality.

Figure 3: Ratio of top 10 percent of incomes to bottom 10 percent[6]

UK	France	Germany	US
13.5	9.1	6.9	15.9

6: Panic, 2007.

But not only is the level of inequality higher than under continental capitalism, it has also resumed its rise under New Labour. "Income inequality is slightly higher under most measures than it was in 1996-7".[7] Figure 4 shows how the most widespread measure of inequality, the Gini coefficient, continued rising in the early Blair years. It then fell slightly (although only to the highest point under Major) and, after 2004, it started rising again.[8]

Figure 4: The UK Gini coefficient

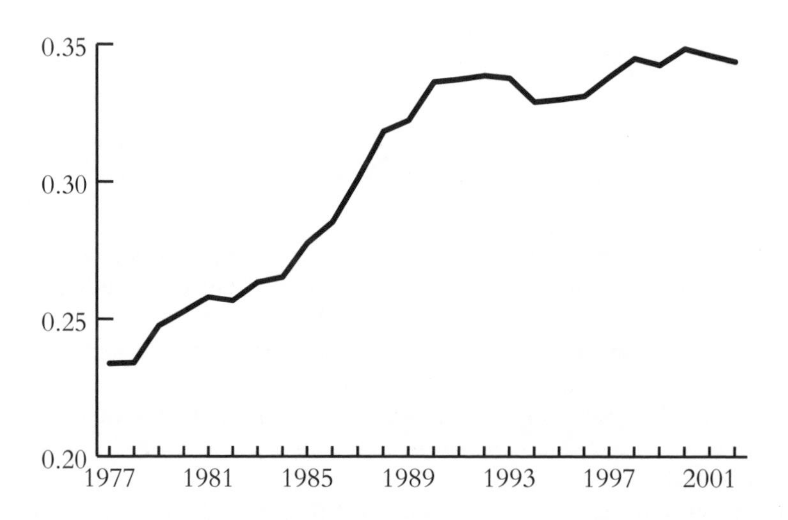

A mood of revulsion against Thatcherism brought New Labour to office in 1997, and in response the new government introduced some mild measures to counter the worst poverty. The combination of slow average household expenditure growth and increased inequality has had the effect of countering these measures. At no point during Brown's spell as chancellor has a serious dent been made in the poverty figures.

7: Institute for Fiscal Studies, 2007.

8: Institute for Fiscal Studies, 2007, p19.

One figure that even normally sycophantic media commentators have been unable to ignore is the numbers of children in poverty. This rose this year by 200,000, after falling a little (by just a sixth) between 1996-7 and 2004-5. Less commented on is that the proportion of working age non-parents in poverty has risen to a level above that of 1996-7.[9] The total number of working age adults on less than 60 percent of the median household income is now 7.1 million, as against 6.8 million ten years ago.

Reducing poverty is claimed as one of New Labour's great achievements. Its other is that it has avoided a recession. This can, however, hardly be ascribed to any economic skills on Brown's part. On taking office as chancellor ten years ago he scrapped one of the few powers left to the government to control the tempo of economic activity by handing control of interest rates to the Bank of England.

During the long boom from the 1940s to the mid-1970s governments claimed they could use a range of measures to influence the economy—controls on bank lending, controls on consumer credit, controls over foreign exchange transactions, changes to consumer taxation, and raising and lowering government expenditure. Most of these measures were abandoned by the Thatcher and Major governments—leading to complaints from left of centre critics that they were "one club golfers", relying on interest rates alone. It was this power that Brown gave up, at the same time as ruling out for the first three years of his tenure any rise in government spending.

So the fact that Britain avoided the backwash of the 1997 Asian crisis and the 2001 US recession can hardly be ascribed to measures taken by Brown. His claim that Bank of England independence played a role should be laughable, since the independent Federal Reserve in the US could neither control the "irrational exuberance" of the dotcom bubble of the late 1990s nor ward off the recession which hit in 2001 (writing off $1,000 billion of new technology investment even before 9/11).

In fact, the most economically devastating feature of the Thatcher and Major years continued unchecked during Brown's time in the Treasury—the destruction of manufacturing jobs. Over the ten years some 1.5 million jobs have gone, a third of the 1996 total. By the beginning of this year there were only 2.97 million jobs in the UK's manufacturing industries.[10] The decline averaged around 3,000 a week during Brown's

9: Institute for Fiscal Studies, 2007, p29.
10: Office for National Statistics figure.

period "running" the economy. His "skills" have not prevented manufacturing from experiencing a stop-go pattern as marked as any in the past. Manufacturing output fell by 4 percent in 1991, only a little less than the 6 percent fall in the recession ten years earlier.

The recovery afterwards brought output back to roughly the same level as ten years ago—and for that matter 20 years ago. There has not been absolute "deindustrialisation". Restructuring has left certain industries intact—and the workers in them as potentially powerful as ever. So while Rover has disappeared and Ford UK shrunk, the Nissan, Toyota and Honda plants produce nearly as many cars as the old firms ever did.[11] British capitalism retains some important manufacturing firms—BAE, Rolls Royce and GlaxoSmithKline, for instance.

But this is little comfort for those who have lost their jobs. They face the same sense of devastation as in the Thatcher-Major period. So "almost a quarter of the workers at collapsed car maker MG Rover are still without jobs...while one in five of those in work were earning the equivalent of the minimum wage".[12] Only "16,000 new jobs have been created in former colliery areas against a target of 42,000 by 2012 after 250,000 jobs disappeared... Average household incomes are £50 a week lower than regional averages and more than 250,000 people in coalfields are claiming incapacity benefits".[13]

The decline of employment in the old industrial sectors finds expression in the secret story of Britain's unemployment figures. According to the official story, the unemployment rate was 5.5 percent in March this year, with 1.69 million unemployed. In every one of Brown's budget speeches in recent years this has been contrasted with figures in countries such as France, with its 9 percent rate.

However, what is missing from the official figures is something Labour made much of when in opposition—the number of people thrown out of work who have been put on to disability benefits by dole office managers under orders to keep their figures down. In 2002 they accounted for 7 percent of the workforce (as compared to 0.2 percent in France). Studies suggest about a third of them "want work" but cannot get it. If these were included, Britain's unemployment rate would increase "by 1.5 percent in the lowest unemployment areas, rising to 4.2

11: Car production reached an all-time peak of 1,750,000 in 1999; it is now down to just over 1,500,000. See SMTT, 2006, and Harper, 2006, table 5.2.

12: According to an Amicus survey of 1,750 union members. See Milner, 2007.

13: Report by SQW consultants, summarised in *Financial Times*, 3 March 2007.

percent in the highest unemployment areas".[14] This would still produce an unemployment rate a little lower than the French one, but not massively lower.

The main difference would seem to be that unemployment in France is more concentrated among the young, with 20 percent unemployed; in Britain the youth unemployment figure is closer to 10 percent, with half a million 18 to 24 year olds out of work, 70,000 more than in 1998.[15] At the same time Britain has a higher level of real (even if unmeasured) unemployment of around one million among those aged over 50.

For all Brown's boasts about the "dynamism" of the British economy compared, for instance, to the French, "British business consistently spends less on R&D than its competitors in the US, France and Germany. In 2002, as part of its Lisbon Agenda, the European Council established a target for R&D investment in the EU of 3 percent of GDP by 2010. In 2003 the UK spent only 1.9 percent of GDP, a fall since the early 1990s, when it was around 2.1 percent of GDP".[16]

But what explains the failure of job losses and recessions in manufacturing to feed over into the rest of the economy as they did in 1974, 1980 and 1991?

Here again, the "skills" of Brown are not responsible, nor are the wonders of deregulation and "labour market flexibility". The major driving force has been the unexpected capacity of London to emerge as the major financial hub mediating between the US, Europe and the Far East. The slowdown in industrial accumulation in North America, Europe and Japan over the past 30 years has seen a flourishing of all sorts of speculative activity centred on stock exchanges, debt and, most recently, hedge funds. London's geographic position has made it an ideal base for this.

"Finance and business services made up almost a third (33.0 percent) of the UK economy in 2004 with gross value added of £344.5 billion",[17] and by 1999 new investment in this sector was already three or four times higher than in manufacturing and other industries.[18] Spending on financial skyscrapers and computers was deemed much more important than on producing goods that might satisfy human needs.

14: Webster, 2002.
15: Field, 2007.
16: Nesta, 2006.
17: ONS, 2006.
18: See the chart in Millward, 2003, p 249.

One by-product of this was an in increase in the number of jobs in this completely non-productive sector of the economy. "Financial and business services now account for about one in five jobs in the UK, compared with about one in ten in 1981".[19] "Finance" refers to those who work directly for the banking sectors, and "business services" to a mix of related tasks such as legal, advertising, insurance, office cleaning, leasing, call centres, personnel and recruitment, and security.

Effectively, over the past ten years 1.5 million manufacturing jobs have disappeared, while between one million and 1.5 million "financial and business services" jobs have been created. Catering for the needs of these new workers has in turn provided a market for a host of other services—taxis, fast food outlets and sandwich bars, city centre pubs, and so on—many of them offering jobs at pay scales little better than the minimum wage. The new jobs on offer are rarely in the same locations as the old industries that have shrunk. Hence the expansion of employment in London and some provincial cities, while the old industrial areas have usually continued to decline. But even in London the jobs do not solve the problems of much of the old workforce.

An inflow of £53 billion in foreign direct investment into London (31 percent from the US and 16 percent from India)[20] has not stopped much lower than average levels of employment in boroughs such as Tower Hamlets, Hackney, Haringey, and Barking & Dagenham, and an unemployment rate for London as a whole of around 2 percent above the national average.[21] Those who put their trust in what one is tempted to call "the permanent finance economy", including those who work for the mayor of London's office, are ignoring its contradictory impact. It has served to veil a level of industrial employment decline greater than in most other advanced countries. But it is questionable whether it can do so when the next global recession takes place.

Industrial production proceeds by ups and downs. But it is through finance that the ups get turned into apparently magical bubbles that suddenly collapse overnight.

Foreign direct investment (FDI) accounts for more than a quarter of London's economy and "foreign owned companies had created 42 percent of the capital's economic growth between 1998 and 2004", but "FDI companies are continually re-evaluating their presence here. More

---

19: ONS, 2002.

20: *Financial Times*, 27 April 2007.

21: Seager, 2005.

than half review their global strategy every three to five years, and 13 percent do so every year".[22]

But it is not only London that is dependent on "finance and business services" in this way; so too are many provincial cities. The only way New Labour knows of reacting to this dependence is by shaping all its policies around catering for those who make the investment decisions.

Back in the mid-1990s, while still in opposition, Gordon Brown proclaimed that there was an alternative to old Keynesian attempts to use state intervention to smooth out the ups and downs of capitalism. He said the remedy lay in "post-neoclassical endogenous growth theory". Such theory really amounts to the contention that all governments can do to ensure that capital accumulation takes place, and with it the growth of the economy and the "creation" of jobs, is to lubricate the wheels of the system through "supply side measures". That entails deregulation, softening up the labour force through "labour market flexibility", and training the potential workforce from the moment they are born to provide a pliant "human capital" input for production.

So instead of government intervention being able to ease the pain of capitalism through the mechanism of "demand management", as was suggested by social democratic theorists of 50 years ago such as Anthony Crosland and John Strachey, it is to subordinate the whole lives of the mass of people to the system. Hence the exam assembly line for school students; the imposition of payment by results, and continual appraisal and inspections, on teachers and lecturers; the pressure on single parents, mothers of young children and disabled people to join the million and half people looking for jobs. Hence too the pressure to cut back by one means or another those services for the mass of the population that are unproductive in capitalist terms—care for old people and the long term sick, legal aid and quality education for those to be slotted into unskilled jobs.

So it was that Brown did not only keep to Tory public spending plans for two years, as promised in 1997, but for three years.[23]

New Labour has, however, had one difficulty over the past ten years. Pushing through such "reforms" is difficult for any government trying to rule with a degree of consensus rather than force. Concessions have to be made that cut across the immediate interests of capital, if only to stand

22: Michael Charlton, chief executive of Think London, an FDI agency, quoted in the *Financial Times*, 27 April 2007.

23: See Emmerson and Frayne, 2002.

a chance of re-election. It is sometimes forgotten that New Labour lost three million votes in the 2001 election (*before* the mass disillusion over the war), essentially because holding back public expenditure created disaffection over the attacks on single parents and disabled people, and especially the NHS.

So Blair promised before the 2001 election to raise the percentage of GNP going on the health service to the European average. After the election Brown did finally boost public spending in an attempt to deal with the aftermath of the US recession, raising the percentage of GNP going to the NHS by 2.3 percent over four years.[24] But the implementation aimed to keep sections of capital on side through lucrative public-private partnership schemes, while the re-establishment of the internal market limited the degree to which resources were able to meet the needs of patients. In effect, with New Labour under pressure to deliver real reform, Brown insisted it was combined with neoliberal counter-reforms—and still left the percentage of GNP spent on health about 1.2 percent behind France and Germany.

But this is in the past. Many of the problems Brown managed to evade for ten years could be closing in on him as he takes over the premiership from Blair. Inflation levels are beginning to create panic within the Monetary Policy Committee of the Bank of England, with four interest rate increases between August and May, and more expected. Someone who paid the average national price for a house five years ago will already have seen their repayment rise by about £20 a week over the past year.

The cost of finding any place to live at all is hitting manual and white collar working class and lower middle class people hard, with house prices quadrupling since 1996 and now six times average earnings—20 percent higher than before the last British housing crisis in the early 1990s.

People with mortgages have often managed to cope so far by borrowing still more. Debt to disposable income ratios in the UK are currently at 162.9 percent compared to 137.3 per cent in the US. There are already signs of the US house bubble bursting, with some mortgage lenders going bust, threats to repossess some two million homes and fears in the business press of a new recession. Further increases in interest rates could lead to the same danger here.

The government has left itself with only one weapon capable of placating the Monetary Policy Committee and restricting further interest

---

24: Office of Health Economics press release, 26 February 2007.

rises—holding back public expenditure. Hence the pressure on NHS trusts to cut back, with the sacking of nurses and the shortage of jobs for newly qualified doctors. Hence too the attempt to impose a 2 percent limit on wage increases in the public sector at a time when the retail price index is over 4 percent, and likely to go higher with increased mortgage costs.

The "miracle", like every other in Britain since the 1970s, is likely to end in tears. Let us hope they are not ours but Gordon Brown's.

References

Brown, Gordon, 2004, budget speech, 17 March 2004, http://news.bbc.co.uk/1/hi/uk_politics/3520514.stm

Croft, Nicholas, 2007, "Recent European Economic Growth: Why Can't it be a Return to the Golden Age", *National Institute Economic Review*, January 2007.

Emmerson, Carl, and Christine Frayne, 2002, "Giving us a Steer", www.cipfa.org.uk/publicfinance/search_details.cfm?News_id=13437

Field, Frank, 2007, the *Guardian* website, http://commentisfree.guardian.co.uk/frank_field/2007/05/new_deal_or_no_deal.html

Giles, Chris, 2007, "Brown's Paradox: a Tale of Two Economies", *Financial Times*, 20 March 2007.

Harper, David (ed), 2006, "Economic Trends Annual Supplement", Office for National Statistics, www.statistics.gov.uk/downloads/theme_economy/ETSupp2006.pdf

Institute for Fiscal Studies, 2007, "Poverty and Inequality in UK: 2007".

McMorrow, Kieran, and Werner Roeger, 2007, "Analysis of European Growth Rates", *National Institute Economic Review*, January 2007.

Milner, Mark, 2007, "A Quarter of Rover Workers Still Unemployed", the *Guardian*, 5 February 2007, http://business.guardian.co.uk/story/0,,2005863,00.html

Millward, Robert, 2003, "The Rise of the Service Economy", in Roderick Floud and Paul Johnson (eds), *The Cambridge Economic History of Modern Britain, volume three* (Cambridge University Press).

Nesta, 2006, "The Innovation Gap", October 2006, www.nesta.org.uk/informing/policy_and_research/highlights/innovation_gap_report.aspx

ONS, 2002, "The Jobs People Do", www.statistics.gov.uk/cci/nugget.asp?id=11

ONS, 2006, "Spending on Eating Out Overtakes Meals at Home", www.statistics.gov.uk/pdfdir/ioa0806.pdf

Panic, M, 2007, "Commentary", *Cambridge Journal of Economics*, January 2007.

Seager, Ashley, 2005, "London Revealed as Britain's Worst Employment Blackspot", the *Guardian*, 28 October 2005, http://money.guardian.co.uk/work/story/0,1456,1602343,00.html

SMTT, 2006, "UK New Car Registrations at Q2/2006", http:// smmtlib.findlay.co.uk/articles/industryanalysis/IndustryAnalysisAutomotiveTrends/ACF3030.pdf

Webster, David, 2002, "Unemployment: How Official Statistics Distort Analysis and Policy, and Why", *Radical Statistics* 79/80 (summer/winter 2002), www.radstats.org.uk/no079/webster.htm

José Carlos Mariátegui: Latin America's forgotten Marxist

Mike Gonzalez

José Carlos Mariátegui was born into a society in crisis, a Peru deeply divided between a coastal sector where most of Peru's capitalist class was concentrated, an emerging mining industry in the central valley between Lima and Huancavelica, and a mountain region which Mariátegui described as "semi-feudal". Here 40 percent of the population lived in small, isolated communities, eking a precarious living on the high Andean slopes. They were forced to give their labour to the powerful local landowning class which administered the region without any real influence from Lima, the capital of a weak state.

A brief period of prosperity in the mid-19th century was based on the export of the natural fertiliser guano and the extraction of nitrates, with British capital entirely controlling trade in both commodities. During the 300 years of colonial rule mining had been the central source of wealth in the region. With the rise of guano and nitrates the focus of the economy shifted towards the coast and foreign trade. Peru's small, emerging bourgeoisie grew in the shadow of the foreign capital on which it was wholly dependent. In the sierra the century saw an expansion of often huge landholdings (or latifundia) into what had been communal, indigenously owned lands.

> The emerging state, therefore, was an expression of the symbiosis of the interests of these large and medium landowners, for whom the institutions of the state served the principal function of legitimising the pillage of the small

producers and the definition of the peasant masses as a source of labour, taxes and cannon fodder.[1]

The growing costs of public administration were met by borrowing from European banks, while imports grew to four times the value of exports. At the same time, foreign capital was also sustaining the growth of coastal export agriculture, particularly sugar and later cotton. In the sierra the latifundios' expansion occurred in order to cover local demand as well as to provide a steady stream of cheap and exploited indigenous labour. As the century advanced Peru was entering into a relationship with the global economy, which only emphasised and deepened the already enormous gulf between the modern coast and a mountain world of non-Spanish speaking and racially oppressed indigenous peoples. Where they fought back, they were repressed with exemplary brutality.[2]

The so-called Pacific War of 1879-84 was catastrophic for the Peruvian bourgeoisie. It lost the port of Tacna and most of the nitrate-producing areas to Chile, and the resulting economic collapse left it, as Mariátegui put it, "bleeding and mutilated", and with no resources with which to resist the effective transfer of the economy into foreign hands. The contract for the Central Valley Railway, for example, went to the British based Grace Corporation, and mining came under the direct control of the Peruvian Corporation and the Cerro del Paso Corporation. The main banks were British owned, and foreign interests like the Gildemeisters or Peruvian capital working in combination with external investors such as the Larcos assumed control over agriculture. In the cities, and in particular in Lima and Cuzco, the ancient Inca capital, new industries were emerging as a result of this new economic activity—in particular textiles.

Yet the original inhabitants of Peru experienced increasingly exploitative conditions, which were unmitigated by the developments taking place on the coast. On the contrary, their exploitation intensified as the modern sector of the Peruvian economy developed. It was one of Mariátegui's important insights that these two phenomena were interdependent: that modernisation not only could, but actually needed to, maintain the backwardness of the sierra and the forms of servile labour that persisted there—like the enganche, obligatory labour, and yanaconazgo, a form of debt peonage.

1: Yepes del Castillo, 1972, pp41-42.

2: The rising at Huancané in 1866 was so brutally crushed that a "Society of Friends of the Indians" was formed by white sympathisers, the forerunners of the "indigenist" schools of writers and artists of the early 20th century.

There was resistance, of course. Indigenous rebellions and anarchist led trade unions were two forms of it. There was also a middle class movement, directed against the old landed aristocracy and their control and manipulation of the state, which found political expression in civilismo, founded in the mid-1870s by Manuel Pardo. This was a movement seeking to create a strong state committed to modernisation. But by the beginning of the 20th century it had split into two wings, one compromised with the old elite and committed to the continuation of economic growth based on foreign investment, the other more committed to modernisation, an end to corruption and a strategy of national growth. The individual who came to represent this more radical wing was Augusto Bernardino Leguía y Salcedo, though Leguía never questioned the central role of foreign capital in the process.[3] He was elected to the presidency for the first time in 1908 and would return to power again in the momentous year of 1919.

In fact the most trenchant critique of the old order came from the poet Manuel González Prada. He exposed the moral degeneration of the old ruling class and set it against a picture of "Indian Peru", which was both romantic and idealised. Yet for a new generation his work turned their attention to the hitherto silent and invisible native Peruvian peoples—and laid the groundwork for Mariátegui and his generation. Despite his reputation as a defender of the indigenous population, however, González Prada clearly saw the decay of Peruvian society as corrupting both rulers and ruled; though he laid the responsibility firmly with the powerful, he never saw the indigenous people as potential subjects of history, capable of bringing about change through their own actions.

It was into this society that Mariátegui was born, in Moquegua in 1894. Growing up in Lima, Mariátegui found himself drawn to artistic and cultural forms of dissent. In 1909, at the age of 15, he became a printer's apprentice; within five years he was writing regular columns of social commentary in the newspaper *La Prensa* under the pseudonym Juan Croniqueur. He was also associated with the group of artists around Abraham Valdelomar and the magazine *Colónida*, whose influence was far greater than its four issues would suggest. There is no sign yet that Mariátegui's radicalism was political. He did not associate himself, for example, with the anarchist organisations that led the nascent urban working class movement.

It was essentially an artistic dissidence that drew Mariátegui towards the Bohemians who "strolled" along Lima's avenue of artists, the Jirón de la Unión, just as Baudelaire had strolled along the streets of Paris—"flaneurs"

3: See Garrett, 1973; Yepes del Castillo, 1972, chapter 10; and Kapsoli, 1976.

without direction driven by a world weariness that the great French poet had called "spleen". Mariátegui's writings on artistic modernism found there the scepticism of an avant-garde pressing against received wisdoms. But while many of his Bohemian colleagues remained buried in an aesthetic twilight, Mariátegui began to seek out the links between the artistic and the political vanguard.

By 1916 Peru was changing. In Lima the new factories, most importantly in textiles, were creating a permanent labour force, which was forging trade unions under the influence of anarchism.[4] The first general strike, in support of the workers of the important Vitarte textile plant, took place in April 1911. Although it failed, a new law relating to accidents at work was passed in the same year, the right to strike (though under limited circumstances) conceded in 1913 and the eight-hour day won by the workers of the port of Callao a year later. Attacks on living standards in 1915 and 1916, as raw materials were exported rather than finished goods and profits fell, produced new waves of strikes and demands for a shorter working day.

At the same time new struggles were developing in the countryside. The expansion of the export sector in agriculture displaced the peasantry and increased the rapacious search for labour.[5] The risings that culminated in Puno (the Rumi Maqui revolt) in 1915-6 showed a different aspect of the indigenous communities—as collective fighters against the brutal mode of production prevailing in the Andean mountains. And Puno was not the only rising. In the central Mantaro valley there were repeated confrontations, drawing Mariátegui and one of his colleagues to the area in 1918.

That year Mariátegui founded a new journal, *Nuestra Epoca*, which expressed his movement from the artistic avant-garde towards a growing political radicalism. The name of the journal, "Our Times", referred to more than a spirit of the age; it was a historical moment of change and struggle. "*Nuestra Epoca* did not have a socialist programme, but it must be seen as a move in that direction, both ideologically and in propaganda terms".[6]

Significantly, it lasted only two issues; it was banned after publishing an article by Mariátegui criticising the armed forces. Early the following

4: See Pflucker, 1978, and also Pflucker, 1973, her undergraduate thesis on the important anarchist newspaper *La Protesta*. See too Kapsoli, 1976, and Denis Sulmont's work in general, particularly Sulmont, 1978.

5: This is the theme of a number of the early "indigenista" narratives by writers such as Ciro Alegría.

6: Martínez de la Rosa quoted in Checa, 1964, p116.

year Mariátegui set up *La Razón*, a newspaper whose unambiguous purpose was to support people in struggle. It was the first major watershed in his development as a Marxist and a working class leader.

The year 1919 was a turning point. The cost of living for workers had almost doubled since 1913, and the previous two years had seen a series of strikes in Lima and elsewhere for wage rises and a shorter working day. The first general union, the Federación Local Obrera de Lima, was formed in 1918, and the premature creation of an organising committee for a Socialist Party reflected the generally militant atmosphere rather than any serious political advance. The year began with a strike of bakers, which rapidly became general, under the leadership of anarcho-syndicalists. The government conceded the eight-hour day, but refused wage rises. The Comité Pro-Abaratamiento (for a lowering of prices of basic goods) formed in April, bringing together a wide range of organisations in a series of protests, and in May new strikes paralysed the city, leading to the arrest of three union leaders. The declaration of a state of emergency and the arrest of the movement's leaders did nothing to lessen the level of popular protest, which now coalesced around support for the return of former president Leguía, in the belief that he would challenge the old ruling class and introduce measures to modernise the Peruvian state.

Leguía took power on 4 July and immediately released the imprisoned workers' leaders. The triumphant demonstration that paraded them through the streets stopped outside the offices of Mariátegui's *La Razón* and invited him to join the head of the march. The Leguía honeymoon, however, was brief. By August Leguía was already repressing working class action. *La Razón* was suppressed, and Mariátegui and his co-editor, César Falcón, were "invited to leave the country" with a grant to study abroad. In October they left for Europe. Later Mariátegui would be accused of taking the king's shilling, of surrendering to Leguía. His own explanation is that his activity was restricted as Leguía assumed increasingly dictatorial powers, and that the working class movement was still too weak and disoriented for him to operate successfully within Peru. Leguía offered him the alternative of exile and Mariátegui accepted.

The protests that returned Leguía to power were joined by a growing student movement based mainly in the southern city of Cuzco. This was a pale reflection of the hugely important university reform movement that had begun in Córdoba, Argentina, in 1918. While Mariátegui's activities were restricted to the workers' movement in Lima, his contemporary Victor Raúl Haya de la Torre was emerging as the leader of the student movement. Haya would come to represent an alternative political direction in Peru, and indeed throughout Latin America, enshrined in Apra, the organisation he later founded.[7] While at this stage Haya claimed to be a Marxist, and criticised Mariátegui for leaving Peru, it would become clear that his project for modernisation involved an alliance with "progressive" sections of both the national and the international bourgeoisie, led by the middle class. Thus there was no contradiction for him in working with Leguía in setting up the Universidades Populares, a programme for the education of workers, in 1920. Three years later, however, Haya too would be sent into exile by the increasingly dictatorial Peruvian president. While today Apra is identified with corrupt regimes pressing for neoliberal strategies, in the 1920s Haya's claim that it was a new revolutionary creed did win him some adherents, though its philosophy, with its mix of Marxism, indigenism and an intense personalism around the figure of Haya, in fact made its programme very difficult to follow. Yet at this early stage Mariátegui continued to work with Haya's supporters in common projects, and continued to do so until Haya, from Mexico, announced the formation of his Peruvian Nationalist Party, which later became Apra.

The road to Europe and back

Mariátegui had left Peru with an established reputation within the country's working class movement, an important body of journalistic work and some knowledge of Marxism.[8] His trip to Europe clearly had as one purpose the development and deepening of that understanding. Having spent a little time in France, he went to Italy where, as he later put it, he "acquired a wife and some ideas".[9] He was present at the founding conference of the Italian Communist Party at Livorno in 1921 and learned much of his

7: Apra, the Latin American Popular Revolutionary Alliance, currently holds the presidency of Peru in the person of Alan García. It was, from the moment of its formation as a party in 1924, the main political antagonist of Mariátegui, especially when Mariátegui finally broke with Haya in 1928. Despite the break, many subsequent writers have attempted to claim Mariátegui for Aprismo!

8: According to Redondez, 1982, Mariátegui had been introduced to Marxism already by one professor Maúrtua.

9: His experiences in Europe, largely published in newspapers and journals at home, were later collected as *La Escena Contemporánea*, volume one of the *Obras Completas* (Mariátegui, 1959-) and his Italian writing as *Cartas de Italia*, volume 15 of the same collection. See too Vanden, 1986. The main writer on this aspect of Mariátegui's work is the Italian scholar Antonio Melis. See for example Melis, 1994.

Marxism during this period.[10] Arriving after the Italian factory occupations, his articles and essays reflect his immersion in the debates around the issue of hegemony. More importantly, Mariátegui saw at first hand how the political weakness of the bourgeoisie and the vacillations of reformism could permit the emergence of fascism—and these would be the central themes in his lectures and classes on the world situation which he gave at the Universidad Populares after his return to Peru,[11] and in a subsequent series of articles in various newspapers in 1923-4, published later under the title "Figures and Aspects of International Life".[12]

A great deal has been written about the various influences on Mariátegui's Marxism, and his voracious reading and reviewing of a wide range of European writers has encouraged that. The key point, however, is that his contemporary writings show a very clear recognition of the world-historical significance of the Bolshevik Revolution of 1917 and a consistent admiration for Lenin; a dedicated reading of current Marxist debates; and at the same time a consistent reflection on his own reality from the perspective not so much of Europe as of the international situation:

> Mariátegui's insistence on the need for an internationalist perspective is not the negation of nationalism so much as its supersession... It is a dialectical negation but not in the sense that he condemns or disqualifies nationalism as a historical necessity at a given moment in time.[13]

He returned from Europe in 1923 a "convinced and committed Marxist" ("Marxista convicto y confeso") with a developed critique of the Second International's version of Marxism, which waited passively for the development of capitalism automatically to open the way to socialism.[14] What this meant for him was demonstrated in the activities that would absorb the remaining six and half years of his life. First, the publication of *Amauta*, a magazine that would provide a platform for political debate between all the currents of thought within the socialist

10: While he frequently mentions Antonio Gramsci's name in connection with his Italian experiences, he makes no special mention of him, though Mariátegui's wife later said that the two men had spoken on several occasions.

11: These lectures are collected in *Historia de la Crisis Mundial*, volume eight of Mariátegui, 1959-. Some of these are available in English from www.marxists.org/archive/mariateg/works/

12: Volumes 16, 17 and 18 of Mariátegui, 1959-.

13: Quijano, 1986, pp44-45.

14: Most cogently expounded in his *Defensa del Marxismo* (in volume five of Mariátegui, 1959-), which was not in fact published until after his death.

movement in Peru and beyond, and second the working out of the key ideas that would inform his work as a trade union and party organiser in the late 1920s.

Seven Essays

Published in several stages in his magazine *Amauta*, Mariátegui's key work is his *Seven Essays*.[15] The central themes of his analysis of Peruvian history and society are developed in a pathbreaking materialist account that goes beyond any previous historical work, while setting out the framework of his activism and the political work that would absorb the last two years of his life. It is a book drawing on the work of several years, which confirms that economics must provide the foundation of a Marxist understanding, but also develops the concerns and questions that Mariátegui has identified as central to understanding the specificities of Peruvian history. These will shape his organisational methods, his exploration of the class struggle and his definition of the national reality. For some commentators, hostile in principle to his dialectical method, this definition consigns Mariátegui to the camp of revolutionary nationalism at best. For others, he remains locked in a kind of irrationalism which belies his insistence on locating the development of class consciousness in particular material circumstances. And for the functionaries of the late 1920s Comintern pursuing Stalin's ultra-left "class against class strategy", it suggested that Mariátegui was guilty of heterodoxy and indiscipline. Yet none of these judgments are justified by his work, either his theoretical writing or his practical engagement with the organs of class struggle.

The seven essays of the title cover religion, education, regionalism and (the longest essay) the development of Peruvian literature. The three key pieces, however, which open the work, provide a historical narrative that informs and explains his political strategy. For Mariátegui was always, first and foremost, a strategist of revolution—and his writings the foundation and explanation of that strategy. Analysing the Peruvian economy, he contrasts the colonial economic system with what went before. Under Spanish imperial rule Peru was a source of mineral wealth, its population locked in a system of ruthless exploitation within a structure of authoritarian control centred on the dominant colonial class. Its religious and secular institutions were informed and sustained by an ideology of racial

15: *Siete Ensayos de Interpretación de la Realidad Peruana* (Seven Interpretive Essays on Peruvian Reality) to give it its full title, volume two of Mariátegui, 1959-. There is also an English translation of this work—Mariátegui, 1971.

superiority ("pura sangre"—pure blood) which legitimated that exploitation. It was central to Mariátegui's vision that this contrasted dramatically with the pre-colonial, Inca, society structured around the ayllu system of kinship based collectives. Critics have been quick to point out that these communal organisations functioned within a centralised theocracy that was also highly repressive. Mariátegui acknowledges as much in an extensive footnote in the essay on "The Problem of the Indian"[16]—and he admits that those traditions have suffered disruptions and transformations through three centuries of colonial rule.

His argument, however, is that there is a cultural continuity and an ideological one which has ensured the maintenance of a collective consciousness in the indigenous communities of Peru. For Mariátegui that tradition of collective solidarity resonates with socialist ideas, and it is the task of socialists in that society to build on that synthesis. The importance of that "natural socialism" as Mariátegui himself described it, however, is not because of some romantic nativism, some sense on Mariátegui's part that socialism was the result of cultural processes. He insisted over and over again that ethnic characteristics were inextricably interwoven with class—and that the indigenous community was defined by its economic relationships with the ruling class.

When Peru won its independence from Spain that structure was maintained—and indeed reinforced—as he describes in the opening essay, "The Structure and Evolution of the Economy". The struggle for independence was led by a nascent bourgeoisie anxious to break the Spanish trading monopoly rather than challenge economic dependence on foreign trade altogether. The ruling class that emerged from the independence wars built the new economy around guano, the natural fertiliser deposited by seabirds on the coastal islands, which was exported exclusively to Britain. And the colonial system of exploitation, particularly in the mountain regions, far from being challenged by the new dispositions, was reinforced and later exploited as a source of cheap and pliant labour. This socio-economic structure is defined in the essays that follow—"The Problem of the Indian" and "The Problem of the land"—as gamonalismo:

> [The term gamonalismo] designates a whole phenomenon. It encompasses a far-reaching hierarchy of officials, intermediaries, agents, parasites. Even the assimilated Indian is transformed into an exploiter of his own race when

16: This essay is currently available online—www.ilstu.edu/class/hist127/docs/jcmindio.html

he places himself in its service. The central factor of the phenomenon is the hegemony of the large estate in the politics and mechanism of the state.[17]

It is based on forms of servitude and debt peonage, explained by racist stereotyping—a clear example of the interweaving of race and class. The critical consequence of this analysis was that the post-independence economy developed in subordination to external interests, and maintained the forms and structures of colonial exploitation. The Peruvian bourgeoisie, in the age of guano, and later when the dynamic sector of the economy moved to the mines and the coastal agricultural estates after the the Pacific War, remained dependent upon foreign capital. It had no independent national project of its own. And in his exploration of education, religion and culture Mariátegui found the same characteristic parasitism and lack of independence—though he also identified the points of resistance and struggle, whether in the history of indigenous rebellion or in the echoes in Peru (faint though they were) of the university reform movement that had begun in Cordoba, Argentina, in 1918.

Although the *Seven Essays* offered a fairly comprehensive analysis, each of them was clearly intended as the foundation for a deeper and more extensive exploration, which was precluded by Mariátegui's early death. But they were part of a political project, rather than a theoretical one, in the sense that conclusions were drawn from them in revolutionary practice.

His call to the workers on 1 May 1924 is a key to understanding his strategy.[18] Calling for a "united front" he emphasised that "we are still too few to split into different parts". In the working class movement the influence of a declining anarchism was still significant, generating a suspicion of revolutionary parties; among the students and the social movements, the influence of Haya's democratic nationalism was still considerable; and in the world of the sierra, where resistance was the stuff of everyday life, other, more local, traditions provided the points of reference. And yet, as Mariátegui would increasingly emphasise in his studies of Peruvian reality, and in particular in his *Seven Essays*, that ideological separation belied the role that each played in a unified economic structure integrated into the international market.

17: Mariátegui, 1971, p27.

18: "El Primero de Mayo y el Frente Único", in *Ideología y Política*, volume 13 of Mariátegui, 1959-, pp107-110.

> The working class movement in this country is still too young for us to contemplate dividing or splitting it. Before the time of division comes, and I suppose it is inevitable, we have a great deal of common work to do, in a spirit of solidarity. We have to awaken in the Peruvian proletariat a class consciousness and a feeling for their class; and that is a task for socialists and communists, communists and libertarians equally. It is up to all of us to win workers away from their "official representatives" and to struggle together against repression. It is up to all of us to defend the workers' press and workers' organisation. It is up to all of us to support the demands of the oppressed and enslaved indigenous race. And as we fulfil these historic responsibilities, we shall be doing our basic duty, our roads will merge and run together whatever our final objectives.[19]

Any socialist strategy must of necessity build a united front of forces, while within that unity political debate should continue to develop and advance the centrality of Marxist ideas. But it was clear that Mariátegui was extremely anxious to avoid sectarian splits. In fact he was operating consistently with the positions adopted at this stage by the international Communist movement, although, as Messeguer suggests, he may not have been aware of the discussions taking place in the Comintern. This drive for unity explains too his continuing relationship with Haya de la Torre and his newly formed Peruvian Nationalist Party, later to morph into Apra. It was an alliance that continued with the founding of *Amauta* in 1926 and lasted until the definitive break with Haya's group in 1928.

It was no coincidence, therefore, that in the extraordinarily busy year of 1928 Matriátegui founded the newspaper *Labour* in November as a paper for a growing working class movement. This was in clear anticipation of the formation of the Peruvian Congress of Workers (CGTP), which he would be central in setting up in May of the following year. By this time the labour force consisted of some 58,000 industrial workers (mainly in Lima but also in the southern city of Cuzco) and some 28,000 miners. About a third of the urban workforce was unionised; in the mines, the building of trade unions was much harder, since the foreign mining companies immediately dismissed (or worse) anyone who attempted to set up a union.[20] It was critical, however, to also acknowledge that some

19: Mariátegui, 1959-, volume 13, p108.

20: For a glimpse of the atmosphere that prevailed in the mines see the translation of Ciro Alegria's famous novel *Broad and Alien is the World* (Alegria, 1983), which includes several chapters set in the mining areas (these were not included in early translations).

1.5 million people remained within the rural and indigenous communities or were recent migrants into agriculture or indeed into mining.[21] The implications of that social structure for political organisation had been a central and recurring concern in Mariátegui's writings throughout the late 1920s. For while, as a Marxist who knew and read Lenin, Mariátegui recognised the leading role of the working class, he argued fiercely that a socialist movement in Peru must of necessity address the question of building a united front of struggle that could embrace and mobilise the majority of the exploited in that society. His insistence on that central issue was what produced Mariátegui's particular and original contribution to the development of Marxism in Latin America.

It was the collective traditions and natural solidarity of the indigenous communities, as he depicted them, which would ensure the resonance of socialist ideas in the particular conditions of Peru. But that connection could only be made consciously and deliberately by Marxists. It was this question that he would address in the essays collected in *Peruanicemos el Perú*,[22] though it was discussed and debated in the pages of *Amauta* throughout its existence. As he argued in a debate with the leading Aprista intellectual Luis Alberto Sánchez in 1927:

> No one...can be surprised by the confluence of indigenismo and socialism. Socialism orders and defines the demands of the masses, of the working classes. And in Peru those masses are four-fifths indigenous. Thus our socialism must declare its solidarity with the native people.[23]

It was Mariátegui's conviction that revolutionary socialism must of necessity connect with local traditions and conditions that would very soon bring him into confrontation with the Communist International. Yet if Mariátegui insisted on the "nationalisation"—or rather the adaptation to the real historical experience of each society—of Marxism, he remained emphatically internationalist in his perspectives and relentlessly committed to building the trade union movement as well as, in the same hyperactive year, to the setting up of a Peruvian Socialist Party in which, once again, he would play the leading role. Yet this again would bring him into conflict with the Comintern and its Latin American representatives.

The period between the beginning of 1929 and his death in April

21: These figures are from Chavarría, 1979, p156.

22: *Peruanicemos el Perú* (We must Peruvianize Peru), volume 11 of Mariátegui, 1959-.

23: Mariátegui, 1959-, volume 13, p217.

1930 was overshadowed by the gathering clouds of a disagreement with the Communist International.[24] Early in 1929 a Comintern representative visited Peru to invite Mariátegui's group to send delegates to two upcoming conferences—the trade union conference in Montevideo and the first congress of Latin American Communist Parties, to be held in Buenos Aires in May and June. Mariátegui himself was unable to travel to either—the osteomielitis that dogged his short life was worsening—but he briefed the delegation of four who did attend. They included Hugo Pesce, the young doctor who would later make such an impression on the young Che Guevara and suggest his first readings of Marx, and Julio Portocarrero, a young worker from the important Vitarte textile plant in Lima. Portocarrero was in fact elected to the executive of the Latin American Trade Union Federation (CSLA). Yet "to some extent these meetings represented a showdown between the path being followed by the Peruvian cell and the official line of the Comintern".[25]

Ostensibly the dispute centred on the question of whether or not the new party would be called "socialist" or "Communist". To the last Mariátegui was adamant that it should be a socialist party and resisted the Comintern's mounting pressures. There was never the slightest doubt as to the character of the new party. Its statutes declared the party's affiliation to the Communist International and its commitment to what it described as "militant Leninism". Its six-point programme was equally uncompromising. It argued for the expropriation of the landed estates and their redistribution to communal organisations or small peasants, with guarantees of technical and financial support. It called for the expropriation of all foreign enterprises as well as those belonging to big Peruvian capital. It demanded an immediate renunciation of the foreign debt and all imperialist controls and called for the immediate enactment of the eight-hour working day, as well as the immediate arming of workers and peasants and the dissolution of the armed forces and police into the militias. Its sixth point called for establishment of "workers, peasants and soldiers municipalities" as the organs of power in the new society.[26] By no stretch of the imagination could this be described as a reformist programme, still less as lacking a clear revolutionary impulse.

24: Galindo, 1980, explores this conflict in detail. It should be read in conjunction with Martínez de la Torre's *Notes Towards a Marxist Interpretation of Peruvian History* (Torre, 1958). Torre was one of Mariátegui's closest collaborators, who broke with the Communist Party after his death. His two volume history is invaluable because it reproduces so much primary material—leaflets and pamphlets, as well as correspondence.

25: Chavarría, 1979, p158.

26: Galindo, 1980, p87.

The fact that the Socialist Party did not call for soviets but for municipalities did not affect the fact that these were clearly organs of workers' power similar in character and structure to the soviets.

If there was so little ideological difference, however, why did Mariátegui stick so stubbornly to the "socialist" label? In my view there are several reasons, but they are all tied to his sense that within the framework of revolutionary Marxism each national struggle must find its particular articulation of the local and the international. This was clearly a principle with Mariátegui. Another factor is that he had been briefly arrested and jailed at the beginning of 1928 after the "discovery" by President Leguía of a "Communist plot" to bring down his regime. The reality of the plot was open to severe doubt, but it provided the pretext for a repressive response. It may be that Mariátegui was anxious to avoid a similar response to the foundation of his party which, he hoped, would operate legally as far as possible.[27] Beyond that, however, and of much more fundamental significance, was his conception of the "united front". The party, as its founding programme demonstrated clearly, was intended to appeal to workers, to peasants and indigenous communities, and to the anti-imperialist sectors of the middle classes.

These latter layers were people to whom Haya de la Torre's Apra had appealed, with some success, in the earlier part of the decade—and using some of the same language of "unity" as Mariátegui had. The pages of the journal *Amauta* were an open forum in which the supporters of Apra participated freely. But Mariátegui's September 1928 editorial "Aniversario y Balance" in the journal marked a clear and definitive break with the Apristas:

> *Amauta* now enters its second period, when it no longer needs to describe itself as a vanguard or left journal. To be faithful to the revolution, it is enough that it be socialist... The very word revolution can lend itself it to ambiguities. Its meaning needs to be clear. The Latin American revolution can be nothing other than a stage, a phase of the world revolution. It will be, quite simply, a socialist revolution.[28]

Haya's announcement from Mexico in 1928 of the formation of a party of his own provoked Mariátegui's trenchant response. Up till then he had regarded Apra as a "front" with whom joint work was still possible, despite a continuing debate and a widening ideological gulf. The formation

27: He later insisted, for example, that the CGTP should register under Leguía's labour laws, despite their restrictive character.

28: "An Anniversary and an Accounting", volume 13 of Mariátegui, 1959-, p247.

of the party, however, precipitated matters—for Mariátegui had made his criticisms of Apra clear in *Amauta* and elsewhere. Where Apra argued the possibility of a broad front in alliance with elements of the bourgeoisie, Mariátegui's formulation of the nature of the united front clearly argued for a unity of the working classes and indigenous communities led by socialists. Haya de la Torre, by contrast, had always argued that Peru's backwardness meant that leadership must necessarily fall to middle class elements and the progressive military. While these arguments could be conducted in the context of broad movement of activists, Mariátegui may well have seen the building of a socialist party as a lesser priority. Now, however, the socialist vision of the united front which he propounded required a clear political expression.

Mariátegui's consistent and withering critique of Second International Marxism and reformism provided the political groundwork for this. His studies of the Peruvian economy, particularly in the *Seven Essays* explored the consequences of the weakness of the Peruvian bourgeoisie and its incapacity to carry through an independent national project. The tasks of economic development and growth would therefore have to be carried through by a socialist movement. The concept of the united front and what was clearly an evolving theory of "permanent revolution", although never couched in those terms, seemed to suggest at least some awareness of Leon Trotsky—and there seems to have been some direct contact between Mariátegui and the Trotskyist groups around Naville during 1929.

But this does not seem to be the primary reason for the deep and growing hostility of the Comintern representatives in Latin America. Rather, it derived in the first place from Mariátegui's resistance to calling his party Communist. And that in turn seems to have been interpreted as an indication of a deeper deviation, prioritising race over class and nation over the international movement. Mariátegui's response was to send with the Peruvian delegates to the May-June Congress three key documents addressing those areas of concern: "The Problem of Race in Latin America", "The Anti-imperialist Perspective" and "Antecedents and Developments of Class Struggle".[29]

Final days

Since his days at *La Razón* Mariátegui had been a tireless campaigner, organiser, writer and provider, through *Amauta*, of a platform for socialist debate. As the 1920s drew to a close his level of activity did not diminish,

29: All three appear in the first section of *Ideología y Política*, volume 13 of Mariátegui, 1959-.

despite his deteriorating physical condition and increasing financial difficulties at home. His Wednesday evenings at home in Calle Washington, Lima, brought the movement to him—and the respect he had earned ensured that the movement did visit. His correspondence—aside from his hundreds of articles, reviews and documents—reveals an activist as engaged with comrades elsewhere in the continent as with those in Peru.[30] The amputation of his right leg meant that he would conduct his activity in this final period from a wheelchair.

His letters from this time to his friend Samuel Glusberg in Buenos Aires, reveal that the political tensions in Peru were becoming increasingly difficult to handle and the pressures on him mounting; just before his death he began to make arrangements to move to Buenos Aires where he felt the atmosphere would be less oppressive and he would feel his isolation less. In May-June 1929, however, he was unable to travel and it was Pesce and Portocarrero who would once again present his documents to the Comintern.

But the frosty reception given to the publication of his *Seven Essays* gave Mariátegui some sense of the hostility his ideas might meet at the conference. Codovilla, secretary of the Argentine Communist Party and the representative of the Comintern at the conference, argued fiercely that Mariátegui's analysis of the specificity of the Peruvian situation was a concession to nationalism. Peru, he argued, was more than adequately described by the general thesis on semi-colonial nations, and by extension could not therefore be an exception to the general "class against class strategy" laid down by the Third International.

Yet Mariátegui's documents did not argue Peruvian exceptionalism; they discussed the application of revolutionary strategy in the particular conditions of Peru. Thus his document "The Anti-imperialist Perspective" is a fierce condemnation of Apra's anti-imperialism, because "even if it were able to mobilise the national bourgeoisie and the peasant masses (a possibility we have discounted) this would not cancel conflicts of class". He uses the experience of the 1910-17 Mexican Revolution (about which he wrote extensively) as a warning. In Mexico the revolutionary movement represented most clearly by Emiliano Zapata had produced a bourgeois nationalist regime whose first act had been to attack the peasant revolutionaries. Mariátegui argued, "Our mission is to explain to the masses how only the socialist revolution can offer real opposition to the advance of imperialism." It is hard at this distance to understand why this position should have generated such opposition from Codovilla and others. But in the context

30: For his correspondence, see Mariátegui, 1984.

of the Stalinist turn of the Third International towards an ultra-left policy of treating all non-Communists as counter-revolutionaries, even "social fascists", it becomes easier to understand.

Mariátegui's second paper on the "problem of race" met with equally obstinate resistance. Returning to the arguments that he had made in *Seven Essays* and elsewhere, Mariátegui reminded the conference that four-fifths of Peru's workforce were still peasants or semi-rural workers (for example in the mines) with conflicting allegiances. By mobilising the solidarity and collective action embedded in indigenous traditions, he argued, socialism could take root among the majority of the exploited in Peru. The Comintern line, by contrast, was to see this as a national question and to argue for the "self-determination of the indigenous peoples". It was ironic that Mariátegui's insistence on the interlacing of race and class, and that the situation of the indigenous peoples had to be understood ultimately in terms of the economy, should have been rejected in the name of Marxism!

The consequence of the Buenos Aires conference, given the authority of the Comintern representatives, was that Mariátegui's authority and leadership came under immediate attack. Eudocio Ravines, a sinister character who had moved from Apra into the offices of the Third International in Paris, was now sent to Peru to implement the decisions of the conference and form a Communist Party. Mariátegui's letters to Glusberg reveal a man of failing health increasingly frustrated by events at home. Ironically, Mariátegui welcomed Ravines when he arrived in Peru early in March 1930 and agreed that he should take over the leadership. A month later Mariátegui was dead and the city of Lima stopped all activity for five minutes in his honour. His funeral was a massive demonstration of the affection in which he was held.

By May the Peruvian Communist Party had been formed—on the basis that Mariátegui's project for a united front had been too broad, admitting intellectuals and petit bourgeois elements.[31] Within a year a disastrous armed rising in the indigenous highlands isolated the communities and brought down on them the most severe repression. By the mid-1930s much of Mariátegui's patient work in the trade union movement had been undone, and his ideas systematically misrepresented to the succeeding generation. By then, of course, the Third International had turned back to many of his positions—without acknowledgment, of course.

Perhaps it is appropriate to leave the last word with Gregory Zinoviev:

31: Chavarría, 1979, pp165-167.

> Mariátegui has a brilliant mind; he is a true creator. He does not seem like a Latin American; he does not plagiarise, he does not copy, he does not parrot what the Europeans say. What he creates is his own.[32]

In his own time, that originality was his undoing. Today, it is the reason to rediscover his work.

References

Alegria, Ciro, 1983, *Broad and Alien is the World* (Merlin).

Chavarría, Jesús, 1979, *José Carlos Mariátegui and the Rise of Modern Peru 1890-1930* (University of New Mexico Press).

Checa, Genaro Carnero, 1964, *La Acción Escrita* (Lima).

Galindo, Alberto Flores, 1980, *La Agonía de Mariátegui* (Desco).

Garrett, Gary R, 1973, "The Oncenio of Augusto B. Leguia: Middle Sector Government and Leadership in Peru, 1919-1930" (University of New Mexico).

Kapsoli, Wilfredo, 1969, "Luchas obreras en el Peru" (Lima).

Mariátegui, José Carlos, 1959-, *Obras Completas* (Amauta, Lima).

Mariátegui, José Carlos, 1971, *Seven Interpretive Essays on Peruvian Reality* (University of Texas).

Mariátegui, José Carlos, 1984, *Correspondencia*, in two volumes (Amauta).

Melis, Antonio, 1994, *Leyendo Mariátegui* (Lima).

Pflucker, Piedad Pareja, 1973, undergraduate thesis, Universidad Católica (Lima).

Pflucker, Piedad Pareja, 1978, *Anarquismo y Sindicalismo en el Peru: 1904-1929* (Lima).

Quijano, Aníbal, 1986, *Introducción a Mariátegui* (ERA).

Redondez, Raimundo Prado, 1982, *El Marxismo de Mariátegui* (Amaru Editores).

Sulmont, Denis, 1978, *El Movimiento Obrero en el Peru: 1900-1956* (Lima).

Torre, Ricardo Martínez de la, 1948, *Apuntes para una Interpretación Marxista de la Historia Social del Perú*, in two volumes (Lima).

Vanden, Harry, 1986, *National Marxism: J C Mariátegui's Thought and Politics* (Boulder).

Yepes del Castillo, Ernesto, 1972, *Perú 1820-1920: un Siglo de Desarrollo Capitalista* (Lima).

32: Chavarría, 1979, p162.

At an impasse? Anti-capitalism and the social forums today

Alex Callinicos and Chris Nineham

The international movement against capitalist globalisation has been globally visible for nearly a decade now. It started with the Chiapas rising of January 1994 and the French public sector strikes of November-December 1995, and exploded onto the global stage at the Seattle protests in November 1999. It then enjoyed a period of dynamic expansion through the launch of the World Social Forum (WSF) in Porto Alegre, Brazil, in January 2001, the massive confrontation at the G8 summit in Genoa in July 2001, and the first European Social Forum in Florence in November 2002. The culmination was the enormous demonstrations against the war in Iraq between February and April 2003. Subsequently, however, there has not been the same forward impetus. Indeed, increasingly centrifugal pressures and even a degree of disarray have become evident.[1]

The seventh World Social Forum, held in Nairobi, Kenya, in January 2007, may have marked a turning point. The forum was far from being a disaster, despite the questionable decision to hold it in a country with weak social movements. Some 46,000 people participated, the majority from Kenya itself and around a quarter from the rest of Africa—no mean achievement, given the poverty and vast distances of the continent. The coming together of activists involved movements from across Africa and

1: For background on the movement in its initial phase, see Harman, 2000; Charlton and Bircham, 2001; Callinicos, 2003; Mertes, 2003; and Tormey, 2004.

the rest of the Global South, as well as from the North, generated some of the energy on display at the earlier world and European forums. And the opening and closing marches, from the slum settlements of Kibera and Kariobongi respectively, did offer a vivid sense of the convergence of global struggles, even if they were relatively small.

Nevertheless, the forum was also crippled by internal controversy. Many local and foreign activists expressed the view, summarised by one of the organisers, Onyango Oloo, national coordinator of the Kenya Social Forum, that "the event gave rise to disturbing and negative tendencies such as commercialisation, militarisation and authoritarian and undemocratic decision-making".[2] Particular anger was caused by the sponsorship of the forum by a mobile phone company, the high entrance fees charged to Kenyan participants, the dominance of catering by elite local hospitality firms such as the Windsor and Norfolk, and the pervasive presence of the police and military. The tensions climaxed when a coalition of Kenyan slum-dwellers and foreign activists led by Trevor Ngwane of the South African Anti-Privatisation Forum stormed the Windsor restaurant, owned by John Michuki, minister of internal security (and known by Kenyans as Kimendeero, the crusher, because of his role for the British colonial regime during the 1950s Mau Mau rebellion), and redistributed its contents. Oloo paints a damning insider's portrait of the undemocratic way in which the forum was run. He tells of "a political evaluation of the WSF" by "perhaps the most high profile member of the organising committee" which refers to "glue-sucking urchins from Korogocho" (a slum in northern Nairobi), while dismissing most of the critics of the process as "condescending Trotskyites from the North".[3] The Filipino intellectual and activist Walden Bello, one of the movement's most consistent strategic thinkers, writes, "There was a strong sense of going backward rather than forward in Nairobi".[4]

Italian trade unionist Bruno Ciccaglione criticises what he calls "the tendencies...to transform the WSF into a folklorist/commercial event", but argues that these are only symptoms. "The real problem" is the divergence in what is happening to the different movements that were the driving force in the WSF process:

2: Oloo, 2007, p1.
3: Oloo, 2007, p3.
4: Bello, 2007.

> On the one side the European movements, able to produce large mobilisations and concrete victories in past years, are today in a deep crisis and do not look capable to have unitary and common mobilisations at a continental level, and, sometimes, like Italy, even at a national level. On the other side the Latin American movements, very strong at the moment, are living an interesting and successful period...but they are a lot more concentrated on their own continent rather than on a worldwide perspective.[5]

This loss of impetus can be traced in the trajectory of the most powerful anti-capitalist organisation in Europe, Attac France. Founded in 1998 to campaign for the regulation of financial speculation, it initially grew explosively, attaining a membership of 30,000 by 2001, and spawning affiliates in many other countries. However, Attac's membership stagnated in 2002-4 and then started to decline, falling to 21,000 in 2006. This reflected an increasingly bitter internal crisis that drove Attac to the verge of a split by the end of last year.[6]

There are in fact a number of issues that we need to analyse to begin to understand this sense of crisis in the European movement. There are inherent difficulties with common mobilisations, there are weaknesses in the methods and practices of the social forum movement, and there are political problems that have emerged in the process of developing the wider movements. This article aims to help develop this understanding. Its focus is largely on Europe because this is the region that we know best and it is here that the crisis in the anti-capitalist movement is most visible.

The dialectic of national and global

Global capitalism is subject to what Leon Trotsky called the law of uneven and combined development. So too are the movements that resist it. The anti-capitalist movement developed certain key national bases during its initial phase of dynamic expansion. The Al Qaida attacks on New York and Washington on 11 September 2001 crippled the North American coalition of activists that had been responsible for the Seattle protests and had expanded rapidly thereafter. Fortunately, an axis had already developed through the first WSF in Porto Alegre between Attac in France and a coalition of Brazilian NGOs and social movements (notably the MST landless labourers' movement and the CUT trade union federation), which gave the movement a stable global framework. A powerful third partner came

5: Ciccaglione, 2007.
6: Wintrebert, 2007, figures from pp69-71.

from the explosive development of the social forum movement in Italy, under the inspiration of the WSF and hugely accelerated by the confrontation at the Genoa G8 summit in July 2001.[7] Others played an important role—for instance the Indian organisers of the most successful WSF to date, in Mumbai in January 2004—but the most politically important relationships were between these three partners.

Relations within the Franco-Italian-Brazilian trinity were never exactly harmonious. Neither Attac nor its partners in the Brazilian based WSF organising committee were happy about the high profile involvement of the Partito della Rifondazione Comunista (the Refounded Communist Party) in the Italian movement. Bernard Cassen, first president of Attac, was openly critical of the emphasis on the war at the first European Social Forum in Florence in November 2002.[8] That emphasis also drew the Italians closer in 2001-3 to the emerging anti-war movement in Britain—the object of much mistrust from both Attac and various autonomists because of the role of the radical left in its leadership. Nevertheless, these tensions were relatively easy to manage till after Florence and the anti-war protests of early 2003.

Greater internal polarisation became visible in 2003-4, reaching a crescendo at the third European Social Forum in London in October 2004. In part it involved a natural process of political differentiation. As the movement developed, it confronted increasingly demanding questions about how to pursue the struggle both against neoliberalism and against the imperialist offensive mounted by the United States and its allies. The diverging responses led to the crystallisation of distinct political tendencies within the movement—a reformist right wing, focused on Attac and its international network, seeking a return to a more regulated capitalism; autonomists who claimed to be transcending traditional debates on the left and building localised alternatives to capitalism in the here and now; and a radical left seeking to get rid of capitalism altogether. Such a clash of different political perspectives was inevitable, though debate was often obfuscated by the tendency of the right wing to use autonomist language and even (as at the London European Social Forum) to ally with the autonomists against the left.[9]

But the subsequent evolution of the movement has shown it has other problems. A key characteristic of the anti-capitalist movement has been its transnational character (hence it was always a misnomer to call it

7: For a wildly biased and inaccurate but interesting account of this process by one of the founders of Attac, see Cassen, 2003a.

8: Cassen, 2003b.

9: For a more extended discussion of the process of political differentiation, see Callinicos, 2004a; on the European Social Forum in London, see Callinicos, 2004b.

the "anti-globalisation movement", since it has from its inception been the most international of movements: for those reluctant to apply the label "anti-capitalist", "the movement for another globalisation" and "altermondialiste movement" are much better alternatives). But this poses the problem of how it pursues a genuinely transnational struggle. International mobilisations against G8 summits and World Trade Organisation meetings are one answer, but these are intermittent and artificial events, and are too vulnerable to the contingencies of location (which tend, precisely because of the protests, to be ever more remote) to be the basis for a sustained movement.

Opposition to the war in Iraq offered a genuinely universal unifying issue. No wonder, then, that 15 February 2003 represents a historic peak of global mass protest. But the bulk of the movement did not persist with anti-war mobilisation once Baghdad had fallen on 9 April 2003. There were a variety of reasons for this. As we have seen, one very influential actor, Attac, regarded the war as a diversion from the real priority of opposing neoliberal globalisation. Moreover, in much of continental Europe the peace movements also gave up serious anti-war campaigning. This reflected their origins as pacifist groupings campaigning against nuclear weapons during the Cold War. Ideologically and temperamentally they were ill-equipped to respond to a conflict pitting American imperialism against enemies it portrayed as "Islamo-fascist", and so threw in the towel with some relief.

In the US itself the luxury of not talking about the war wasn't available, and the US anti-war movement has mobilised on a very impressive scale. A series of historic demonstrations and the stand of anti-war troops and their families have helped to turn US opinion overwhelmingly against the war, a feat many had felt was impossible. But from the start the anti-war movement was divided. There was Answer, led by pro-North Korean Stalinists who have subsequently themselves split, and there was the much broader and more mainstream United for Peace and Justice. Many of this organisation's leaders and supporters allowed themselves to be diverted into John Kerry's presidential campaign in 2004, in the vain hope that even a pro-war Democrat would be better than George Bush. The distraction was doubly damaging because of the demoralisation caused by Kerry's defeat. It is only in the past year or so that the American anti-war movement has begun to recover from these setbacks.

There were, of course, exceptions to the pattern of dropping the issue of the war once it had started. The Spanish anti-war movement, though never well coordinated at a national level, played an important role in turning the tragedy of the Madrid train bombings into a rout for the warmongering Aznar government in March 2004. The movements in Turkey and Greece have continued to make an impact on their national political scene. But the most important exception has been the Stop the War Coalition in Britain, a new kind of anti-war movement founded specifically to oppose the "war on terrorism", whose radical left leadership has been able to sustain a broad coalition with considerable popular support and mobilising power.

At an international level, Focus on the Global South, whose roots lie in the 1990s campaigns against trade and debt from which the anti-capitalist movement emerged, has shown a very clear understanding of the connections between neoliberalism and imperialism and has devoted considerable effort to maintaining a global anti-war network. The annual Cairo Conference has built powerful links between the opposition in the most important Arab state and some Northern anti-war coalitions. But, important though these different initiatives are, and despite the fact that there is deep seated popular opposition everywhere to Bush's "long war", the fact remains that there is currently no real *global* movement against the war.

No other issue has emerged to replace the war as a transnational mobilising focus. The idea was floated at a meeting in Genoa in July 2003 of building "a social 15 February". It was a wonderful idea, but, in the circumstances, utopian. Everyone, wherever they were, could campaign against the war in Iraq. But neoliberal attacks necessarily unfold on a national terrain. Even when they reflect global or (within the European Union) continental initiatives by capital, the timing and content of their implementation are shaped by the nation-state concerned. Taking up what in the European movement has come to be called "the social question" therefore has a centrifugal logic.

Now in many ways this is a welcome development. The old establishment taunt at the anti-capitalist movement was that it was an elitist travelling circus. But the movement has in fact sunk real, national roots in some parts of the world. In Europe this has happened in a number of countries, notably France, Italy, Germany, Greece and Britain. But this has produced diverging political priorities in different countries.

For example, there has been a long-running debate between the movements in France and Britain over the relative priority of the war and "the social question". In part, this reflects real political disagreements arising from different appreciations of the relationship between neoliberalism and imperialism.[10]

10: For a brief summary of these differences, see Callinicos, 2004a, pp98-106.

At the same time, the different socio-political realities of the two countries mean that the issues differ in their mobilising power. France is the European country that has witnessed the most sustained resistance to neoliberalism, with social explosions in 1995, 2003, 2005, and 2006. In Britain, perhaps because neoliberalism was imposed here first and most comprehensively under the Thatcher government in the 1980s, there is a degree of popular fatalism about the possibility of stopping or reversing the inroads of the market that has, for example, made it difficult to mount effective mass agitation against the Bolkestein Directive aimed at privatising public services in the European Union. The war in Iraq has, by contrast, generated enormous popular anger that continues to bring large demonstrations onto the streets.

These difficulties have not made cross-border mobilisations against neoliberalism impossible. On the contrary, respectable altermondialiste contingents took part in protests in Brussels in March 2005 and Strasbourg in February 2006. But the reach of these mobilisations was limited to north western Europe and participants numbered in thousands, not tens or hundreds of thousands. This pattern will no doubt change with the further development of social resistance to neoliberalism—Britain included, since increasing pressure on living standards may lead to a revival in workers' struggles here—but this future prospect doesn't alter the present limitations of the movement.

The troubled return of politics

Greater engagement by the movements with their national realities has a further complicating effect. The more anti-capitalist coalitions find themselves operating in a national arena, the harder it is to evade the political field. But one of the founding myths of the movement is its separation from political parties, reflected in the famous ban on their participation in social forums in the WSF Charter of Principles. This was a symptom of what Daniel Bensaïd has aptly called:

> A "social illusion"...an illusion in the self-sufficiency of social movements reflected in the experiences after Seattle (1999) and the first World Social Forum in Porto Alegre (2001). Simplifying somewhat, I call this the "utopian moment" of social movements, which took different forms: utopias based on the regulation of free markets; Keynesian utopias; and above all neo-libertarian utopias, in which the world can be changed without taking

power or making do with counter-powers (John Holloway, Toni Negri, Richard Day).[11]

The ideology of autonomous social movements developed during the 1970s and 1980s, as the left and the organised working class suffered serious defeats. It is therefore not surprising that it should be a major influence on activists mobilising against neoliberalism. Many of them were veterans of these defeats. They are often based in non-governmental organisations (NGOs) that, by virtue of their social role, have a complex relationship of both distance from and dependence on official politics, or, as in France and Italy, they are based in the broad activist coalitions through which the altermondialiste movement began to develop in the course of the 1990s.[12] As time has gone on, this ideology has become a growing obstacle to the further development of the movement.

This can be seen in all three countries of the dominant trinity. In Brazil the ban on parties in the Porto Alegre charter was hypocrisy from the start. The WSF depended on a tacit understanding between its founders and the Workers' Party, which was, at the time of the WSF launch, in opposition at the federal level but in control of the city of Porto Alegre and the state of Rio Grande do Sul of which it is the capital. The election of Workers' Party leader Lula as president in October 2002 posed an acute problem for the movement both locally and internationally, since he stuck to the neoliberal economic policies of his predecessor, Fernando Henrique Cardoso.

The increasing integration of the Workers' Party leadership in Brazilian capitalism caused revulsion among many activists and intellectuals previously loyal to the party.[13] The Porto Alegre WSF in January 2005 was marked by a visible polarisation, with Lula addressing the forum at its start and Hugo Chávez speaking to a huge rally of the young at its end. That put the Porto Alegre charter on life support and dramatised the choice facing the left in Latin America between a regional version of Blairism and the search for 21st century socialism.

In France the pressure of the political field has been both more complex and more demanding. Probably the most important single impact that the anti-capitalist movement has had in a national arena was

11: Bensaïd, 2007, pp139-140.

12: See Nineham, 2006. Wintrebert, 2007, offers an interesting account of the role of such coalitions in the emergence of French altermondialisme—see chapter 1.

13: See the damning analyses in Oliveira, 2003 and 2006.

the role altermondialistes played in the campaign that defeated the neoliberal European Constitutional Treaty in the French referendum of 29 May 2005. Considerable credit must go to the leadership of Attac for identifying the issue of the constitution as a major challenge to the movement. But a decisive role in that movement was played by the traditional political organisations of the left, despite the contribution of Attac and other altermondialiste groups.

The French Socialist Party split as its rank and file rebelled against its leadership—a development that was matched in the CGT, the biggest trade union federation. A leading role within the national network of 29 May collectives was played by the Socialist Party left (and not so left) alongside the Communist Party and the Ligue Communiste Révolutionnaire (LCR). This was, as Stathis Kouvelakis put it, "the triumph of the political": "The real significance of the referendum process was the popular mobilisation which took hold of political questions on a scale not seen since the early 1970s".[14]

Building on this victory has, alas, proved very difficult. A strong will developed after the referendum to continue the coalition that had delivered the No vote and to give it a political expression by running a unitary anti-neoliberal candidate in the presidential elections of April-May 2007. This was, however, sabotaged by the two most important political organisations of the radical left, though they did so by pursuing opposed strategies. The Communist Party sought to embrace and indeed in many cases take over the 29 May collectives in order to gain their support for the candidacy of the party's general secretary, Marie-George Buffet. The LCR, by contrast, kept aloof and concentrated on preparing the presidential campaign of its candidate, Olivier Besancenot, a stance it justified on the grounds that the collectives had failed to rule out in principle participating in a social-liberal coalition government headed by the Socialist Party.

The result was chaos, rancour and division in the collectives. Instead of a unitary anti-neoliberal candidate running in the first round of the presidential elections on 22 April, the political fragmentation on the radical left actually increased compared to the first round five years before, with José Bové running as the candidate of the rump of the collectives against Buffet, Besancenot and two other Trotskyist candidates. The cohesion of the organised left has also been weakened, with powerful minorities in both the Communist Party and the LCR opposed to their parties' official positions.

14: Kouvelakis, 2005, p10.

The behaviour of the political organisations has increased hostility to parties and thereby strengthened the ideology of autonomous social movements. Besancenot's success in coming fifth in the first round with over 4 percent of the vote, well ahead of Buffet and Bové, salvaged something from this debacle, but it places a heavy responsibility on the LCR to take the initiative in building a genuinely united radical left.

The crisis of the French radical left also affected Attac. The replacement in 2002 of Cassen as president of Attac France by his chosen heir Jacques Nikonoff marked the beginning of an increasingly bitter faction fight. It pitted the two of them against a loose left that saw Attac as an important ingredient in a broader coalition of social movements rather than, as Susan George (sponsor of the opposition slate for the Attac leadership) put it, "a hierarchical, top-down pyramidal organisation with a strong executive, able to give orders to its troops and eventually to serve their private political ambitions on the French left".[15]

Cassen and Nikonoff made an abortive attempt to run an altermondialiste list in the European parliamentary elections in May 2004 and sought unsuccessfully to keep Attac local committees out of the collectives formed to oppose the European Constitution a year later. But, as Raphaël Wintrebert has documented in his important study of Attac, the shockingly autocratic methods used by Cassen and particularly by Nikonoff were an important factor in the developing polarisation. After the referendum victory Attac imploded into a fierce internal struggle that became worse after the National Administrative Council elections held in June 2006 were denounced by the defeated left opposition on grounds of fraud (their claims were upheld by two internal inquiries). The opposition won the restaged elections the following December but Cassen and Nikonoff showed their intention to continue the struggle by forming their own network, Avenir d'Attac.[16]

It was in Italy that the troubling question of the political representation of the social movements has had the most disastrous consequences. Fausto Bertinotti, general secretary of Rifondazione, closely identified his party with the social forums during their heady expansion between Genoa and Florence. He brilliantly used the abstract and ambiguous vocabulary of autonomism to give the impression that Rifondazione fully identified with the most radical ambitions of the anti-capitalist movement, without committing himself to anything very definite. But, as the

15: George, 2006.
16: Wintrebert, 2007, Part III.

social forums lost impetus, Bertinotti turned back towards mainstream politics.

He prepared the way for the party's return to the centre-left (from which it had broken in 1998) with a campaign in 2004 committing Rifondazione to pacifism and opposition to political violence. The logical culmination of the process was Rifondazione's entry into the centre-left government formed by Romano Prodi after he narrowly won the Italian general election in April 2006. Ironically, in the light of Bertinotti's earlier pacifist professions, this led to Rifondazione voting to support Italy's participation in the Nato military mission in Afghanistan and expelling a far left senator who abstained in one parliamentary division on this issue.

The effect on the anti-war movement in Italy, hitherto the largest in Europe, was nothing short of catastrophic. Piero Bernocchi of the left union Cobas described the situation at the end of 2006:

> There is now a big split in the Italian anti-war movement. A first part doesn't give to the occupation of Afghanistan the same importance as the occupation of Iraq; to avoid going against Prodi's government, it didn't want to organise anything when the government decided to maintain the troops in Afghanistan and this part is for the Italian troops in Lebanon. The second part is for withdrawal from Afghanistan but not from Lebanon. The third part, in which Cobas are, is for the end of all the Italian war missions (Afghanistan, Lebanon, Kosovo, etc).[17]

The consequences of these divisions were visible on the streets of Rome. On the first anniversary of the invasion of Iraq in March 2004 a million people had marched in Rome. Three years later only 30,000 demonstrated. Given the central role that the Italian social forums had played for the anti-capitalist movement globally at the time of Genoa and Florence, this was a disastrous development.

If the French case showed the difficulty in gaining political representation for the social movements and of overcoming the divisions among the established left organisations, the Italian situation highlighted the dependence of movements on parties. Despite all the talk of autonomous social movements, when Bertinotti moved rightwards, he pulled the Italian movement along with him, fragmenting it in the process. Both examples illustrate, unfortunately in negative terms, that movements seeking to challenge neoliberalism and imperialism cannot escape the political field.

17: Bernocchi, 2006.

Fragmentation and drift

These political divisions were greatly reinforced by the increasingly dysfunctional way in which the anti-capitalist movement organises itself. From Seattle onwards the principle has prevailed that decisions are taken in assemblies open to all and on the basis of consensus. This method of decision making did have some advantages in the early phase of the movement's development. Giving everyone a veto helped to build trust in a new coalition involving actors from very different backgrounds and it bypassed the problem of deciding how to weigh the votes of different organisations, which would have been raised by a system of delegate democracy.

Nevertheless, there are very high costs to this supposedly "horizontal" form of democracy. It is subject to what was long ago identified in the American women's movement as "the tyranny of structurelessness": in the absence of formal structure, informal elites emerge to ensure that the movement actually functions.[18] This has been very visible in the European Social Forum (ESF) process, where an alliance of the French and Italian altermondialiste coalitions has largely dominated decision making.

From the start, securing consensus has frequently involved backdoor bargaining to arrive at compromises; recalcitrant minorities have sometimes been bullied into not exercising their right to veto decisions; chair-people, seeking to manage difficult and often lengthy meetings, have always sought to steer discussion, sometimes in a very directive way. Moreover, the quickly established procedure of taking decisions at the European Preparatory Assembly, whose venue shifts each time from one European city to another, tended to ensure the dominance of large organisations—trade unions, NGOs, the different branches of Attac, political parties—with the resources to send delegates to these meetings.

Instead of recognition of these defects, leading to a serious attempt to improve the democratic functioning of the process, there has been a marked degeneration. In the lead-up to the London ESF, Italian and to a lesser extent French delegates persistently intervened to support the opposition of a fairly marginal grouping of autonomists to the British coalition responsible for bringing the forum to London, and acquiesced in the attempts violently to disrupt the forum and the closing rally. Subsequently, however, the situation became substantially worse.

The Athens ESF, held in May 2006, had to contend with deep

18: Freeman, 1972.

political divisions. On one side was the Greek Social Forum, a coalition of far left sects sponsored by the radical left party Synaspismos and by the Franco-Italian axis, and on the other was Genoa 2001, involving the Greek Socialist Workers Party and the Greens, and linked to the Greek trade union federation. The result of a bitterly contested preparatory process was the smallest ESF to date, where even the large concluding demonstration was marred by a row over the order of march that saw violent attacks by Greek Social Forum "stewards" on the anti-war contingent.

None of this stopped the dominant forces in the ESF process from proclaiming Athens a success. But the difficulties that they have faced in finding a viable national coalition willing to host the fifth ESF were symptomatic—it took till April 2007, nearly a year after Athens, to reach agreement that the next Forum will take place in Scandinavia in September 2008, and even then the venue—either the Danish capital, Copenhagen, or the Swedish city of Malmö—remains undecided. No wonder attendance at European Preparatory Assemblies has dwindled, as many participants have voted with their feet, leaving the Franco-Italian hard core and their hangers on to dominate. Despite the growing evidence of crisis, however, this group has, ever since the London ESF, responded by seeking organisational solutions, reflected by a growing obsession with "methodology" that has spawned yet more all-European meetings and thereby made the decision-making process even more opaque and unaccountable.

The same preoccupation with procedure was evident in the faction fight inside Attac, where the leaders of the opposition (many of them, such as Pierre Khalfa, prominent in the ESF process) made what Wintrebert calls the "important 'strategic' error" of arguing that "it wasn't fundamental problems that divided the leading members [of Attac], but only a problem of the 'style of leadership'." This conceded the initiative to Nikonoff and Cassen, who were much more willing to introduce political issues, such as their defence of French republican "laicity" against the Muslim veil.[19]

The problems created by this kind of organisational overload were reinforced by the increasing influence of the conception of the social forums advanced by Cassen and another of the founders of the WSF, the Brazilian Chico Whitaker. For them, the social forums do not belong to a movement, or even the "movements of movements". Rather, they are "a socially horizontal space" where different actors can converge to discuss and share

19: Wintrebert, 2007, p261.

perspectives.[20] In particular—and this is a constant source of puzzlement to participants in social forums who are uninitiated into these mysteries—the international forums don't take decisions. This risks alienating activists who want to be part of the movement's decision-making process and who are often radicalised partly by the way neoliberalism has hollowed out democratic political forms at national level. It is also off-putting because it can turn the social forums into talking shops pure and simple. An interplay between discussion, decision and mobilisation is the lifeblood of any real movement.

The left within the movement has sought to bypass the problem by inventing the Assembly of the Social Movements, where different social movements get together at the end of each social forum and adopt an action plan of mobilisations. The device immediately attracted the hostility of Whitaker, Cassen and others on the right of the movement. Their response has involved celebrating "diversity" by fragmenting social forums around different "thematic priorities". Thus the fifth WSF in Brazil in January 2005 was spread along the banks of the river Guiba in Porto Alegre with the division of the site into 11 distinct "thematic terrains". As we wrote at the time:

> Space A was devoted to autonomous thought, B to defending diversity, plurality, and identities, C to art and creation, and so on. The effect was tremendously to fragment the forum. If you were interested in a particular subject—say, culture or war or human rights—you could easily spend the entire four days in one relatively small area without coming into contact with people interested in different subjects.[21]

Even though European activists reacted negatively to that WSF, the drive to fragment the Social Forums was used to justify the absence of any unifying events at the Athens ESF. Even figures generally on the left of the movement gave way to the new cult of diversity. Piero Bernocchi argued at an European preparatory meeting in Istanbul in September 2005 that the altermondialiste movement was a "rainbow coalition" that could not take decisions over priorities. But the very strength of the movement from Seattle onwards lay in the convergence of different coalitions in a common struggle against neoliberalism and war. Had the view Bernocchi expressed in Istanbul prevailed before Florence, 15 February would never have happened.

20: See, for example, Whitaker, 2003.

21: Callinicos and Nineham, 2005.

Fragmentation reached the level of caricature in Nairobi. Cramped physical conditions and organisational chaos meant that there was no repetition of the physical partition into "thematic terrains". But the official programme concluded with "big forums of struggles and alternatives" meeting separately to discuss 21 different themes, followed by "a tree-planting event". The left successfully insisted on ending instead with an unscheduled Assembly of the Social Movements, which at least agreed on a common schedule of future mobilisations.

But the assemblies are organised within the prevailing ideology of autonomous social movements and therefore reflect the weaknesses already discussed. As in other cases, the method of consensus decision making tends to ensure the dominance of "insiders" with resources and connections. The agenda and order of speakers are fixed in advance by meetings that, though theoretically open to all, are run by veterans and those with the greatest resources and stamina. There is very rarely any real discussion at the assemblies themselves—and never any voting. This rules out the possibility of any serious popular discussion or development of strategy. They do serve a real function and represent a sincere effort by those who organise them to give some coherence to the movement. But they don't provide the kind of democratic decision making the movement needs.

Many activists have grown increasingly impatient with the fragmentation and drift that have come to prevail. At last year's WSF in Bamako, Mali, Samir Amin of Egypt and François Houtart of Belgium initiated an appeal. It "aims at consolidating the gains made" at the social forums by "defining and promoting alternatives capable of mobilising social and political forces. The goal is a radical transformation of the capitalist system".[22]

Amin, a leading radical dependency theorist in the 1960s and 1970s, has been a key figure in pressing for a much greater strategic focus for the anti-capitalist movement:

> There is no room for self-congratulation about these successes [of the movement]. They remain insufficient to shift the balance of social and political forces in favour of the popular classes, and therefore remain vulnerable to the extent that the movement has not moved from defensive resistance to the offensive... Progress is and will be difficult. For it implies (i) the radicalisation of struggles and (ii) their convergence in diversity...in common action plans, which imply a strategic political vision, the definition

22: Amin et al, 2006. See Sen and Kumar (eds), 2007.

> of immediate and more distant objectives (the "perspective" that defines the alternative). The radicalisation of struggles is not that of the rhetoric of their discourses, but their articulation of an alternative project with which they propose to replace the prevailing systems of social power...convergence can only be the product of a "politicisation" (in the good sense of the word) of the fragmented movements. This necessity is resisted by the discourse of "apolitical civil society", an ideology imported directly from the United States, which continues to exert its ravages.[23]

Amin, who goes on to criticise "the theorists of autonomist currents [who] affirm that we can change the world without taking power", for denying the necessity of a strategic convergence of struggles, also notes that the Bamako Appeal had "irritated the WSF 'Secretariat'." Indeed a seminar on the appeal in Nairobi saw a fierce clash when Chico Whitaker objected strongly to Trevor Ngwane's critical defence of the appeal and criticisms of the fragmentation and absence of strategy in the WSF. But it was clear that large numbers of activists were worried about the lack of direction of the movement. The response of the WSF international council was to issue a call for worldwide mobilisations to coincide with the big business World Economic Forum in January 2008—a decision that both contradicted the ideology of the social forums as simply "spaces" and implied that a summons to action from the stratosphere could somehow magically give unity and impetus to the movement.

Moving forward

It is important not to take too cataclysmic a view of the current condition of the anti-capitalist movement. Above all, the other side isn't in too good a state. The World Trade Organisation's Doha round, launched in November 2001 and intended radically to deepen global capitalism's reach into national economies and to demonstrate the unity of the world's ruling classes after 9/11, has run to a halt. True, the anti-capitalist movement can't claim the chief credit for this, which lies with the deep and persisting divisions between the United States and the European Union and the emergence of a new bloc of powerful Third World states, the Group of 20. Moreover, both Washington and Brussels are seeking to bypass the deadlock by negotiating bilateral economic partnership agreements with individual countries. Nevertheless, the disarray in the World Bank with Paul Wolfowitz's sacking symbolises the larger difficulties faced by the neoliberal camp.

23: Amin, 2007.

The plight of the imperialist offensive launched by the Bush administration after 11 September 2001 is, of course, much more serious. US failure to impose its will on Iraq led to the administration's defeat in the mid-term elections in November 2006 and goaded Bush into ordering a military "surge" that shows no signs of succeeding. America and its Nato allies are mired in a long-term guerrilla war in Afghanistan that may prove equally intractable. There is a crisis of legitimacy for US global hegemony that will limit Washington's ability to exercise "soft" ideological power as well.

A poll of 26,000 people in 25 countries for the BBC World Service in January 2007 revealed that 73 percent disapproved of the Iraq War, while "majorities across the 25 countries also disapprove of US handling of Guantanamo detainees (67 percent), the Israeli-Hezbollah war (65 percent), Iran's nuclear programme (60 percent), global warming (56 percent), and North Korea's nuclear programme (54 percent)". 49 percent of those polled said that the US is playing a mainly negative role in the world.[24] This erosion of America's global standing has real effects. Commenting on US secretary of state Condoleezza Rice's shift towards a more compromising position on issues such as North Korean nukes, the *Financial Times* explained:

> Ms Rice has been forced by America's drastically compromised situation in Iraq into making changes from a position of weakness. "When you have a hammer, everything looks like a nail," said a former senior diplomat in the Clinton administration. "But, because of Iraq, these guys don't have much of a hammer any more".[25]

The weakening of US hegemony isn't just a consequence of the ham-fisted arrogance of the Bush administration. It is an achievement of those who have opposed the global state of exception proclaimed by Bush after 9/11. Pride of place here must go to the resistance in Iraq itself, but the international anti-war movement can claim a share of credit.

Washington's descent into the Iraqi quagmire has in turn created a space in which resistance can develop elsewhere. The most important case in point here is Latin America, especially in Venezuela and Bolivia where the interaction between mass movements and political leaders has produced governments that have begun, in however hesitant and inconsistent a way,

24: BBC World Service, 2007.
25: Luce, Barber, and Dinmore, 2007.

to pursue a logic that breaks with neoliberalism.

None of these very positive features of the present situation alter or remove the difficulties that we have discussed above. What they do cast into question is any suggestion that the balance of forces is shifting decisively to the right or that the cycle of struggles that began in the mid-1990s is drawing to a close. Even in Europe, where the movement is in greatest trouble, we are barely a year away from the massive revolt by French students and trade unionists that smashed the CPE law reducing the rights of young workers. The persistence of the neoliberal offensive will undoubtedly produce more social explosions, particularly if France's new right wing president, Nicolas Sarkozy, carries out his threat to drive through market "reforms".

The critical issue is that posed by Samir Amin when he asks: "Does the World Social Forum benefit popular struggles?" In other words, what is the relationship between the anti-capitalist movement as an organised force and mass resistance to neoliberalism and imperialism? The honest answer is that is pretty variable and is likely to remain so. The organisational implosion of the European movement does not make one especially optimistic about the ESF. If the next forum does indeed take place in Scandinavia, this will be in a region where anti-capitalist resistance has been at a comparatively low level (with the exception of the protests at the Gothenburg EU summit in June 2001). A Scandinavian ESF will probably be the most right wing yet, dominated by NGOs and the local branches of Attac.

The same need not be true of the WSF. Even in Nairobi there were, as we have already suggested, hints of the explosion of energy that can be generated by the convergence of different movements. Unfortunately, as we have seen, the dominant forces in the WSF process are pushing in the opposite direction, and promoting fragmentation rather than what Amin calls "convergence in diversity". It is the duty of the left within the anti-capitalist movement firmly to resist these tendencies. This resistance, however, needs to be accompanied by an alternative strategy that is informed by an understanding of the strengths and weaknesses of the movement to date.

This understanding has to involve an open break with the ideology of autonomous social movements. Too often the left has taken its stand within the framework of that ideology, whether for tactical reasons or from principled agreement. But a break is required by an honest appreciation of the interplay between political parties and social movements. The truth is that cooperation between the two actually strengthens both. However much retrospect is coloured by Bertinotti's subsequent right turn, the high points of the European movement at Genoa and Florence were informed by this cooperation, involving not merely Rifondazione but also smaller parties of the radical left such as the LCR and the Socialist Workers Party as well as more radical elements of Italy's centre-left Left Democrats.

The same is true at a global level. The peak so far reached by the WSF took place, not at any of the Porto Alegre Forums, but in Mumbai in January 2004, infused as it was by both a strong anti-imperialist consciousness and the movements of India's vast poor. But the two key organisations of the Indian left—the Communist Party (Marxist) and the Communist Party of India—alongside various Maoist organisations, played a critical role both in making the forum possible and in restraining themselves from trying to dominate the forum or competing too openly among themselves.

An honest reappraisal of the relationship between parties and movements would allow the social forums to play to their strengths. The two most successful forums—Florence and Mumbai—were ones where opposition to the "war on terror" was a dominant theme. Saying this does not mean returning to the tedious and sterile argument—either the war or the "social question". Opposition to both neoliberalism and war are constitutive themes of the anti-capitalist movement. But recognition of both the principled significance and the mobilising power of anti-imperialism needs to be built into how the social forums operate. This was proved by the success of last year's "polycentric" WSF in Caracas, Venezuela. It was taken for granted among the tens of thousands of mainly Latin American activists assembled there that the US poses a real and present threat to the gains being made by movements in Bolivia, Venezuela and Ecuador. President Hugo Chávez echoed many others when he spoke there of the importance of the movement against the Iraq war in weakening the US's ability to act in what it regards traditionally as its own backyard.

Yet the Caracas forum also showed up the limitations of the WSF process. It should have been possible, for example, to launch a very high profile, high powered campaign from the forum calling on all the movements round the world to pledge defence of the gains of the Chavista experience so far. Many present were suggesting it. But because of the autonomist principles so jealously guarded by the WSF leadership, no such centralised initiative was taken.

In breaking out of this impasse, it will be necessary to define precisely what the radical left is within the movement. This is no simple matter. The big Indian Communist parties, despite the very positive role they played in the Mumbai WSF, participate in neoliberal coalitions at the all-India and state levels: the Left Front government in West Bengal has violently clashed with workers and peasants in recent months. The sorry record of Rifondazione has already been discussed. A much more principled organisation, the LCR, has kept aloof from the anti-capitalist movement as an organisation, because of its acceptance of a version of the ideology of autonomous social movements (although individual LCR members such as Christophe Aguiton, Pierre Rousset and Sophie Zafari have played important roles in the movement at global and/or European levels).

Documents of the left within the movement tend to espouse versions of radical reformism. The Bamako Appeal's first plank is, "For a multipolar world founded on peace, LAW and negotiation".[26] Amin's pronouncements are sometimes redolent of nostalgia for the high tide of Third World nationalism between the 1950s and 1970s: "The reconstruction of a 'front of the countries and peoples of the South' is one of the fundamental conditions for the emergence of 'another world' not based on imperialist domination".[27] Another important figure on the left of the movement, Walden Bello of Focus on the Global South, shows a similar approach in his calls for "deglobalisation".[28] Such formulations do not sufficiently address the reality that confronting imperialism as a system will require global social transformation based on the collective power and organisation of the oppressed and exploited in the North as well as the South.

None of this should prevent cooperation among different forces on the left seeking to give the anti-capitalist movement a more coherent and strategically focused direction. Such cooperation is essential. But it needs to be accompanied by open debate about the nature of the enemy that we are confronted with and of the alternatives that we should be seeking.[29] Striking the right balance between disagreement and cooperation once again requires a break with the ideology of autonomous social movements.

This ideology conceives social movements as a neutral space somehow

---

26: Amin, et al, 2006. For a critical take on such slogans, see Miévelle, 2005.

27: Amin, 2007.

28: Bello, 2002.

29: See, for example, Callinicos, 2003, and Callinicos, 2006.

beyond politics. But fighting neoliberalism and war is necessarily a highly political affair, and nowhere is free of the antagonisms of wider capitalist society. The development of the movements necessarily generates political disagreements that cannot be kept separate from party organisations. The emergence of new anti-capitalist political formations that are at least partly the product of movements of resistance—Portugal's Left Bloc, the Left Party in Germany, Respect in Britain—shows the extent to which activists recognise the need for a political voice as part of the development of opposition to neoliberalism and war.

We believe that the concept of the united front, developed by the revolutionary Marxist tradition, provides a better guide to building democratic, dynamic movements than does the model that has prevailed so far. A united front involves the coming together of different forces around a common but limited platform of action. Precisely because they are different, these forces will have disagreements about political programme; they may also differ over how to pursue the common actions that have brought them together. But so long as they come together round limited and relatively specific aims, such alliances can be politically inclusive and maximise the chances of practical campaigning agreement. Because they are focused round action, they can be a testing ground for different tactics and strategies. This is the way to break movements away from abstract position taking or sectarian point scoring, so providing a framework in which political debate and practical organising can fruitfully interplay.

Constructing such united fronts is not easy: it requires initiative and clear leadership on the one hand, and openness and humility on the other. But at a time when the anger against neoliberalism is growing everywhere and so many people are reassessing their political loyalties, it seems to us that the anti-capitalist left needs urgently to try such methods if it is to reach out and connect with its potential audience.

There is unlikely to be agreement between the different tendencies in the movement in the short or medium term over general political alternatives. But we can reach constructive agreement on the many issues—opposition to neoliberalism and war—that unite a large spectrum of forces. It is precisely this kind of unity in action that many people are looking for in the current situation. Through the experience of such campaigning, new political coalitions can emerge. Moreover, the left within the movement, whether revolutionary or reformist, should working together in order to fight to give the movement a more strategic and focused direction.

Many of the ideas and arguments of the anti-capitalist movement have gone mainstream in the seven long years since Seattle. Neoliberalism has been widely discredited. The world's "hyper-power" is in the process of a terrible humiliation in the Middle East that will have major repercussions for its ability to intervene and shape geopolitics. In these circumstances the left has a responsibility to examine the weaknesses as well as the strengths of the anti-capitalist movement as it has functioned up to now, and not allow the movement to be trapped in an impasse.

References

Amin, Samir, 2007, "Le Forum Social Mondial est-il utile pour les luttes populaires?", 1 February 2007, www.forumsocialmundial.org.br/noticias_textos.php?cd_news=349

Amin, Samir, et al, 2006, "The Bamako Appeal", 18 January 2006, www.openspaceforum.net/twiki/tiki-read_article.php?articleId=66

BBC World Service, 2007, "World View of US Role Goes from Bad to Worse", 23 January 2007, http://news.bbc.co.uk/1/shared/bsp/hi/pdfs/23_01_07_us_poll.pdf

Bello, Walden, 2002, *Deglobalisation: Ideas for a New World Economy* (Zed).

Bello, Walden, 2007, "The World Social Forum at the Crossroads", *Foreign Policy in Focus*, 5 May 2007, www.fpif.org/fpiftxt/4196

Bensaïd, Daniel, 2007, "The Return of Strategy", *International Socialism 113* (winter 2007), www.isj.org.uk/index.php4?id=287&issue=113

Bernocchi, Piero, 2006, email circulated on European Social Forum list, 5 December 2006 (English lightly edited), http://lists.fse-esf.org/pipermail/fse-esf/2006-December/001399.html

Callinicos, Alex, 2003, *An Anti-Capitalist Manifesto* (Polity).

Callinicos, Alex, 2004a, "The Future of the Anti-Capitalist Movement", in Hannah Dee (ed), *Anti-Capitalism: Where Next?* (Bookmarks).

Callinicos, Alex, 2004b, "Building on the Success of the London ESF", 26 November 2004, circulated by email, www.resist.org.uk/reports/archive/esf2004/esf04_07.php

Callinicos, Alex, 2006, "Alternatives to Neoliberalism", *Socialist Review*, July 2006, www.socialistreview.org.uk/article.php?articlenumber=9793

Callinicos, Alex and Chris Nineham, 2005, "Critical Reflections on the Fifth World Social Forum", 8 February 2005, www.forumsocialmundial.org.br/dinamic.php?pagina=bl_Callinicos_vfsm_i

Cassen, Bernard, 2003a, *Tout a Commence à Porto Alegre* (Mille et une nuits).

Cassen, Bernard, 2003b, "On the Attack", *New Left Review 19* (January-February 2003), http://newleftreview.org/A2431

Charlton, John and Emma Bircham (eds), 2001, *Anti-Capitalism: A Guide to the Movement* (Bookmarks).

Ciccaglione, Bruno, 2007, "WSF in Nairobi: Urgent to relaunch the social movements", circulated by e-mail on the European Social Forum list, 13 February 2007 (English lightly edited).

Freeman, Jo, 1972, "The Tyranny of Structurelessness", The Second Wave, volume 2, number 1, www.jofreeman.com/joreen/tyranny.htm

George, Susan, 2006, "A New Beginning for Attac France", *Transnational Institute*, 28 December 2006, www.tni.org/detail_page.phtml?&page=archives_george_attacnewbeginning

Harman, Chris, 2000, "Anti-Capitalism: Theory and Practice", *International Socialism 88* (Autumn 2000), http://pubs.socialistreviewindex.org.uk/isj88/harman.htm

Kouvelakis, Stathis, 2005, "France: The Triumph of the Political", *International Socialism 108* (autumn 2005), www.isj.org.uk/index.php4?id=134&issue=108

Luce, Edward, Lionel Barber and Guy Dinmore, 2007, "How Rice is Learning to Play a Weaker US Hand", *Financial Times*, 23 April 2007.

Mertes, Tom (ed), 2003, *The Movement of Movements* (Verso).

Miéville, China, 2005, *Between Equal Rights* (Brill).

Nineham, Chris, 2006, "Anti-Capitalism, Social Forums, and the Return of Politics", *International Socialism 109* (winter 2006), www.isj.org.uk/index.php4?id=161&issue=109

Oliveira, Francisco de, 2003, "The Duckbilled Platypus", *New Left Review 24* (November-December 2003).

Oliveira, Francisco de, 2006, "Lula in the Labyrinth", *New Left Review 42* (November-December 2006), http://newleftreview.org/?page=article&view=2642
Oloo, Onyango, 2007, "Critical Reflections on WSF 2007 Nairobi", CADTM, 19 March 2007, www.cadtm.org/article.php3?id_article=2544
Sen, Jai, and Madhuresh Kumar (eds), 2007, *A Political Programme for the World Social Forum?* (Indian Insitute for Critical Action & University of KwaZulu-Natal Centre for Civic Society), www.cacim.net/bareader/home.html
Tormey, Simon, 2004, *Anti-Capitalism: A Beginner's Guide* (Oneworld).
Whitaker, Chico, 2003, "Notes about the World Social Forum", 17 March 2003, www.forumsocialmundial.org.br/dinamic.php?pagina=bal_whitaker_ing
Wintrebert, Raphaël, 2007, *Attac, la politique autrement?* (Editions La Découverte).

France at the crossroads

Antoine Boulangé and Jim Wolfreys

Prior to the presidential election of April/May 2007 France seemed to epitomise both the crisis facing mainstream politics in Europe and the potential of the developing movement against neoliberalism, which had scored a number of important victories. However, the election, when it came, appeared to confound such assumptions. Not only did the three mainstream parties (the Gaullist UMP, the Socialists and the centre-right UDF) win three quarters of the first-round vote, up from less than 50 percent in 2002, but in the second round Nicolas Sarkozy won a resounding victory over the Socialist candidate, Ségolène Royal.

The right wing *Figaro* newspaper wrote that with Sarkozy's victory "France is embarking on a neo-conservative turn of the same type as those experienced in their time by Margaret Thatcher's Great Britain, Ronald Reagan's America, José Maria Aznar's Spain, or even Silvio Berlusconi's Italy".[1] The radical left, meanwhile, emerged from the election in a fragmented state, with three of the principal figures of the successful 2005 campaign against the EU constitution—the Communist Marie-George Buffet, the LCR's Olivier Besancenot, and the *altermondialiste* activist José Bové competing with Lutte Ouvrière's perennial candidate Arlette Laguiller for a share of the vote. Their scores were squeezed by the pressure to avoid a repeat of the 2002 debacle, when far right leader Jean-Marie Le Pen beat the Socialists into third place. Only Besancenot, who won around 1.5 million votes, was able to improve on his 2002 performance.

1: Wolton, 2007.

The others achieved disappointing results, with the Communist electorate amounting to little more than the family and friends of its 80,000 members.

Table: First round, presidential election, 22 April 2007
Source: French interior ministry

Candidate	Votes	Percentage
Nicolas Sarkozy	11,448,663	31.18
Ségolène Royal	9,500,112	25.87
François Bayrou	6,820,119	18.57
Jean-Marie Le Pen	3,834,530	10.44
Olivier Besancenot	1,498,581	4.08
Philippe de Villiers	818,407	2.23
Marie-George Buffet	707,268	1.93
Dominique Voynet	576,666	1.57
Arlette Laguiller	487,857	1.33
José Bové	483,008	1.32
Frédéric Nihous	420,645	1.15
Gérard Schivardi	123,540	0.34

What should we make of all this? Most of the Western media has concluded that the 2007 election represented a revival of mainstream parties and an end to French exceptionalism, presaging the "modernisation" of the French economy along neoliberal lines, and the reconfiguration of both right and left in, respectively, neo-conservative and Blairite guises. As for the radical left, some have argued that its failure to achieve either a unity candidacy or an improvement on its 2002 score was because it had overestimated the significance of the vote against the EU constitution in May 2005, and had therefore exaggerated the opportunities open to it.[2] Others have claimed that France has simply shifted to the right.

This article will argue that the election does not mark a fundamental

2: Zappi, 2007.

break with the political situation opened up by the struggles of 1995, but is an expression of the ongoing process of polarisation that has been a characteristic of this period. In a context of political reconfiguration it is the mainstream right under Sarkozy that has been able to claw back the initiative, with the Socialist Party in disarray and the radical left still struggling to come to terms with the choices and responsibilities incumbent upon it.

French exceptionalism: myths and reality

A constant refrain of the British media is that France needs to "modernise". Simon Heffer, writing in the *Daily Telegraph*, offers a typical generalisation: "While much of the rest of the world moves on through the application of free-market economic disciplines, France is demoralised, impoverished, overtaxed and in despair".[3] On the eve of the second-round poll he compared the choice of Sarkozy or Royal to that between Margaret Thatcher and James Callaghan faced by British voters in 1979.[4]

But this image of a France that is immune to neoliberalism and aloof from a globalising economy is a myth. The past two decades have seen wholesale privatisation of public services by governments of the left and right alike, and the opening up of the domestic market to international competition. France is ranked second only to Britain worldwide in terms of foreign direct investment.[5] Between 1993 and 2003 the number of subsidiary firms owned by foreign capital tripled, with one employee in seven now working for foreign concerns, compared to one in ten British or German workers.[6] The proportion of major industrial firms that are foreign owned stands at roughly 50 percent in France, while for France's competitors the rate is between 10 percent and 25 percent.[7] Twelve of the top 40 French firms have less than a quarter of their workforce based in France, with 66 percent of the activity of leading firms conducted abroad. Alcatel, for example, is listed on nine major stock exchanges across the world, while 95 percent of Total's profits were made abroad in 2005.[8]

What is really at stake is not whether France can adapt to the world market, but more specifically, whether those who hold power can face down opposition to neoliberal reform. As Philippe Marlière argues, "Over

3: Heffer, 2006.
4: Heffer, 2007.
5: *Les Echos*, 20 February 2007.
6: *Alternatives Economiques*, winter 2006.
7: *AGREP*, 2 May 2006.
8: *L'Express*, 30 March 2006.

the past 15 years, French workers have successfully defeated the greatest attacks on their welfare state. This is unique in the West. This French exceptionalism angers those who feel that neoliberal economics are not politically and ideologically driven, but the best science can offer".[9]

It is true that over the past decade the proportion of GDP taken up by public debt has grown at a faster rate in France than in any pre-enlargement EU country. Much was made of this debt during the campaign—one current affairs show put a debt counter on its screen for the duration of the election, while the British media lazily and repeatedly echoed widespread misconceptions about France's "bloated public sector".[10] What none of them acknowledged was the fact that public debt in France amounts to less than the total sum paid out to companies every year in subsidies—65 billion euros, more than the entire education budget. Nearly a third of this figure is taken up with the cost of exonerating companies from making social security contributions.[11]

It is also true that for each of the past ten years the French economy has grown at a slower rate than the average for the OECD countries. Yet total profits for major firms rose by 218 percent in the ten years to 2005 (by 42 percent for smaller companies), reaching 84 billion euros.[12] Profits represent 40 percent of annually created wealth in France, against 33.5 percent in the US and 31.5 percent in Britain. Despite the fact that almost half the profits made in France are paid out in dividends to shareholders,[13] it was the question of productivity that became a central question of the campaign. French workers are more productive per hour than US or British workers, but they work fewer hours.[14] Sarkozy's response was to target the 35-hour week, which he intends to demolish by scrapping the extra charges incurred by firms when employees work overtime, along with the bonuses paid to workers who do so. Fatuously claiming to be speaking on behalf of "the France that gets up early", he claimed this would allow those who wanted to work more to earn more. But in reality, as Olivier Besancenot pointed out throughout the campaign, the scrapping of overtime bonuses meant that people would instead be working more and earning less. Meanwhile, Royal, despite defending the principle of

9: Marlière, 2007.

10: During the election this phrase appeared in the *Guardian*, the *Daily Telegraph* and the *Times*, as well as the *New York Times* and the *Washington Post*.

11: *La Documentation Française*, 2007.

12: *Economist*, 28 October 2006.

13: *L'Express*, 8 October 2006.

14: OECD, 2005.

the 35-hour week, made the need for French people to be "reconciled" with business values a cornerstone of her campaign. An editorial in the *Economist* in autumn 2006 summed up how those who hold such values view the French economy:

> The government...has been paralysed ever since street protests forced it to withdraw a modest labour market reform in the spring... France matters. It is the world's sixth biggest economy, a permanent member of the UN Security Council and a declared nuclear power. It was a founder of today's European Union... It is in part thanks to France's paralysis that the union itself is so uncertain of its direction... It will always be hard to get reforms past the gauntlet of France's street protesters. But at least the government is not hobbled by the scratchy coalition politics that bedevils all attempts at reform in Germany and Italy... The real issue is not whether France is reformable—for the answer must be yes. It is whether there is a Madame Thatcher who has the courage to take on vested interests.

The recipe for reform envisaged by the *Economist* is a familiar one: cuts in public services and social security, privatisation, deregulation, a longer working week, health service and pension reform. What stands in the way of this is the failure of successive governments to take on and beat the labour movement.

Sarkozy has positioned himself as the champion of a "clean break": an end to the compromises and retreats that right wing governments have been forced into over the past decade and a half. As he put it in his own blunt words during the campaign, "We must liquidate the heritage of May 1968".[15] His immediate targets are those who defeated his predecessors. He plans to get a version of the neoliberal EU constitution, which the public rejected two years ago, adopted by parliament. The lifting of restrictions on overtime will effectively end the 35-hour week. He plans to reduce the number of fixed term contracts by introducing a single contract for the workplace modelled on the right wing Villepin government's CPE labour legislation, which will make it easier for workers to be sacked. His attacks on unions include the imposition of secret ballots after eight days of strike action in the public sector, schools and universities, and the obligation on transport and other public sector workers to provide a "minimum service" during strikes. His ministry of "immigration and national identity" will fix quotas on the numbers of immigrants to France, and decide who

15: *Le Figaro*, 30 April 2007.

among them has "a vocation" to become French. Repeat offenders will be subject to a policy of "three strikes and you're out", resulting in an automatic maximum penalty, and the treatment of minors will begin to be aligned with that of adult offenders. The unemployed will be denied benefits if they turn down more than two jobs for which they are qualified. Despite the traditional inclusive noises made by Sarkozy on the night of his election, his presidency will accentuate the polarisation of domestic politics and, on the world stage, push French foreign policy in a more pro-US, pro-Israel direction.

On the face of it, then, Sarkozy represents the *Economist*'s "chance" for France: a neo-conservative hybrid of Napoleon Bonaparte and Margaret Thatcher. His victory is a serious setback for the movement against neoliberalism. But the scale of resistance constrains his room for manoeuvre. During the CPE protests last year, for example, voices on the right urged the Villepin government to hold out against the movement, evoking Thatcher's stance against the miners. Sarkozy, having initially taken a hard line, was one of the voices urging a compromise solution to the crisis. The right, as the defeat of each of its governments for nearly three decades prior to 2007 demonstrates, has nowhere near the popular support enjoyed by Thatcher, which means that its every attempt to take to the offensive has only reinforced its isolation from the rest of the population. Sarkozy's own victory was only achieved by distancing himself from Villepin and Chirac in order to present himself as an outsider figure.

Royal is also constrained by the general crisis of the political establishment, but her position is further complicated by the decline of the Socialist Party. So, while the party leadership would have liked to implement neoliberal attacks on the labour movement in the name of "modernisation", it also had to seek electoral support from a constituency whose outlook remains significantly to the left of the party, and which deserted it in 2002 and in the 2005 referendum on the EU constitution. These contradictions plagued Royal's campaign. Sensing that her "social liberal" (ie social and free market) message was undermining popular support for the Socialists, party leader François Hollande announced that the party would increase the tax burden on those taking home more than 4,000 euros (£2,300) a month—80 percent of employees in France take home less than half this amount. Royal responded that, on the contrary, she had no intention of reversing the tax breaks for the rich introduced by the right, despite the fact that these amounted to 120 billion euros a year, higher than either France's social security or pension deficits.[16] A week later Sarkozy, the candidate who pays the most wealth tax, made a speech proclaiming himself the champion of working men and women. Royal's reaction was to unveil a 100-point programme in February that was far to the left of anything she had previously proposed. "She was losing support both from the establishment of the party and from the left, so she's going back to the socialist orthodoxy," was how one economist explained her plans to raise the state pension and the minimum wage and to renationalise the electricity industry.[17]

Such incoherence from the Royal entourage, combined with various mishaps (her campaign spokesperson told a national television audience that Royal's only defect was her husband, Hollande), undermined her credibility. But the basic problem facing Royal was that, whereas Tony Blair was able to benefit from opposition to 18 years of Thatcherism while pursuing his own market-driven agenda, the Socialists have shared power with the right for the past 25 years and can no longer automatically win votes from those who know what "social liberalism" in office means. Despite being one of the weakest Socialist parties in Europe, the French Socialist Party has been in government for 15 of the past 25 years. Over this period the party's activist base has steadily eroded. The reliance on polls and outside agencies as a substitute for activism should not, as one recent study of the party points out, just be seen as a consequence of the influence of television and the media; it is also a reaction to the shrinking of active party membership. This decline manifests itself in many ways, from the contraction of the party's activist networks to the weakening of the organised currents that structured internal party competition and debate. In this sense Royal is the logical candidate of a party in decline. She has never led a current within the party, or contributed to its "theoretical" review, and symbolises the "fickle choices of the party's elected representatives, the disarray of its activists, and the discredited view of the party held by its most loyal voters".[18]

The radical left

Despite the failure to inflict decisive and lasting defeats on workers over the past quarter of a century, there has been a constant drive to claw back the social and welfare concessions made during the post-war boom. Disparities of wealth and income are stark. Unemployment has not dropped below 8 percent for over 20 years, and stands at over 20 percent among young

16: *Le Monde*, 12 January 2007.

17: Stewart, 2007.

18: Lefebvre and Sawicki, 2006, p28.

people. Although the French labour movement has not suffered the same heavy defeats inflicted on British workers during the 1980s, the cumulative effect of the ruling class offensive has been to drive significant sections of the working class into relative poverty, their atomisation reflected in a process of "disaffiliation" from political and trade union organisation, opening up a space for racist ideas to gain a foothold among the most isolated elements of the workforce.

The decline of the traditional institutions of the labour movement, notably the Communist Party, has contributed to this process, and limited workers' scope for action. Thus, despite the rise in struggle since 1995, the total number of strike days remains low compared with the 1975-85 period. The weakness of trade unions has had an impact. The forms of struggle to have emerged since 1986, based on rank and file activity organised through strike committees or "coordinations" and mass meetings, have allowed movements to grow rapidly and spontaneously, but these struggles have a significant weakness. They are relatively ephemeral and have not yet found a means to compensate for the permanent organisational capacities provided for workers by strong trade unions.

But while the mass organisations of the labour movement are weaker, the working class itself is going through a process of transition and regeneration and has grown numerically stronger since the 1970s. Most serious studies of working life in France estimate that workers, employees and "intermediary professions" makes up around 75 percent of the active population of some 25 million people.[19] Sectors new to struggle—teachers, employees in the service industries, immigrant and fixed term contract workers—have adopted radical forms of action.

Thus, while the total number of strike days has remained low in the decade since 1995, there has been a significant rise in street demonstrations. Moreover, groups of workers that were previously difficult to organise, such as part time or fixed term contract staff, have begun to engage in struggle—the recent offensive six-week strike by PSA car workers in Aulnay being a good example. A recent study by the French ministry of employment bears out this picture of a new working class in the process of finding the means to organise itself. It found that although only 7 percent of workers are unionised, in single establishment firms with between 100 and 499 employees union presence now stood at 10 percent. Trade union structures are also developing in firms employing more than 20 people, 38 percent of which had at least one union representative in

19: Artous, Wilno, Fortino and Cuperty, 2005, p55.

2004-5, up from 33 percent in 1998-9. In firms that had union reps 62 percent of employees considered their role to be "irreplaceable".

The present situation, then, is one in which aspects of the past—notably the weight of defeats suffered in the 1980s and their effect on organised labour—coexist with an often uneven process of working class recomposition and regeneration. So far political forces to the left of the Socialists have been unable to build a political home for those who no longer recognise themselves in social democracy. The principal issue at stake today, then, is the disconnection between the social and the political field.

This is not an abstract theoretical question. There is a powerful anti-capitalist current in France. Not only have millions mobilised on various occasions in the recent past, but networks of activists exist all over France as a result of struggles going back 20 years, from the student movement of 1986, and the health, railway and postal workers' strikes of the late 1980s, to the mobilisations of students and public sector workers in recent years. Each successive movement has nourished these networks, leaving them stronger going into the next wave of protests, and making France, along with Italy, the country where the anti-capitalist movement has developed furthest.

One of the most significant indications of this development is the way the terms of the debate about the relationship between the social and the political have changed. Following the emergence of the so-called social movement in the late 1990s, various representatives of grassroots associations, along with a number of trade unions and intellectuals including Pierre Bourdieu, issued a public statement proclaiming the autonomy of the movement from political parties, anxious to avoid it becoming reappropriated by political forces, notably the Communist Party.

Following the drama of the 2002 election, and the defeated movement against pension reform in 2003, came the biggest anti-capitalist protest yet seen in France, when 300,000 gathered in Larzac in support of Bové. By now the question was posed differently: how could the hiatus between the social movement and its political expression be overcome?

It was a question the revolutionary left was not in a position to answer at that stage, substituting rhetorical statements about being the only alternative to neoliberalism, and proclamations about the need for "a big anti-capitalist force", for an authentic political engagement with the movement.[20] The campaign against the EU constitution offered a way out of this dichotomy. Political forces—the Communist Party, the LCR and a left-leaning current within the Socialist Party known as the PRS—played a leading role in the movement,

20: See Kouvélakis, 2004.

equipping it with arguments, propaganda and an activist core. It was a role that was supplemented by the work of the grassroots associations and non-aligned activists, but one whose worth all those involved could appreciate. The importance of political parties to the movement, something which had been openly contested within the anti-capitalist movement at the European Social Forums in Florence in 2002 and Paris in 2003, was now broadly accepted.

The campaign against the EU constitution has already been detailed in this journal.[21] The key, and potentially contradictory, aspects of its success were the break of broad sections of the left from social liberalism, and the desire for unity. The need for unity was a lesson learnt and imprinted on the minds of all who had participated in the struggles of the previous decade and there was a tangible sense of recognition every time it was invoked on the platforms of the campaign. The most prominent Socialist figure in the "no" campaign, Jean-Luc Mélenchon, has conveyed the mood of the campaign very well:

> Writing these lines, the emotion comes back to me. I see the good people of the Aisne region, so marked physically, meeting in a packed room with their MP... While I was speaking, denouncing all the great minds who were promising them more privatisation of public services—the only lasting inheritance in the room—and ever more "free and undistorted" competition, I ended up shouting: "Punish them! Vote to punish!", which was clearly excessive, and later denounced by many upstanding figures who also noted the class hatred that it revealed. But I was astonished to see the whole room rise and stand, some saluting with clenched fists, others clapping in rhythm and I don't know what besides... And all this brought back to me a reality of stifled fears and vengeful rages to which I'd opened the door and which I saw had us all pinned down...this time of contained suffering and impotent humiliation. If we don't understand that...then we fail to grasp the carnal reality of this No to a neoliberal Europe.[22]

The impetus of the campaign meant that the collectives formed to organise it remained active, meeting to discuss how to translate their effectiveness into something more permanent. This in itself was a further example of how the movement was reaching for political tools independently of the parties themselves: just as the Attac movement for global justice had been transformed from a network established to campaign around the issue of financial speculation into something much broader, so, once it had reached the limit of

21: Wolfreys, 2005, and Kouvélakis, 2005.

22: Mélenchon, 2005.

its effectiveness, attention turned to another tool that could be fashioned into something fulfilling the functions usually assumed by a political party.

The attempt to nominate a unity presidential candidate for the anti-neoliberal left was a process which offered for the first time the chance of a political alternative emerging to challenge the dominance of reformist politics (whether Communist or Socialist) over social movements. It allowed for discussion, on a wider scale than at any time since the late 1970s, of the possibility of a break with the reformist management of capitalism. The discussions which took place across France involved between 20,000 and 30,000 activists. The Communist Party attempted to manoeuvre its leader, Marie-George Buffet, into a position where she would be adopted as the candidate of the collectives. Whatever the degree of bad faith that lay behind the actions of the Communist leadership, this marked a significant shift in strategy. Having participated in the plural left coalition under the premiership of Lionel Jospin between 1997 and 2002, the Communist Party had now moved onto the terrain of the radical left and was seeking the nomination of a movement explicitly opposed to social liberalism. But instead of taking the leadership's line at face value in order to hold it to account before its membership, the LCR, in abstaining from the process on the grounds that the Communists could not be trusted, severely limited the prospect of meaningful dialogue with the many thousands of activists who genuinely believed in the possibility of a radical left alternative emerging.

Once the attempt to find a candidate who the collectives could unite around had failed, José Bové, who had withdrawn from the process at an earlier stage, declared himself a candidate, pulling—at least initially—a number of activists from the LCR into his campaign. In the event his campaign was overshadowed by Besancenot, the only candidate of the radical left who was able to rally a significant number of votes around the aspirations of the movement. That nearly one in ten young people voted for him is a testimony to the dynamism of the LCR's campaign. But the lesson of the election for the radical left is nevertheless that, united, the whole remains greater than the sum of its parts.

Conclusion

The European radical left is at a crossroads. As Daniel Bensaïd has pointed out, the failure of the social movement in Italy to defeat attacks on public services and social protection has led expectations to drift towards electoral solutions, with the result that Rifondazione Comunista now offers support to the social liberal government of Romano Prodi.[23] In France the victory over the CPE youth employment law in 2006 generated realistic hopes that the movement would find a political voice in the elections. The articulation between the movement and the collectives is not straightforward, however, and there was no direct or automatic translation of that victory into a qualitative regeneration of the collectives. This, coupled with the absence of the LCR leadership from the deliberations over a unity candidate, gave the Communist Party scope to exert its still considerable institutional muscle.

The failure of the process has led some to conclude that organisations remain an obstacle to unity, as if the LCR, a vital and consistent component of the struggles of the past decade, can be placed on an equal footing with the Communist Party and its history of compromise and betrayal. But it is the struggle against neoliberalism, and not the decisions taken by the organisations of the radical left, which initiated the drive for unity. For this reason, the possibility of a united radical alternative to compromise with social liberalism will remain on the agenda, but not indefinitely.

We are still in the early stages of a recomposition of the French labour movement. The election of Sarkozy presents it with a more daunting challenge than any faced since 1995. When Chirac became president in that year he did so on a vow to heal France's "social fracture", a promise that undermined his subsequent attempts to attack the public sector. Sarkozy has been unequivocal in his desire to pursue these attacks and now has a mandate to do so. But his victory is not primarily the result of his ability to wrest control of the UMP party from Chirac and unite it around an authoritarian project. It is above all a consequence of the failure of the Socialists to capitalise on the unpopularity of the right, which has governed since 2002.

Of the six issues which voters considered the most important in making their choice in the presidential election, all, aside from law and order, were themes that traditionally favour the left: unemployment, spending power, education, exclusion/poverty and pensions.[24] Sarkozy cannot rely on positive widespread popular backing for a neoliberal programme. His success underlines the fact that options are narrowing for mainstream parties, a further indication, as was argued in this journal following the 2002 election, that the centre cannot hold.

This is obvious when we consider the state of the Socialist Party. In the mid-1990s Jospin was able to put together a "plural left" coalition that wed the Communists and Greens to the compromises with the market

---

23: Bensaïd, 2006. On the Italian situation see Trudell, 2006.

24: Ipsos/Dell, 2007. See also Dalem, 2007.

pursued by his government. The effect of this has been to demolish the electoral base of both coalition partners. The principal figurehead for the left in the Socialist Party today is Laurent Fabius, an enthusiastically pro-market prime minister under Mitterrand who has now undergone an unconvincing makeover as a committed socialist. The scope for a credible left reformist project emerging from within the party and pulling other forces into its orbit is clearly diminishing. More strident voices within the party want it to form an alliance with part of the right wing UDF coalition.

The UDF's presidential candidate, François Bayrou, a mild mannered party functionary and a minister in the right wing Balladur and Juppé governments of the 1990s, took advantage of the licence given by the personalised nature of the election to recast himself as a rustic gentleman farmer of the "centre". Although millions of voters saw him as a more credible alternative to Sarkozy than Royal, the UDF will be unable to sustain the illusion that it represents a middle way between left and right: following Sarkozy's election 22 of its parliamentary group of 29 deputies pledged their unhesitating allegiance to the new president. The last time the Socialists experimented, in a more limited form, with opening up to the right, under the Michel Rocard premiership from the late 1980s, the experience proved disastrous, wrecking Rocard's career as a front-line politician and leading to the Socialists' worst ever electoral results in the early 1990s.

In this context, the radical left can have a crucial influence on the pace and nature of political regroupment. An anti-neoliberal alternative to the mainstream will not simply materialise as a natural by-product of the decline of the Communist Party and the rightward drift of the Socialist Party. The inherently conservative political instincts of those who lead left currents in the Socialist and Communist parties mean that they are likely to remain in them long after these parties have ceased to function as meaningful tools for their political aspirations. The LCR has now proved incontrovertibly and impressively that it can punch far above its weight in presidential elections; it can also play a major role in the regroupment of forces outside its ranks.

Two elements underpinning the success of the Besancenot campaign have a significance that goes beyond the election. First, the profile of the campaign chimed with the aspirations of the radical left as a whole. Besancenot's standing as one of the figureheads of the referendum campaign, the *altermondialiste* tone and mood of the meetings, the solidarity expressed with the revolt of the impoverished suburbs and the confidence and élan of his attacks on the mainstream candidates, media and Medef employers' association alike, meant that he was able to become a repository for the aspirations of the radical left. This limited the damage done by the debacle over the unity candidate. Second, the campaign provided compelling proof that a class-based revolutionary party of struggle can win a significant audience despite competition from other forces, and even achieve a greater echo among activists than parties more than 20 times its size, like the Communist Party. In other words, the potential for a small revolutionary party to play a pivotal role in the regeneration of the left, at a time when the traditional institutions of the labour movement are in deep crisis, is clear.

As we have seen with the urban riots of November 2005 and, to a lesser degree, the sporadic confrontations between youth and police following Sarkozy's election, opposition to his neoliberal authoritarianism will find the means to express itself through rage and frustration in the absence of a more coherent political focus. In the months ahead the resistance of the movement, and the anger of those on its fringes, are going to be challenged by a right that has been given time to regroup. The LCR's presidential campaign proved the organisation's capacity to draw together a broad spectrum of forces around an anti-neoliberal platform. Its ability to translate this achievement in building effective, united opposition to Sarkozy will play a crucial role in the outcome of the struggles to come.

References

Artous, Antoine, Henri Wilno, Sabine Fortino and Patrice Cuperty, 2005, *Classe ouvrière, salariat, luttes de classe*, Les cahiers de critique communiste, "Arguments et mouvements" (Editions Syllepse).

Bensaïd, Daniel, 2006, "The return of strategy", *International Socialism 113* (Winter 2006), www.isj.org.uk/index.php4?id=287&issue=113

Dalem, Alexis, 2007, "Comment on perd une élection", *Le Monde*, 9 May 2007.

Heffer, Simon, 2006, the *Daily Telegraph*, 9 May 2006.

Heffer, Simon, 2007, the *Daily Telegraph*, 5 May 2007.

Ipsos/Dell, 2007, exit poll, 22 April 2007, www.ipsos.fr/presidentielle-2007/pdf/ssu.pdf

Kouvélakis, Stathis, 2004, "Some hypotheses on the reasons for a (not merely) electoral defeat" and "A new political cycle", International Socialist Tendency *Discussion Bulletin 5*, July 2004, www.istendency.net

Kouvélakis, Stathis, 2005, "France: the triumph of the political", *International Socialism 108* (Autumn 2005), www.isj.org.uk/index.php4?id=134&issue=108

La Documentation Française, 2007, "Rapport sur les aides publiques aux entreprises: mission d'audit de modernisation", Ministère délégué à l'Industrie, Janvier 2007, www.finances.gouv.fr/directions_services/cedef/bibliotheques/finances-publiques.htm

Lefebvre, Rémi, and Frédéric Sawicki, 2006, *La société des socialistes: Le PS aujourd'hui* (Editions du Croquant).

Marlière, Philippe, 2007, "Strategy sell-out", the *Guardian* website, 7 May 2007, http://commentisfree.guardian.co.uk/philippe_marlire/2007/05/strategy_sellout.html

Mélenchon, Jean-Luc, 2005, "La dimension invisible du 'non'", *La Revue socialiste*, July 2005.

OECD, 2005, www.oecd.org/dataoecd/28/17/36396820.xls

Stewart, Heather, 2007, "Can the French carry on living like this for ever?", the *Observer*, 18 February 2007, www.guardian.co.uk/france/story/0,,2015460,00.html

Trudell, Megan, 2006. "Rifondazione votes for war", *International Socialism 113* (winter 2007), www.isj.org.uk/index.php4?id=284&issue=113

Wolfreys, Jim, 2005, "How France's Referendum Caught Fire", *International Socialism 107* (summer 2005), www.isj.org.uk/index.php4?id=121&issue=107

Wolton, Thierry, 2007, "Avec Nicolas Sarkozy, la fin de l'exception française", *Le Figaro*, 7 May 2007, available from www.lefigaro.fr

Zappi, Sylvia, 2007, "L'échec de la gauche antilibérale", *Le Monde*, 29 April 2007.

The superpower's shopfloor

Kim Moody is the author of a new book on the American working class: US Labor in Trouble and Transition. He spoke to Martin Smith and Chris Harman about his research

Martin Smith: Can you give us an overview of the state of the American working class, its organisational strength, its mood and so on?

Let me start with an anecdote. Before I left New York I was teaching at a class of apprentice electricians. These are very conservative workers, mainly white and so on. It was on the eve of the transit strike—the whole bus and subway system was out for three days—and I invited a friend of mine who is an activist in the union, a black worker in his fifties with a long political background, to come to speak to these apprentices. He started off by saying, "You have to understand I'm from a generation of trade union activists that have only known retreat. That's why I think there will be a strike." In other words, people were fed up. This was a situation where discipline was just unbelievable: there were 35,000 workers and in one year there were 15,000 disciplinary actions by the management.

And they did strike—although it was clear that the union leaders did not want them to strike even though the leadership reluctantly called the action. Not only did they strike, but they rejected the first contract offer. They didn't win a clear victory, but my point is that there was anger there. This is a group of workers that is racially mixed—black, white, Latino—with a strong union and a tradition, and they fought back.

The point is that the situation for the organised working class has been one of decline and retreat for quarter of a century. Union density is 13 percent now, 8 percent in the private sector, the lowest its been since the start of the 20th century. But the retreat is not without resistance—at every point there has been an effort to fight back. There have not been a lot of unofficial strikes, unlike the 1960s and 1970s. Most of the strikes are forced on the unions or sometimes even positively led by some unions. But generally the level of strike action is not rising, even if it has gone up a little bit in the past couple of years.

Some of the strikes stand out more than others. The 1997 UPS strike by the Teamsters was extremely important because it was well prepared by both the leadership and the rank and file, and the strike was successful.

In the 1990s there were about 20 strikes at individual plants run by General Motors, which revealed the power of local activists. They found that if you close down one plant the whole system comes to a halt from Canada to Mexico because of the just-in-time production methods. Almost all those strikes won their immediate demands for more workers, for an increase in the workforce. But the national leadership of the union never pulled this movement together, never made use of this power.

The first effort to do something at the top of the union movement was the attempt in the 1990s to change the direction of the AFL-CIO union federation in response to rank and file activity. As a result John Sweeney was elected as president of the AFL-CIO in 1995, but has spent subsequent years squandering that victory, unable to come up with anything resembling a new strategy. The rhetoric was that we should "organise the unorganised". The failure to deliver this was not only due to his own political failings, but also because of the resistance from a lot of unions that don't really see it that way.

If anyone was going to do the organising it had to be rank and file activists in the labour movement. It could not be done by the army of professional organisers that the SEIU—the Service Employees International Union—and some of the others try to do it with.

The failure of Sweeney eventually led to a split in the AFL-CIO in 2005 with the formation of the rival Change to Win coalition of unions. Since then nothing much has changed. The SEIU—the major force in the Change to Win coalition—is more aggressive in organising than any other union, along with the Teamsters, who are also in Change to Win. But then the Communication Workers who are still in the AFL-CIO are also organising. So the division was not one of principle or politics or "vision". It's hard to say what it was really about. I was teaching classes in New York with activists from the unions involved in the split; almost to a person they had no idea it was going on. It was all done at the top. At root the split seems to have been about money and power—for the leaderships, that is. Some unions thought they were wasting money paying dues to the AFL-CIO, which was not altogether wrong. The new Change to Win federation structure is very bare bones.

The problem with the approach taken by some of the unions in Change to Win is that they have combined the organising push with two other practices. The first of these is they have merged union locals (branches). So now you have local unions that cover six or seven states, with members hundreds of miles apart. It is impossible to have meetings. They are run by a huge staff and are basically administrative units. They are not really democratic workers' organisations at all. For decades we have talked about the "labour bureaucracy", but this goes far beyond what we used to think of. A lot of people are inclined to forgive that because the SEIU does organise workers. But the rate at which it does that has slowed down, and one reason for this is the way they do it. They plan these organising drives years in advance and don't deviate from the plan. Even if another group says we want to join, they say, no, sorry. I'm not exaggerating.

The second problem, which is very much part of the Change to Win thing, and particularly the SEIU, is the whole concept of "partnership". Andy Stern, the SEIU leader, says things like, "We can't have class conflict any more. We have to work with the employers to help them succeed." They promise this in the organising drives—in a sense they are almost trying to organise the employer rather than the employees. In the Health Maintenance Organisations on the west coast they are explicitly saying they will restrain their members if it will help the business. This has always been an aspect of "business unions" but now it is being turned into an explicit ideology.

One of the things that made SEIU famous was their Justice for Janitors campaign in 1990. When I was doing research for my book I looked at the wage settlements they have done and they are horrible. In 15 years they have not even made up lost real wages.

You can't say all the Change to Win unions are for partnership and all the AFL-CIO unions are against it. Unfortunately many of the leaders promote this idea, which is a little different from the union-management cooperation stuff of the 1980s and 1990s. Maybe they are trying to copy the European social partnership idea.

MS: But lots of people come to Britain and talk about the SEIU recruitment drives, and they sound very exciting. In New York or Seattle you see SEIU union people everywhere with their purple union baseball caps.

They mobilise members for demonstrations when they need them—and demobilise them when they don't. The caps and T-shirts are near universal, but that's more of an American thing. The SEIU have a term for it—the purple army—they are very concerned with image and this is part of it.

However, they do lead some interesting struggles. They are organising among workers who desperately need organisation. They are organising in industries that do not face international competition—what are sometimes called landlocked industries, like hospitals or building cleaners, that cannot be moved abroad. Their biggest growth now is among security guards. What gives the union some vibrancy is that many of the workers are immigrant workers and come from places like El Salvador and Mexico, and bring with them radical political ideas and traditions. That was very much the case with Justice for Janitors. The first people they recruit, who become the rank and file organisers, are political people.

There are 12 million immigrant workers in the US. They come overwhelmingly from Latin America. It took the unions a long time to realise this was an important constituency. The immigrant demonstrations and strikes on May Day 2006 were spectacular. The strikes closed down whole industries. It enabled us to see where these workers could have an impact. It's not just in landscaping or building maintenance: they closed down half the food processing industry, the ports on the west coast and construction in California.

There has been enormous repression since the May Day strikes. Also, the Catholic church, which played a big role in 2006, got scared by what it had unleashed. This year there was no national drive so you didn't get the same kind of thing. But in Chicago you still got 150,000 demonstrating—on a workday—and in Los Angeles 35,000. There are hundreds of local organisations and maybe half a dozen national coalitions, ranging from the conservative to the radical, concerned with this, and some are doing union organising on their own. There are stories about how the Laborers' Union sent organisers into the South to organise a meatpacking plant and the organisers said, "When we got there we discovered the union was there before the union. They had organised themselves. All the union had to do was distribute union cards."

The unions are going to have to make a breakthrough in the South. So much economic activity has gone there in the past 30 years—not just the food processing industry, which is massive, but also the automobile industry. There are now two automobile industries in the US. There is the old one, General Motors, Ford, Chrysler and so forth, which is in crisis. Then there is the new one, in the South, owned by Mercedes, Nissan,

Toyota, etc, which is doing very well. There are no big layoffs in these plants in the South. This has to be the major organising target if the unions are going to succeed—the plants in the South are 95 percent non-union.

MS: Is there going to be another drive like "Operation Dixie" in the late 1940s and early 1950s?

That was a catastrophe. The CIO unions went down South from 1946 through to the early 1950s with the idea of (a) beating the Communists, because they were the only people to have fought to build unions in the South, and (b) organising the whites, so they wouldn't have to face the race question. Of course they failed on the race question and they got into a big faction fight with the Communists in the steel industry—they ended up with nothing.

I don't think they are that stupid now. There are no Communists in the South, anyway. The unions actually hire any left wingers they can get their hands on. Sweeney was the first one to do this in the 1980s. He asked, "How are we to get some spirit back into this organisation? Well, we will hire all these veterans of 1968." The question is, can they deal with the race issue? It is much more complicated in the South than it used to be, because it is no longer just black and white; it is black and white and Latino and some Asians, etc. The South has changed. It's much more industrial, even if it is still pretty backward.

The SEIU, despite some rhetoric, is not interested in organising in the South. It still has zillions of service workers to organise throughout the rest of the country. So it will have to be the job of the former industrial unions—the auto workers, the communications workers—who do have a foothold in the South. The United Auto Workers recently won union ballots in two small car parts plants in the South. It's good but it's not enough.

The unions have to function together, and they have to use those that have strategic power. That was what was right about Operation Dixie: they knew they had to do it as a federation. Now there are two federations and you need unions from both of them to make this thing work. Hopefully they will be able to work together despite this rather pointless split. That has to include the Teamsters, because trucking is the basis of this whole industry in the South. If you control Southern trucking you can pretty well close down anything.

MS: Give us some positive examples of organising workers—we haven't heard much about this in Britain.

There's meatpacking. For example, on 1 May 2006, when they struck, the people who were organising the Smithfield plant called a demonstration of immigrant workers for that day and they came not just from the Smithfield plant but from four or more plants and closed down all the major plants in the state. Recently at Omaha, Nebraska, they have had some success in organising meatpacking plants—that's not in the South but it's an important food processing area.

A key thing in both of these was the alliance with what we now call "workers' centres". These are organisations that have grown up in the past 20 years. They tend to be based in immigrant communities and are called workers' centres because, unlike older community organisations, they focus on the workplace. They are not unions. There are about 130 of them around the country, mainly in the South. They have played a role at Smithfield and in North Carolina generally.

Sometimes they get financial support from the unions, but there's tension between the two. Union leaders come across something they don't control—immigrant workers who organise themselves on a community basis and usually on a nationality or ethnic basis as well—and they don't know what to do with them. The union leaders have learnt some things in recent years and now the AFL-CIO has said that it wants workers' centres to affiliate. The Laborers' Union actually set up a workers' centre themselves.

The workers' centres have played a big role in the organising drives. One of the problems historically in the United States—perhaps in Britain as well—was that 30 or 40 years ago you lived in a community next to the plant and you walked to work. That all broke down a long time ago in the US. People now travel routinely over 100 miles to a good job if they can get it.

With the immigrants creating communities that are urban or semi-urban, they are now communities that are close to workplaces. So you have this new connection of the working class community and the workforce, which makes things a lot easier. So there have been successes like in New York City in organising taxi drivers—almost all from the Indian subcontinent. They organised themselves and recently became affiliated to the AFL-CIO. The workers' centres are now pretty much working with the unions in organising. This represents a long term hope.

I am certainly not predicting that we are on the verge of an upsurge. Forces have to accumulate. The growth in organisation does not show up in the numbers yet. The unions are still haemorrhaging more members than they are gaining. The official figures for 2006 say that the unions lost another 300,000 people—this includes a lot of General Motors people and so forth. So the organising has not even got to the point where it is keeping pace with the losses.

I see this as flowing from the fact that the unions have no strategic focus. As I mentioned, the Teamsters could be key to organising the South. They are doing lots of things, but they are all over the place. There is no industrial or geographic focus to it. The same is true of the United Auto Workers. They have spent the past 20 years organising university graduate students and part-time lecturers. It's all very nice but they can't bring about even a minor shift in class power in the country.

MS: You have talked quite a lot about Latinos. What about the black working class? It was the backbone of much of the militancy in the 1960s and 1970s. And what about the white working class?

The black working class have been hit extremely hard, harder than any other section. They became important in the 1960s and 1970s because they had finally carved out a substantial presence in industry. That has been heavily set back, which is why cities like Detroit and Cleveland are devastated. Cleveland 20 years ago was a major industrial city. Now it is the poorest city in the US. The black working class who remain employed are pretty heavily concentrated in the public sector and the service sector now. They are still key in many industries. They are important in a lot of industries in the South and in the automobile industry, North and South.

Part of the problem is a political problem. Although the black working class are not in general as conservative as the white working class, they have been more dependent on the Democratic Party. The Democratic Party is also very dependent on them but does not give them anything. So there has been a long period of political frustration and it has not taken any clear radical direction.

You now also have a big black middle class. One result of the civil rights movement was that more black people could get civil service jobs, white collar work, although the fragility of the black middle class has to be understood—it is very dependent on the public sector.

As for white workers, there are more of them than anyone else, despite all the changes. They are still 75 percent of the workforce. There is a difference between public sector workers, who still have some job security and are generally unionised, at least in the big cities, and the industrial working class, which has been devastated. Whole towns that used to be bastions of unionism are just deserts now. But industry has not gone away entirely, even in the North, in the rustbelt. So the white industrial workers can still be important.

Their consciousness has always been completely contradictory. They were the backbone of the most militant unions in the 1930s and 1940s, and into the 1950s. There has not been a socialist presence in most of these unions for a long time, but they would vote Democrat and think of this as a class thing, even if we would not see it like that. At the same time, though, racism has always been very deep in the white working class. At times, in the heat of struggle, the racism can be put on the backburner. So for a long time, if you are running for office in the local union of, say, the Auto Workers, the Teamsters or what is left of the steel workers, you would never dream of running an all white slate. So you have a lot of racism, but also an operational sense that we are all in this together.

The other thing which has changed today is that you get a kind of backlash against the unions. People are not in the same plant any more. They are unemployed or working at some crummy job, or they are going to some trade school hoping to learn something. They are not in the same struggle any more. And those who had these good union jobs and lost them, they blame not only management but the union too. They say, "Where was the union? They knew about this and they just let us go."

An anecdotal story shows something. There was an organising drive in northern Pennsylvania, not too far from Pittsburgh. This is part of the country that was very heavily unionised, not just steel but everything. The SEIU were trying to unionise a nursing club and they are not accustomed to losing recognition ballots. But they lost disastrously. Someone did a study, interviewing workers, and they said, "We cannot have faith in you. Look what the unions did to the steel plants. They did not stick up for anybody."

So a lot of people who used to be good union members have bought into this neoliberal ideology or evangelical Christianity. Abortion suddenly becomes important in a way it wasn't. You had always been a Catholic, and a good Catholic, and you were against abortion, but somehow it wasn't the issue. The issues were money and fighting the boss. Now abortion and gay marriage in somewhere like Ohio becomes the issue in the 2004 election—it's incredible. And the union can't challenge that stuff.

Chris Harman: There is the widespread idea, even on the left, that industry has just disappeared from the economically advanced countries. Reading your book, what comes across is that it is much more to do with the move from the north east of the US to the South and the west. The figures you give are quite interesting. There is a net loss of just two or three million out of 20 or 30 million workers.

The manufacturing job losses are heavily concentrated in four industrial sectors. Textiles and clothing have virtually all gone abroad; metal working has not totally gone. Iron ore mining and all the things that go with it are down. The other thing that went down in the 1990s is chemicals, which was a well organised industry. But many other industries are still there—they've just moved within the US. There will be more losses of manufacturing jobs, no doubt about it. Some will move to China, Mexico or Brazil. But there are some things it is just not economical to produce far away. Those things will still be produced for the local and national market.

The idea that society is no longer composed of material things is, of course, nonsense. You have only to look around you. These things have to come from somewhere and some come from China, or India even, but they have not got rid of all the ones produced in the US by any means. The irony of it is that the way they have restructured has caused some forms of traditional manual work like trucking and railroads to increase in importance. This is true even of dock work, despite the new technology. What they call "logistics" now has become key to the new structure of industry. They can't use the Panama Canal now—it's not big enough for their ships—so they bring stuff to the east coast or west coast and run it across the country by truck or rail. So those industries have influence and power. It's yet to be demonstrated. The Teamsters under their present leadership are not likely to do much to show it.

MS: At the time of the big anti-capitalist protest at Seattle in 1999 there was talk about the Teamsters and Turtles (a reference to young environmental activists) coming together. What sort of impact did that have? Was there an anti-capitalist mood inside the unions? The other thing which must have had an effect was 9/11.

9/11 more or less kicked two of the three legs from under the impact of Seattle. There hasn't been a demonstration of that character in the US since. There have been anti-war demonstrations that have been bigger, but they don't have the same effect.

But Seattle did have an impact. It was interesting not just because the AFL-CIO decided to take people there—they took 30,000 people. They tried to prevent them joining the young people in the street but they were not completely successful. The people who broke away to go down there were striking steel workers from Oregon, who had an alliance with environmentalists in their part of the country, and the west coast longshore people, who are in a traditionally left wing union. They have it in their contract they can stop work once a month for a "meeting". They chose that day to stop work. And there were Teamsters from the reform movement—Seattle is a big centre of that. They were mostly white workers from these progressive local unions who had been radicalised and had moved beyond the consciousness of workers who put the blame on imports "taking the jobs away". These more progressive groups of workers had been educated by people like us in *Labor Notes*, who had worked with them for many years building networks from Canada, US and Mexico around the issue of the North American Free Trade Agreement. So there was a small layer of workers who went to Seattle and when they saw a confrontation they liked it. It was very interesting to see people coming back from Seattle saying, "Next time we're on strike I want those anarchists coming down."

After Seattle the unions changed their minds on a lot of these questions. Not completely: the steel workers are still very protectionist. But at the same time they do more work of an international kind in Latin America, etc.

CH: You've talked a few times about the Teamsters. Tell us about the debate inside this union.

Since the mid-1970s there has been an opposition group in the Teamsters, Teamsters for a Democratic Union (TDU). It was started by people who were at that time in the International Socialists, but it brought in regular teamsters and it grew over the years. They built, not particularly by running people for elections, which you could not do in that union for a long time, but through workplace organising with strikes and that sort of activity. By the 1980s they were pretty strong. A door was opened for them in a way that nobody would have expected. The Reagan administration intervened with a legal suit over corruption—they were going after the mob. They were clearly interested in weakening the Teamsters and were out to put the union under government control. TDU said, "No. Don't take over the union. If you are going to do anything, have an election for officers." The union did not have elections previously. Leaders were chosen at the convention, which was rigged. For some reason that nobody understands, the government said it would supervise the election but not run it.

TDU were not powerful enough to run on their own, so they forged an alliance with some reform-minded people who were not quite as radical as them. Ron Carey was president of a big Teamster local in New York City based in UPS. He had a good reputation and so TDU supported him, and they won because the old guard split and ran against each other. No one was quite sure what Carey would do. He was certainly not under the control of TDU—influenced, yes, but not under control. But what he did was begin the process of cleaning up the union, or reorganising the divisions to have contract fights instead of just caving in, as they had for decades. The first ones he did were not all that successful, but as time went on they became stronger and the 1997 UPS strike was successful.

Working with the TDU and other forces they changed the culture of that union. It was the most remarkable thing I have ever seen. There are still a lot of corrupt big city Teamster locals and they still have enormous power, with the old guard under Hoffa junior back in charge at the top.

In 1997 there was a fight inside the Carey camp before the union election. Carey was beginning to go the way of all flesh. He was now on the board of the AFL-CIO, hobnobbing with all these big shots, Democrat politicians and so forth, and he became convinced the way to win the election was to do it they way the Democrats try to win elections and so he hired these Democratic Party consultants. TDU opposed that, saying, "Run a rank and file campaign. You are not going to raise enough money to equal Hoffa." He said, "OK, if you want to do the rank and file stuff, that's fine, but I'm going to do the professional stuff." There was a money laundering scheme that was clearly illegal. Carey was charged—he was found innocent by a jury a couple of years ago, but he was removed from office in the union. The reform forces were in disarray and without a candidate with name recognition.

When you are running a rank and file movement or a reform movement, you have a certain amount of time to demonstrate what you can do, and if you mess up, as Carey clearly did, you lose your chance for a long time. The turnout in votes now is low and it is hard to convince people we can make a big change. People say, "We thought this guy Carey was an honest guy, but they are all crooks." It was a big, big setback.

But Hoffa junior has not been able to undo all the things that were done. He's undone some, so he's giving his friends two or three salaries; he's not organising strike preparation—he called a very disastrous strike at the Overnight Trucking Company that Carey was starting organising meticulously. Hoffa got talked into calling a strike before most of the workers were properly organised, firing all the organisers who were Carey or TDU supporters, and the strike dragged on disastrously for a couple of months.

MS: You talk about how the strategy at the top of the unions is to merge unions and so on. The other strategy has been to work through the Democratic Party. Is that still carrying on?
There is no section of the American labour movement bureaucracy that is not totally committed to the Democratic Party. You get some rhetoric about "we're not going to depend on them again", but unfortunately it's not true. Every time an election comes they all fall for it. Everything is put on hold except that.

MS: Did any of the unions back Ralph Nader when he stood for election?
Not the leaderships. In 2000 Nader got three million trade unionists' votes. We were involved. There was a substantial "Labour for Nader" campaign.

It was exciting. But it did not involve the top people at all. In fact, if you were a local official or shop steward and you were supporting Nader, the leadership came down on you—"You put Bush in the White House."

The commitment to the Democratic Party at the top is universal and still very strong. These people are capable of illusions that are mind blowing. They backed Kerry, although he was no pro-labour person. Hillary Clinton, she certainly is not, but they will go for her. Even when the Democrats win, they do nothing for labour. It's not as bad as Bush, but that's all you can say about it.

Beside the fact that they are supporting a capitalist party, the union leaderships have to lie to their members. They can't sell Democrats on the basis of, "We know he's really a jerk and not going to do anything, but he's better than the other guy." No, they have to put out literature: "John Kerry is a friend of the unions, of working people, etc, etc," which is not convincing to the members or anybody else.

The other problem is that they don't have an alternative political strategy at that level at all. All they can ever think of is, "Maybe we will support a few moderate Republicans"—as if that is going to do anything. They don't consider the idea of a new party or of backing someone like Nader. There was an effort in the 1990s to set up a "Labor Party", which was a very good thing. It was very exciting to see that happen. You would go to the convention and it would be a convention for coalminers, nurses from California, Latino farm workers, auto workers—a fantastic mix. Six international unions supported it. But the problem was that even those people, the ones that were willing to take such a step, a mildly radical class conscious step, were still tied to the Democrats. So they had the idea: "We're not going to run candidates." At the beginning they may not have had the strength to run at the national level, but they could run at the local level. But they would not do that. So it had nothing to do. It's still there, the way political things do not disappear, but it has no power and no dynamism.

That's the problem. The labour leadership has no other vision of what to do. They do not even have the notion that maybe the way to move the political agenda a little bit is to do some mass action, something like Seattle. Seattle inspired some people and influenced some union leaders, but it scared others. "Every time we bring people together in numbers they riot," they said. "We can't have this."

I think organising in the South is the key to this. If you think in terms of electoral politics, there's not going to be any change. Either the Republicans are going to triumph or there has to be something new. You can't just win in the North. The South is the basis of Republican dominance now, but its demographics are changing. It is becoming more and more urban, more working class—but workers are not in unions so they act as individuals.

It's nice to see the Republicans got beaten in November's congressional elections. But you can watch these Democrats behaving in Congress and saying, "We're going to put a date for withdrawal from Iraq" and all that, but they are voting Bush hundreds of millions of dollars to conduct this war. And Hillary Clinton is not even against the war.

CH: Can you tell us a bit about ***Labor Notes****?*

I was one of the co-founders of *Labor Notes* in 1979. It is an independent national monthly magazine that goes out to trade union activists. I worked for *Labor Notes* until 2001, when I moved to New York. And when I was in New York I was still on the executive board. Now I am not officially connected, although I stay in touch.

The organisation was set up in the wake of the 1978 miners' strike in the US. What we saw then, and what we felt about the whole period of the 1960s and 1970s, was that one of the problems was that you had these huge rank and file movements—the miners' was the only one that won at the national level—but then things fell apart. We saw this miners' strike and the miners were suddenly going out with auto plants up North and steel plants collecting money, and people organised caravans from the Northern cities to take stuff down to the miners. It occurred to us that one of the problems with the whole era was that what was missing was any kind of institution, political force or publication that brought all this together, giving any kind of class vision, putting it in an analytical context.

We did not have the idea of starting an organisation. Most of us started with the International Socialists at that time, but the idea was that it would not be controlled by the organisation and that it would be independent, which is what by and large has happened, although the staff tend to be socialist for the most part. We were surprised by our own success. The magazine actually took off. I think the circulation is about 8,000 or 9,000. Then we started holding conferences to get people from the different parts of the working class together and those were a huge success—about a thousand people every other year. The problem is it's about the only thing of its kind. It doesn't have the resources to have the sort of impact we would like it to have, although it has some. It's become an important left institution within the trade union movement. Leaderships have been hostile to it, but they have never been able to do anything particularly negative.

The layer of militants in the US is not that different from those in Britain or anywhere else, except in the important sense that socialism as a political idea has not been on a large scale an important part of the labour movement in the US for half a century. That is not to say there are not a lot of socialists. You can go to a lot of, say, these auto workers' demonstrations and pick out somebody who's not in a group and you wouldn't think of as socialist, and you talk to them a little while and you find they are. And you get this other phenomenon I come across all the time. It's a sort of little identity piece—to have an Industrial Workers of the World (IWW) card. You can come across ordinary union people who are attracted to this idea of radical unionism, revolutionary unionism. The IWW as it exists today is really just a political sect. But the idea of it, the history of it, is something that appeals to a certain number of militants. I'm always surprised when someone pulls me aside and says, "I've got a red card."

The rate of profit and the world today[1]

Chris Harman

The "tendency of the rate of profit to fall" is one of the most contentious elements in Karl Marx's intellectual legacy. He regarded it as one of his most important contributions to the analysis of the capitalist system, calling it, in his first notebooks for *Capital* (now published as the *Grundrisse*), "in every respect the most important law of modern political economy".[2] But it has been subjected to criticism ever since his argument first appeared in print with the publication of volume three of *Capital* in 1894.

The first criticisms in the 1890s came from opponents of Marxism, such as the liberal Italian philosopher Benedetto Croce and the German neoclassical economist Eugen von Böhm-Bawerk. But they have been accepted since by many Marxists—from Paul Sweezy in the 1940s to people such as Gérard Duménil and Robert Brenner today.

The argument was and is important. For Marx's theory leads to the conclusion that the there is a fundamental, unreformable flaw in capitalism. The rate of profit is the key to capitalists being able to achieve their goal of accumulation. But the more accumulation takes place, the more difficult it is for them make sufficient profit to sustain it: "The rate of self-expansion of capitalism, or the rate of profit, being the goal of capitalist production, its fall...appears as a threat to the capitalist production process".[3]

1: This article is based on research for a forthcoming book on capitalism in the 21st century. I would appreciate suggestions and constructive criticism. Please email chrisharman@swp.org.uk

2: Marx, 1973, p748.

3: Marx, 1962, pp236-237.

This "testifies to the merely historical, transitory character of the capitalist mode of production" and to the way that "at a certain stage it conflicts with its own further development".[4] It showed that "the real barrier of capitalist production was capital itself".[5]

Marx and his critics

Marx's basic line of argument was simple enough. Each individual capitalist can increase his (or occasionally her) own competitiveness through increasing the productivity of his workers. The way to do this is by using a greater quantity of the "means of production"—tools, machinery and so on—for each worker. There is a growth in the ratio of the physical extent of the means of production to the amount of labour power employed, a ratio that Marx called the "technical composition of capital".

But a growth in the physical extent of the means of production will also be a growth in the investment needed to buy them. So this too will grow faster than the investment in the workforce. To use Marx's terminology, "constant capital" grows faster than "variable capital". The growth of this ratio, which he calls the "organic composition of capital",[6] is a logical corollary of capital accumulation.

Yet the only source of value for the system as a whole is labour. If investment grows more rapidly than the labour force, it must also grow more rapidly than the value created by the workers, which is where profit comes from. In short, capital investment grows more rapidly than the source of profit. As a consequence, there will be a downward pressure on the ratio of profit to investment—the rate of profit.

Each capitalist has to push for greater productivity in order to stay ahead of competitors. But what seems beneficial to the individual capitalist is disastrous for the capitalist class as a whole. Each time productivity rises there is a fall in the average amount of labour in the economy as a whole needed to produce a commodity (what Marx called "socially necessary labour"), and it is this which determines what other people will eventually be prepared to pay for that commodity. So today we can see a continual fall in the price of goods such as computers or DVD players produced in industries where new technologies are causing productivity to rise fastest.

4: Marx, 1962, p237.

5: Marx, 1962, p245.

6: The organic composition of capital was depicted algebraically by Marx by the formula c/v, where c = constant capital, and v = variable capital.

The arguments against Marx

Three arguments have been raised time and again against Marx.

The first is that there need not be any reason for new investment to take a "capital intensive" rather than a "labour intensive" form. If there is unused labour available in the system, there seems no reason why capitalists should invest in machines rather than labour. There is a theoretical reply to this argument. Capitalists are driven to seek innovations in technologies that keep them ahead of their rivals. Some such innovations may be available using techniques that are not capital intensive. But there will be others that require more means of production—and the successful capitalist will be the one whose investments provide access to both sorts of innovation.

There is also an empirical reply. Investment in material terms has in fact grown faster than the workforce. So, for instance, the net stock of capital per person employed in the US grew at 2 to 3 percent a year from 1948 to 1973.[7] In China today much of the investment is "capital intensive", with the employed workforce only growing at about 1 percent a year, despite the vast pools of rural labour.

The second objection to Marx's argument is that increased productivity reduces the cost of providing workers with their existing living standards ("the value of their labour power"). The capitalists can therefore maintain their rate of profit by taking a bigger share of the value created.

This objection is easy to deal with. Marx himself recognised that rises in productivity that reduce the proportion of the working day needed for workers to cover the cost of their own living standards could form a "countervailing influence" to his law. The capitalists could then grab a greater share of their workers' labour as profits (an increased "rate of exploitation") without necessarily cutting real wages. But there was a limit to how far this counter-influence could operate. If workers' laboured for four hours a day to cover the costs of keeping themselves alive, that could be cut by an hour to three hours a day. But it could not be cut by five hours to minus one hour a day. By contrast, there was no limit to the transformation of workers' past labour into ever greater accumulations of the means of production. Increased exploitation, by increasing the profit flowing to capital, increased the potential for future accumulation. Another way to put the argument is to see what happens with a hypothetical "maximum rate of exploitation", when the workers labour for nothing. It can be shown that eventually even this is not enough to stop a fall in the ratio of profit to investment.

7: Clarke, 1979, p427. See also the comment by M N Bailey, p433-436. For a graph showing the long term rise of the capital-labour ration, see Duménil and Lévy, 1993, p274.

The final objection is "Okishio's theorem". Changes in technique alone, it is claimed, cannot produce a fall in the rate of profit, since capitalists will only introduce a new technique if it raises their profits. But a rise in the profit rate of one capitalist must raise the average profit of the whole capitalist class. Or as Ian Steedman put it, "The forces of competition will lead to that selection of production methods industry by industry which generates the highest possible uniform rate of profit through the economy".[8] The conclusion drawn from this is that the only things that can reduce profit rates are increased real wages or intensified international competition.

Missing out from many presentations of this argument is the recognition that the first capitalist to adopt a technique gets a competitive advantage over his fellow capitalists, which enables him to gain extra profits, but that this extra profit disappears once the technique is generalised. What the capitalist gets in money terms when he sells his goods depends upon the average amount of socially necessary labour contained in them. If he introduces a new, more productive, technique, but no other capitalists do, he is producing goods worth the same amount of socially necessary labour as before, but with less expenditure on real, concrete labour power. His profits rise.[9] But once all capitalists producing these goods have introduced these techniques, the value of the goods falls until it corresponds to the average amount of labour needed to produce them using the new techniques.[10]

Okishio and his followers use the counter-argument that any rise in productivity as a result of using more means of production will cause a fall in the price of its output, so reducing prices throughout the economy—and thereby the cost of paying for the means of production. This cheapening of investment will, they claim, raise the rate of profit.

At first glance the argument looks convincing—and the simultaneous equations used in the mathematical presentation of the theorem have convinced many Marxist economists. It is, however, false. It rests upon a sequence of logical steps which you cannot take in the real world. Investment in a process of production takes place at one point in time. The cheapening of further investment as a result of improved production techniques occurs at a later point in time. The two things are not

8: Steedman, 1985, p64; compare also pp128-129.

9: For Marx's argument with a numerical example, see Marx, 1965, pp316-317.

10: For more on this argument, with a simple numerical example of my own, see Harman, 1984, pp29-30.

simultaneous.[11] It is a silly mistake to apply simultaneous equations to processes taking place through time.

There is an old saying: "You cannot build the house of today with the bricks of tomorrow." The fact that the increase in productivity will reduce the cost of getting a machine in a year's time does not reduce the amount the capitalist has to spend on getting it today.

Capitalist investment involves using the same fixed constant capital (machinery and buildings) for several cycles of production. The fact that undertaking investment would cost less after the second, third or fourth round of production does not alter the cost of undertaking it before the first round. The decline in the value of their already invested capital certainly does not make life any easier for the capitalists. To survive in business they have to recoup, with a profit, the full cost of their past investments, and if technological advance meant these investments are now worth, say, half as much as they were previously, they have to pay out of their gross profits to write off that sum. What they have gained on the swings they have lost on the roundabouts, with "depreciation" of capital due to obsolescence causing them as big a headache as a straightforward fall in the rate of profit.

The implications of Marx's argument are far reaching. The very success of capitalism at accumulating leads to problems for further accumulation. Crisis is the inevitable outcome, as capitalists in key sections of the economy no longer have a rate of profit sufficient to cover their investments. And the greater the scale of past accumulation, the deeper the crises will be.

The crisis and the rate of profit

The crisis, however, is not the end of the system. Paradoxically it can open up new prospects for it. By driving some capitalists out of business it can permit a recovery of the profits of others. Means of production can be bought at bargain basement prices, raw material prices slump and unemployment forces workers to accept low wages. Production once again becomes profitable and accumulation can restart. There has long been a dispute among economists who accept Marx's law about the implications of this. Some have argued that the rate of profit will tend to decline in the long term, decade after decade.

11: This point was made by Robin Murray in a reply to an attempt by Andrew Glyn to use a "corn model" to disprove the falling rate of profit (Muray, 1973), and was taken up by Ben Fine and Lawrence Harris in *Rereading Capital* (Fine and Harris, 1979). It now stands are the centre of the arguments put forward by the "temporal single-system interpretation" of Alan Freeman and Andrew Kliman. See, for instance Freeman and Carchedi, 1996, and Kliman, 2007.

Not only will there be ups and downs with each boom-slump cycle, there will also be a long term downward trend, making each boom shorter than the one before and each slump deeper. Others Marxists, by contrast, have argued that restructuring can restore the rate of profit to its earlier level until rising investment lowers it again. According to this view, there is a cyclical motion of the rate of profit, punctuated by intense crises of restructuring, not an inevitable long term decline. So Marx's law should be called "the law of the tendency of the rate of profit to fall and its countervailing tendencies".[12]

There have been periods in the history of the system in which crises got rid of unprofitable capital on a sufficient scale to stop a long term decline in profit rates. There was, for instance, a decline in profit rates in the early stages of the industrial revolution, from very high rates for the pioneers in the cotton industry in the 1770s and 1780s to much lower rates by the first decade of the 19th century.[13] This led Adam Smith and David Ricardo to see falling profit rates as inevitable (with Smith blaming them on competition and Ricardo on the diminishing returns of physical output in agriculture). But profit rates then seem to have recovered substantially. Robert C Allen claims they were twice as high in 1840 as in 1800.[14] His figures (if accurate) are compatible with the "restructuring restoring the rate of profit" argument, since there were three economic crises between 1810 and 1840, with 3,300 firms going bust in 1826 alone.[15]

If crises can always counteract the fall in the rate of profit in this way Marx was wrong to see his law as spelling the death knell of capitalism, since the system has survived recurrent crises over the past 180 years.

But those who rely on this argument assume restructuring can always take place in such a way as to harm some capitals but not others. Michael Kidron presented a very important challenge to this contention in the 1970s. It was based on understanding that the development of capitalism is not simply cyclical, but also involves transformation through time—it ages.[16]

The concentration and centralisation of capital

The process by which some capitals grow at the expense of others—what Marx calls the "concentration and centralisation" of capital—eventually

12: Fine and Harris, 1979, p64. The argument is also accepted by Andrew Kliman, see Kliman, 2007, pp30-31.

13: See the figures in Harley, 2001.

14: Allen, 2005.

15: Flamant and Singer-Kérel, 1970, p18.

16: Hence Kidron's description of present day capitalism as "ageing capitalism", rather than the term "late capitalism" popularised by Ernest Mandel.

leads to a few very large capitals playing a predominant role in particular parts of the system. Their operation becomes intertwined with those of the other capitals, big and small, around them. If the very large capitals go bust, it disrupts the operation of the others—destroying their markets, and cutting off their sources of raw materials and components. This can drag previously profitable firms into bankruptcy alongside the unprofitable in a cumulative collapse that risks creating economic "black holes" in the heart of the system.

This began to happen in the great crisis of the interwar years. Far from bankruptcies of some firms bringing the crisis to end after a couple of years they deepened its impact. As a consequence, capitals everywhere turned to states to protect them. Despite their political differences, this was what was common to the New Deal in the US, the Nazi period in Germany, the emerging populist regimes in Latin America or the final acceptance of Keynesian state intervention as the economic orthodoxy in wartime Britain. Such interdependence of states and big capitals was the norm right across the system in the first three decades following the Second World War, an arrangement that has variously been called "state capitalism" (my preferred term), "organised capitalism" or "Fordism".[17]

The intervention of the state always had doubled edged repercussions. It prevented the first symptoms of crisis developing into out-and-out collapse. But it also obstructed the capacity of some capitals to restore their profit rates at the expense of others.

This was not a great problem in the first decades after 1945, since the combined impact of the interwar slump and the Second World War had already caused a massive destruction of old capital (according to some estimates a third of the total). Accumulation was able to restart with higher profit rates than in the pre-war period, and rates hardly declined, or did so slowly.[18] Capitalism could enjoy what is often now called its "golden age".[19]

17: The latter term is misleading, since it equates mass production methods of exploitation, rising consumer spending and state intervention in industry, as if someone set out to produce all three; rather than the logic of the concentration and centralisation of capital working itself out. The term "post-Fordism" is even more confusing, since mass production methods remain in many sectors of the economy, and there is everywhere a complex interaction between states and capitals.

18: Different measures of profit rates give slightly different pictures in these decades.

19: Mike Kidron ascribed this to the role of arms spending in his two books, Kidron, 1970a, and Kidron, 1974, a view which I endorsed in Harman, 1984. More on this question later in this article.

But when profit rates did begin to fall from the 1960s onwards the system found itself caught between the danger of "black holes" and of failing to restructure sufficiently to restore those rates. The system could not afford to risk restructuring by letting crises rip through it. States intervened to ward off the threat of big bankruptcies. But in doing so they prevented the system restructuring sufficiently to overcome the pressures that had caused the threat of bankruptcy. The system, as Kidron put it in an editorial for this journal, was "sclerotic".[20]

As I wrote in this journal in 1982:

> State intervention to mitigate the crisis can only prolong it indefinitely. This does not mean the world economy is doomed simply to decline. An overall tendency to stagnation can still be accompanied by boomlets, with small but temporary increases in employment. Each boomlet, however, only aggravates the problems of the system as a whole and results in further general stagnation, and extreme devastation for particular parts of the system.

I argued that "two or three advanced countries" going bankrupt might "provide the system with the "opportunity for a new round of accumulation", but that those running the other parts of the system would do their best to avoid such bankruptcy, lest it pulled down other economies and the banks, leading to "the progressive collapse of other capitals". My conclusion was that "the present phase of crisis is likely to go on and on—until it is resolved either by plunging much of the world into barbarism or by a succession of workers' revolutions".[21]

The empirical picture

How does the empirical record of profit rates over the past 30 years measure up to these various arguments? And what are the implications for today?

There have been a number of attempts to calculate long term trends in profit rates. The results are not always fully compatible with each other, since there are different ways of measuring investment in fixed capital, and the information on profits provided by companies and governments are subject to enormous distortions (companies will often do their best to understate the profits to governments, for tax reasons, and to workers, in order to justify low wages; they also often overstate their profits to shareholders, in order to boost

20: Kidron, 1970b, p1.

21: Harman, 1982, p83. This article was reprinted, with minor changes, as chapter three of Harman, 1984.

their stock exchange ratings and their capacity to borrow). Nevertheless, Fred Moseley, Thomas Michl, Anwar Shaikh and Ertugrul Ahmet Tonak, Gérard Duménil and Dominique Lévy, Ufuk Tutan and Al Campbell, Robert Brenner, Edwin N Wolff, and Piruz Alemi and Duncan K Foley[22] have all followed in the footsteps of Joseph Gillman and Shane Mage who carried through empirical studies of profit rate trends in the 1960s.

A certain pattern emerges, which is shown in graphs given by Duménil and Lévy (figure 1) for the whole business sector in the US and by Brenner (figure 2) for manufacturing in the US, Germany and Japan.

Figure 1: US profit rates accounting for (—) and abstracting from (- -) the impact of financial relations[23]

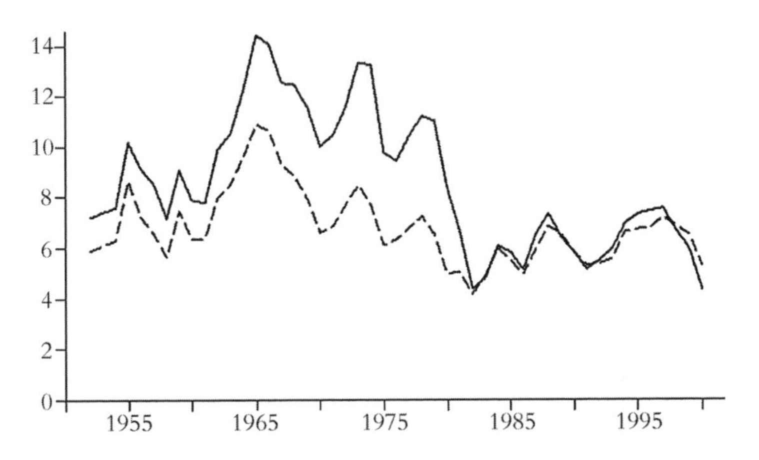

There is general agreement that profit rates fell from the late 1960s until the early 1980s. There is also agreement that profit rates partially recovered after the early 1980s, but with interruptions at the end of the 1980s and the end of the 1990s. There is also an important area of agreement that the fall from the mid-1970s to the early 1980s was not a result of rising wages, since this was the period in which US real wages began a decline which was not partially reversed until the late 1990s. Michl,[24]

22: Alemi and Foley, 1997.
23: Duménil and Lévy, 2005a, p11.
24: Michl, 1988.

Moseley, Shaikh and Tonak, and Wolff[25] all conclude that the rising ratio of capital to labour was an element in reducing profit rates. This conclusion is an empirical refutation of the Okishio position. "Capital intensive" investments by capitalists aimed at raising their individual competitiveness and profitability have had the effect of causing profitability throughout the economy to fall. Marx's basic theory is validated.

Figure 2: US, German and Japanese manufacturing net profits rates[26]

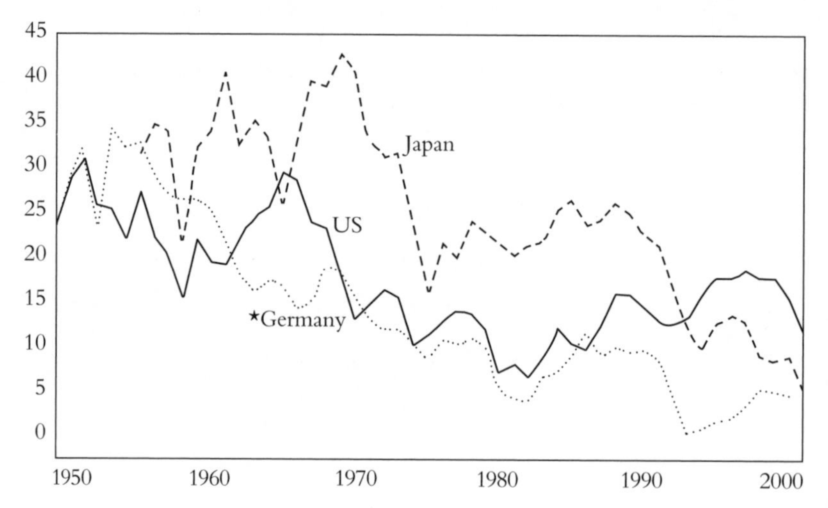

*Profit rate for Germany covers West Germany 1950-90 and Germany 1991-2000

Profit rates did recover from about 1982 onwards—but they only made up about half the decline that had taken place in the previous period. According to Wolff, the rate of profit fell by 5.4 percent from 1966-79 and then "rebounded" by 3.6 percent from 1979-97; Fred Moseley calculates that it "recovered...only about 40 percent of the earlier decline";[27] Duménil and Lévy that "the profit rate in 1997" was "still only half of its value of 1948, and between 60 and 75 percent of its average value for the decade 1956-65".[28]

25: Wolff, 2003, pp479-499.
26: Brenner, 2006, p7.
27: Moseley, 1997.
28: Duménil and Lévy, 2005b.

Explanations

Why did profit rates recover? One important factor was an increase in the rate of exploitation throughout the economy, as shown by the rising share going to "capital" and opposed to "labour" in national output: Moseley showed a rise in the "rate of surplus value from 1.71 in 1975 to 2.22 in 1987".[29]

There was, however, also a slowdown in the growth of the ratio of investment to workers (the "organic composition of capital"), at least until the mid-1990s. An important change took place in the system from around 1980 onwards—crises begin to involve large scale bankruptcies for the first time since the interwar years:

> During the period from World War II through the 1970s, bankruptcy was not a major topic in the news. With the exception of railroads, there were not many notable business failures in the US. During the 1970s, there were only two corporate bankruptcies of prominence, Penn Central Transportation Corporation in 1970 and W T Grant Company in 1975.

But:

> During the 1980s and early 1990s record numbers of bankruptcies, of all types, were filed. Many well known companies filed for bankruptcy... Included were LTV, Eastern Airlines, Texaco, Continental Airlines, Allied Stores, Federated Department Stores, Greyhound, R H Macy and Pan Am... Maxwell Communication and Olympia & York.[30]

The same story was repeated on a bigger scale during the crisis of 2001-2. For instance, the collapse of Enron was, as Joseph Stiglitz writes, "the biggest corporate bankruptcy ever—until WorldCom came along".[31]

This was not just a US phenomenon. It was a characteristic of Britain in the early 1990s as bankruptcies like those of the Maxwell Empire and Olympia & York showed, and, although Britain avoided a full recession in 2001-2, two once dominant companies, Marconi/GEC and Rover, went down, as well as scores of recently established dotcom and hi tech companies. The same phenomenon was beginning to be visible in continental Europe, with an added twist in Germany that most of the big enterprises

29: Moseley, 1991, p96.
30: Mastroianni, 2006, chapter 11.
31: Stiglitz, 2004.

of the former East Germany went bust or were sold off at bargain basement prices to West German firms,[32] and then in Asia with the crisis of 1997-8. On top of this there was the bankruptcy of whole states—notably the USSR, with a GDP that was at one stage a third or even half that of the US. Most of the left held a confused belief that these were "socialist" states. This prevented many commentators from understanding that these states collapsed because the rate of profit was no longer high enough to cover their cost of equipping themselves for international competition.[33] It also prevented them from analysing the impact that writing off these vast amounts of capital had on the world system.[34]

What occurred through these decades was a process of recurrent "restructuring through crisis" on an international scale. However, it was only a limited return of the old mechanism for clearing out unprofitable capitals to the benefit of the survivors. There were still many cases in which the state intervened to prop up very big firms or to pressurise the banking system to do so. This happened in the US with the near bankruptcy of Chrysler in 1979-80,[35] with the crisis of the S&Ls (effectively US building societies) in the late 1980s and the collapse of the giant derivatives gambler Long Term Capital Management in 1998. On each occasion fear of economic, social and political instability prevented the crisis clearing unprofitable capitals from the system. Orlando Capita Leiva tells how in the United States "the state supported...restructuring. In 1970 public investment was only 10 percent of private investment. It increased to 24 percent in 1990 and from then on maintained levels almost double those of 1970".[36]

Official use of the rhetoric of neoliberalism does not preclude a continuing strong element of state capitalism in actual government policy. This is true not just of the US. Governments as varied as those of the Scandinavian countries and Japan have rushed to prop up banks whose collapse might damage the rest of the national financial system—even if, as a last resort, this involves nationalisation.[37] The government of Germany

---

32: Dale, 2004, p327.

33: See Harman, 1977, and Harman, 1990.

34: It took repeated comments by Ken Muller to make me even begin to try to think this through.

35: "In a rare emotional appeal to the House of Representatives, Speaker Tip O'Neill brought a hush to the chamber as he recalled the dark days of the Great Depression and warned that failure to save Chrysler would result in worker layoffs large enough to trigger a new depression. Said he: 'We won't be able to dig ourselves out for the next ten years'." *Time* magazine, 31 December 1989.

36: Leiva, 2007, p 12.

37: See OECD, 1996.

poured billions into the eastern part of the recently unified country after companies found their newly acquired subsidiaries could not be profitable otherwise. And the world financial institutions have reacted to successive debt crises with schemes that protect big Western banks from going under, despite occasional complaints from, for instance, the *Economist* to the effect that this prevents the system from taking the only medicine that will restore its full vigour.

Unproductive labour and waste

Moseley, Shaikh and Tonak, and Simon Mohun have all noted another feature of capitalism's most recent development—one highlighted by Kidron back in the 1970s. This is the growing "non-productive" portion of the economy.

Mainstream neoclassical economics regards all economic activities involving buying and selling as "productive". This follows from its limited focus on the way transactions take place in markets. Marx, like Adam Smith and David Ricardo before him, had a deeper concern—to discover the dynamics of capitalist growth. He therefore further developed a distinction to be found in Smith between "productive" and "unproductive" labour. For Marx, productive labour was that which created surplus value through expanding production. Unproductive labour was that which, rather than expanding production, was simply distributing, protecting or wasting what was already produced—for instance, the labour of personal servants, policemen, soldiers or sales personnel.

Marx's distinction was not between material production and "services". Some things categorised as "services" add to the real wealth of the world. Moving things from where they are made to where they can be consumed, as is done by some transport workers, is therefore productive. Acting in a film is likewise productive insofar as it yields a profit for a capitalist by giving people enjoyment as so improving their living standard. By contrast, acting in an advert whose only function is to sell something already produced is not productive.

Marx's categorisation has to be refined to come to terms with present day capitalism, in which things like education and heath services are much more important than when he was writing. Most present day Marxists would accept that those elements of teaching that increase the capacity of people to produce things (as opposed to merely disciplining children) are at least indirectly productive. Kidron went further and argued that what was productive was that which served the further accumulation of capital. The production of means of production did this, and so did the production of goods that kept workers and their families fit and healthy enough to be exploitable (ie good that replenished their "labour power"). But production that merely provided luxuries for the capitalist class and their hangers-on should not be regarded as productive, nor should that which went into arms.[38]

Unproductive labour is of central importance to present day capitalism, regardless of the exact definition given to it. Fred Moseley estimates the numbers in commerce in the US grew from 8.9 million to 21 million between 1950 and 1980, and the number in finance from 1.9 million to 5.2 million, while the productive workforce only grew from 28 million to 40.3 million.[39] Shaikh and Tonak calculate that the share of productive out of total labour in the US fell from 57 percent to 36 percent between 1948 and 1989.[40] Simon Mohun has calculated that the share of "unproductive" wages and salaries in "material value added" in the US grew from 35 percent in 1964 to over 50 percent in 2000.[41] Kidron calculated that, using his wide definition, "Three fifths of the work actually undertaken in the US in 1970s was wasted from capital's own point of view".[42]

Moseley, Shaikh and Tonak, and Kidron in his later writings[43] had no doubt. The burden of providing for unproductive labour serves as a drain on surplus value and the rate of profit.[44] Moseley, and Shaikh and Tonak, calculated the rate of profit in "productive" sectors (the "Marxian rate of profit"), and then compared their results with those provided for the economy as a whole by corporations and the US government's National

---

38: See the chapter "Waste US: 1970" in Kidron, 1974. See also my discussion of this in Harman, 1984.

39: Moseley, 1991, p126. He mistakenly underestimates the amount of productive and unproductive labour by excluding the public sector from the capitalist economy, see p35.

40: Sheikh and Tonak, 1994, p110.

41: Mohun, 2006, figure 6.

42: Kidron, 1974, p56.

43: Kidron, 2002, p87.

44: However, Duménil and Lévy do not accept that unproductive expenditures necessarily lower the rate of profit. They contend that unproductive expenditures can help the rate of profit through the impact of increased managerial supervision on productivity. They claim this explains the rise in the rate of profit which occurred between the 1920s and the late 1940s. Their argument is doubly wrong. The most obvious cause of that rise was the destruction of capital in slump and war. And increased productivity in itself cannot increase the rate of profit, since its effect, once it takes place right across the system, is to lower the socially necessary labour required to produce, and hence the value of, each unit of output. Their position follows from their inversion of Marx's relationship between productivity and value, which in effect abandons the labour theory of value by denying it is possible to use values as a basis for prices. See my review of their *Capital Resurgent*, Harman, 2005.

Institute of Pension Administrators (NIPA).[45] Shaikh and Tonak calculate that from 1948-89 "the Marxian rate of profit falls by almost a third... The NIPA based average rates even faster, by over 48 percent, and the corporate the fastest of all by over 57 percent. These more rapid declines can be explained by the relative rise in the proportion of unproductive to productive activities".[46] Moseley concludes that "in the post-war US economy through the late 1970s the conventional rate of profit declined even more than the Marxian rate"—by 40 percent as opposed to 15-20 percent. He has argued that the in the 1990s it was mainly the rise in the level of unproductive labour that stopped the rate of profit fully recovering.

Why have unproductive expenditures grown like this, even to the extent of choking off what might otherwise be healthier profit rates? Different factors are involved, but each is itself a reaction to low profit rates (and attempts by firms and governments to keep crisis at bay):

•Capitals pour greater resources into attempts to defend and expand markets in unproductive ways.

•Wave upon wave of speculative investment occurs as capitalists seek easy profits through gambling in money markets, financial adventures, hedge funds and so forth.

•Managerial hierarchies grow in an effort to exert increased pressure on those at the bottom—a typical feature of both the public and private sectors today.

•The costs to the system of trying to maintain social peace increase through both "security" expenditures and minimal benefits for those it cannot productively employ.

•States resort to military adventures as a way to offload the problems faced by capitals within them.

Contradictory effects

There is a vicious circle. Reactions by individual firms and states to the falling rate of profit have the effect of further reducing the resources available for productive accumulation.[47]

But the effect of unproductive expenditures is not only to lower the rate of profit. It can also reduce upward pressure on the organic composition of capital. This was an insight used by Michael Kidron to explain

45: Moseley, 1991, p104.

46: Shaikh and Tonak, 1994, p124.

47: One fault with Moseley's analysis is that he does not see this, but looks for other factors to explain the rising level of waste.

the "positive" impact of massive arms spending on the system in the post-war decades. He saw it, like luxury consumption by the ruling class and its hangers-on, as having a beneficial side-effect for those running the system—at least for a time.

Labour which is "wasted", he argued, cannot add to the pressure for accumulation to be ever more capital intensive. Value which would otherwise go into raising the ratio of means of production to workers is siphoned out of the system. Accumulation is slower, but it continues at a steady pace, like the tortoise racing the hare in Aesop's fable. Profit rates are weighed down by the waste, but do not face a sudden thrust into the depths from a rapid acceleration of the capital-labour ratio.

This account seems to fit the early post-war period. Arms spending at around 13 percent of US national output (and with indirect expenditures, perhaps 15 percent) was a major diversion of surplus value away from further accumulation. It was also an expenditure that the US ruling class expected to gain from, in that it helped their global hegemony (both in confronting the USSR and binding the European capitalist classes to the US) and guaranteed a market to some important productive sectors of the US economy. In this sense, the capitalists could regard arms, like their own luxury consumption, as something to their advantage—very different in this sense to "unproductive" expenditures on improving the conditions of the poor. And if it reduced the rate of accumulation, this was not catastrophic since the restructuring of capital through slump and war had already boosted accumulation to higher trajectory than that known in the 1930s. Domestically, all firms suffered the same handicap, and so none lost out to others in competition for markets. And internationally, in the early post-war years, other countries involved in significant economic competition with the US (such as the old imperial powers of Britain and France) were handicapped by relatively high arms spending of their own.

Today things are very different. Since the early 1960s the re-emergence of major foreign economic competitors has created a powerful pressure for the US to reduce the share of national output going towards arms. Boosting arms spending in the mid-1960s during the Vietnam War and in the 1980s during the "second Cold War" gave only a short term fillip to the US economy before revealing immense problems. George Bush's rise in arms spending from 3.9 percent 4.7 percent of GNP (equal to about a third of net business investment) has exacerbated the US's burgeoning budget and foreign trade deficits.

The effect of all of these forms of "waste" is much less beneficial to the system as a whole than half a century ago. They may still reduce the downward pressures on the rate of profit from the organic composition of capital—it certainly does not rise as rapidly as it would if all surplus value went into accumulation. But the price the advanced capitalist countries pay for this is slow productive accumulation and slow long term rates of growth. Hence the repeated "neoliberal" attempts by capitals and states to raise profit rates by cutting back on what they pay employed workers, the old, the unemployed and the long term sick; the resort to market mechanism to try to reduce costs in education and health; the insistence that Third World countries pay their pound of flesh on their loans; and the US adventure of trying to seize control of the second biggest source of the world's most important raw material.

It is wrong to describe the situation as one of permanent crisis[48]—rather it is one of recurrent economic crises. The economic recoveries of the 1980s (especially in Japan) and 1990s (in the US) were more than "boomlets". Low levels of past profitability do not stop capitalists imagining that there are miraculous profits to be made in future and sucking in surplus value from all over the world to be ploughed into projects aimed at obtaining them. Many of these are purely speculative gambles in unproductive spheres, as with bubbles in real estate, commodity markets, share prices and so on. But capitalists can also fantasise about profits to be made by pouring resources into potentially productive sectors, and so create rapid booms lasting several years. Investment in the US doubled between 1991 and 1999.[49] When the bubble burst it was discovered that an immense investment in real things such as fibre optic telecommunication networks had been undertaken that would never be profitable, with the *Financial Times* writing of a "$1000 billion bonfire of wealth".[50]

That was a period in which there was some real recovery of the rate of profit. But that did not do away with the "irrational exuberance" of expecting speculative profits where they did not exist. Virtually every major company deliberately inflated its profits so as to take make speculative gains, with proclaimed profits around 50 percent higher than real profits.[51]

There are many signs that in the US (and probably Britain) we may be approaching a similar phase now. Investment in the US, after declining

48: It was a mistake on my part to use such a formulation in 1982—although I think excusable as we faced only the second real recession my generation had experienced and did so a mere four years after the end of the first.

49: Leiva, 2007, p11.

50: *Financial Times*, 5 September 2001.

51: The *Economist*, 23 June 2001.

in the last recession, is now back to the levels of the late 1990s.[52] But the US recovery has been based upon massive government deficits, on balance of payments deficits covered by inflows of lending from abroad, and on consumers borrowing to cover their living costs as the share of "employee incomes in US GDP has fallen form 49 percent to 46 percent".[53] This is the background to the upsurge of speculative ventures such as hedge funds, derivatives markets, the housing bubble and, now, massive borrowing for private equity takeovers of very big corporations (very reminiscent of the "barbarians at the gate" issue of junk bonds in the giant takeovers of the late 1980s). Against such a background, corporate profits will be being puffed up until they lose touch with reality, and things will seem to be going very well until overnight it is discovered they are going badly. And, as they say, when the US gets a cold, the UK can easily catch influenza.

For the moment profit rates in Britain appear to be high. According to one calculation they reached 15.5 percent for all non-financial private corporations in the fourth quarter of 2006—the highest figure since 1969. Under New Labour the share of profits in GDP has reached a record of nearly 27 percent.[54] But the figures for average profits rates will have been boosted by the current high levels of profit on North Sea oil and gas. And calculations of profits made by British firms are not the same as profits made in Britain, given the very high dependence of big firms on their overseas activities (more so than in any other large advanced capitalist country). "Service sector" profitability is high. However, profitability in the much diminished but still important industrial sector has fallen from about 15 percent in 1998 to about 10 percent now. As in the US there are currently many enthusiasts for capitalism who fear the good times are about to end as they eventually did in the 1970s, the 1980s and the 1990s.

There are even doubts about the one part of the world system where immense productive investments are taking place—China. Some commentators see this country as the salvation of the system as a whole. Chinese capital has been able plough much more surplus value back into investment—more than 40 percent of national output—than in the US, Europe or even Japan. It has been able to exploit its workers more, and it has not so far been held back by the levels of unproductive expenditure that characterise advanced capitalist countries (although the present real estate boom is characterised by a proliferation of office sky scrapers, hotels and shopping

52: Leiva, 2007, p11.

53: Riley, 2007.

54: All figures on British profit rates are from Barell and Kirkby, 2007.

malls). All this has enabled it to emerge as a major competitor with the advanced capitalist countries in export markets for many products. But its very high levels of investment are already having an impact on profitability. One recent attempt to apply Marxist categories to the Chinese economy calculates that its profit rates as fell from 40 percent in 1984 to 32 percent in 2002, while the organic composition of capital has increased by 50 percent.[55] There are some Western observers who are convinced that the profitability of some big Chinese corporations is very low, but that this is concealed by the pressure on the big state-run banks to keep them expanding.[56]

Speculation about what will happen next is easy, but pointless. The general contours of the system are decipherable, but the myriad individual factors that determine how these translate into reality in the course of a few months or even years are not. What matters is to recognise that the system has only been able to survive—and even, spasmodically, grow quite fast for the past three decades—because of its recurrent crises, the increased pressure on workers' conditions and the vast amounts of potentially investable value that are diverted into waste. It has not been able to return to the "golden age" and it will not be able to do so in future. It may not be in permanent crisis, but it is in a phase of repeated crises from which it cannot escape, and these will necessarily be political and social as well as economic.

55: O'Hara, 2006.

56: For much more on this, see Harman, 2006.

References

Alemi, Piruz and Duncan K Foley, 1997, "The Circuit of Capital, US Manufacturing and Non-financial Corporate Business Sectors, 1947–1993", manuscript, September 1997, http://cepa.newschool.edu/~foleyd/circap.pdf

Allen, Robert C, 2005, "Capital Accumulation, Technological Change, and the Distribution of Income during the British Industrial Revolution", Department of Economics, Oxford University, www.economics.ox.ac.uk/members/gavin.cameron/ipg/solow-5.pdf

Barell, Ray and Simon Kirkby, 2007, "Prospects for the UK economy", *National Institute Economic Review*, April 2007.

Brenner, Robert, 2006, *The Economics of Global Turbulence* (Verso).

Clarke, Peter, 1979, "Issues in the Analysis of Capital Formation and Productivity Growth", *Brookings Papers on Economic Activity*, volume 1979, number 2.

Dale, Gareth, 2004, *Between State Capitalism and Globalisation* (Peter Lang).

Duménil, Gérard, and Dominique Lévy, 1993, *The Economics of the Profit Rate* (Edward Elgar).

Duménil, Gérard and Dominique Lévy, 2005a, "The Real and Financial Components of Profitability", www.jourdan.ens.fr/levy/dle2004g.pdf

Duménil, Gérard and Dominique Lévy, 2005b, "The Profit Rate: Where and How Much Did it Fall? Did It Recover? (USA 1948-1997)",www.jourdan.ens.fr/levy/dle2002f.pdf

Fine, Ben, and Laurence Harris, 1979, *Rereading Capital* (Macmillan).

Flamant, Maurice, and Jeanne Singer-Kérel, 1970, *Modern Economic Crises* (Barrie and Jenkins).

Freeman, Alan, and Guglielmo Carchedi (eds), 1996, *Marx and Non-equilibrium Economics* (Edgar Elgar).

Harley, C Knick, 2001, "Cotton Textiles and the Industrial Revolution Competing Models and Evidence of Prices and Profits", Department of Economic, University of Western Ontario, May 2001.

Harman, Chris, 1977, "Poland: Crisis of State Capitalism", *International Socialism 93* and *94*, first series (November/December 1976, January 1977)

Harman, Chris, 1982, "Arms, State Capitalism and the General Form of the Current Crisis", *International Socialism 26* (spring 1982).

Harman, Chris, 1984, *Explaining the Crisis: A Marxist Reappraisal* (Bookmarks).

Harman, Chris, 1990, "The Storm Breaks", *International Socialism 46* (spring 1990).

Harman, Chris, 2005, "Half-explaining the Crisis", *International Socialism 108* (autumn 2005), www.isj.org.uk/index.php4?id=148issue=108

Harman, Chris, 2006, "China's economy and Europe's crisis", *International Socialism 109* (winter 2006), www.isj.org.uk/index.php4?id=160&issue=109

Kidron, Michael, 1970a, *Western Capitalism Since the War* (Pelican), the first section of this is currently available online: www.marxists.org/archive/kidron/works/1970/westcap/

Kidron, Michael, 1970b, "The Wall Street Seizure", *International Socialism 44*, first series (July-August 1970).

Kidron, Michael, 1974, *Capitalism and Theory* (Pluto).

Kidron, Michael, 2002, "Failing Growth and Rampant Costs: Two Ghosts in the Machine of Modern Capitalism", *International Socialism 96* (winter 2002), http://pubs.socialistreviewindex.org.uk/isj96/kidron.htm

Kliman, Andrew, 2007, *Reclaiming Marx's "Capital": A Refutation of the Myth of Inconsistency* (Lexington).

Leiva, Orlando Capito, 2007, "The World Economy and the US at the Beginning of the 21st Century", *Latin American Perspectives*, vol 134, no 1.

Marx, Karl, 1962, *Capital*, volume three (Moscow), www.marxists.org/archive/marx/works/1894-c3/
Marx, Karl, 1965, *Capital*, volume one (Moscow), www.marxists.org/archive/marx/works/1867-c1/
Marx, Karl, 1973, *Grundrisse* (Penguin), www.marxists.org/archive/marx/works/1857/grundrisse/
Mastroianni, Kerry A (ed), 2006, *The 2006 Bankruptcy Yearbook & Almanac*, chapter 11 available from www.bankruptcydata.com/Ch11History.htm
Michl, Thomas R, 1988, "Why Is the Rate of Profit Still Falling?", The Jerome Levy Economics Institute Working Paper number 7 (September 1988). http://ssrn.com/abstract=191174
Mohun, Simon, 2006, "Distributive Shares in the US Economy, 1964-2001", *Cambridge Journal of Economics*, volume 30, number 3.
Moseley, Fred, 1991, *The Falling Rate of Profit in the Post War United States Economy* (Macmillan).
Moseley, Fred, 1997, "The Rate of Profit and the Future of Capitalism", May 1997, www.mtholyoke.edu/~fmoseley/RRPE.html
Murray, Robin, 1973, *cseBulletin*, spring 1973.
OECD, 1996, "Government Policies Towards Financial Markets", available from www.olis.oecd.org/olis/1996doc.nsf/
O'Hara, Phillip Anthony, 2006, "A Chinese Social Structure of Accumulation for Capitalist Long-Wave Upswing?", *Review of Radical Political Economics*, volume 38, number 3, http://hussonet.free.fr/rrpe397.pdf
Riley, Barry, 2007, "Equities Run Short of Propellant", *Financial News US*, 16 Apr 2007, www.financialnews-us.com/index.cfm?page=uscomment&contentid=2447560990
Sheikh, Anwar and Ertugrul Ahmet Tonak, 1994, *Measuring the Wealth of Nations* (Cambridge University Press).
Steedman, Ian, 1985, *Marx After Sraffa* (Verso).
Stiglitz, Joseph, 2004, *The Roaring Nineties: Why We're Paying the Price for the Greediest Decade in History* (Penguin).
Wolff, Edwin N, 2003, "What's Behind the Rise in Profitability in the US in the 1980s and 1990s?", *Cambridge Journal of Economics*, volume 27, number 4.

Les Demoiselles d'Avignon, *Pablo Picasso* (1907)

A revolution in paint: 100 years of Picasso's Demoiselles

John Molyneux

This year marks the centenary of the painting of *Les Demoiselles d'Avignon* by Pablo Picasso. There cannot be many paintings whose anniversary would occasion an analysis in a journal of socialist theory—an honour usually reserved for revolutions and other great events in the history of the class struggle—nevertheless *Les Demoiselles* certainly repays serious consideration. Aside from its individual stature as one of the outstanding paintings of the 20th century, there is its enormous importance as a turning point in the history of art and, indeed, wider cultural history, and also its powerful resonance today.

Les Demoiselles d'Avignon is an oil painting on canvas begun by Picasso in late 1906 and completed in the summer of 1907. It is eight feet tall, seven feet eight inches wide, and has hung since 1937 in the Museum of Modern Art in New York. The painting depicts five nude women, clearly prostitutes in a brothel. Of the three women on the left, the leftmost is shown side on, apparently drawing back a curtain to reveal the others, and the second and third are shown frontally, staring straight out of the canvass. The depiction of all three women, especially the head of the furthest left, is influenced by Ancient Iberian (pre-historic "Spanish") sculpture that Picasso had seen the previous year in the Louvre. The two women on the right, one standing slightly in the background between curtains, the other squatting in the foreground, have been given heads that resemble the African sculptures or masks that the artist is known to have seen in the Musée d'Ethnographie du Trocadéro. The bodies of all the women are rendered by means of flat, angular planes of colour with little shading or modelling. Jutting out at the centre of the bottom of the painting is a bowl of fruit—a melon, grapes, pear and apple. The painting received its title not from Picasso but from his friend André Salmon in 1916, and it is either, depending on interpretation, euphemistic or ironic for it refers to a brothel or brothels on the Carrer d'Avinyo in Barcelona, of which Picasso evidently had personal experience.

So much for the basic facts. By far the most frequent comment on *Les Demoiselles*, in both journalism and art history, is that it marks "the birth of modern art".[1] Let us first consider the justification for, and truth of, this bold claim.

Les Demoiselles and modern art

The simplest, most widespread, distinction between "traditional art" (by which is meant European art from about 1300 onwards) and "modern art" is that the former was engaged, at a minimum (it did other, more important, things as well) in the attempt to imitate the appearance of people, objects and scenes in the real world, whereas the latter is not. Traditional art is commonly portrayed as representational, naturalistic or "realistic",[2] whereas modern art either wilfully distorts physical appearances or, in abstract art, abandons them altogether. There are numerous problems with this crude distinction, not least the difficulty involved in regarding paintings of Madonnas, angels and Venuses as "realistic", but there is also clearly some truth in it. At least the faces of the Madonnas, the tunics of the angels and the breasts of the Venuses looked like observable faces, tunics and breasts. And while some "traditional" artists (Hans Holbein, John Constable, Gustave Courbet) are more mimetic (imitative) than others (Sandro Botticelli, Hieronymus Bosch, El Greco)

1: See for example, Wullschlager, 2007, or Jones, 2007.

2: I am using "realistic" here in the way it is used in everyday language, the media and mainstream art history, which basically accepts the method of representing the world developed in the Renaissance as true realism, and not in the specific Marxist sense developed by Frederick Engels, Georg Lukács and others. Lukács distinguished between "naturalism", the more or less accurate depiction of surface appearances, and "realism", which penetrated surface appearances to reveal the real driving forces in society. Lukács developed this distinction in relation to literature, so that for him Honoré de Balzac was a great realist, whereas Émile Zola was merely a naturalist, and "the central aesthetic problem of realism is the adequate presentation of the complete human personality" (Lukács, 1948). It can perhaps be applied to some "traditional" (ie European 1300-1900) visual art, so that Rembrandt's "realism" could be contrasted to the "naturalism" of Van Dyke or numerous hack portraitists. But it is very difficult to see how it can cope with post-1900 art, with its divergent phenomena such as geometric and expressionist abstraction, dadaism, Marcel Duchamp and the "ready-made" tradition, pop art, conceptual art, installation art, performance art, etc. And it cannot be used to understand the difference between "traditional" art and "modern" art which is what I am concerned with here.

and some "moderns" (Paul Klee, Wassily Kandinsky) more expressionist or abstract than others (Amedeo Modigliani, Pierre Bonnard), one has only to compare a representative list of traditionals with a similar list of moderns to get the point—on the one hand Van Eyck, Piero della Francesca, Titian, Rembrandt, Diego Velázquez, Thomas Gainsborough, Francisco Goya, Edouard Manet and Vincent van Gogh who, despite the immense differences between them, were all engaged in producing recognisable images of persons and things; on the other hand Georges Braque, Kandinsky, Kazimir Malevich, Piet Mondrian, Max Ernst, Joan Miró, Jackson Pollock, and Mark Rothko who, despite their differences, were not.

The tipping point between the two—the clearest, most decisive assault on the past, the key breakthrough to the new—is indeed *Les Demoiselles d'Avignon*. Before *Les Demoiselles* even Picasso's own work, his blue and rose periods, was clearly a continuation of the mimetic tradition, closer in many ways to Rembrandt, Goya, Manet and Van Gogh than to his work of one, two or three years later. *Les Demoiselles* opens the floodgates, first to cubism and then in rapid succession to futurism, synthetic cubism, expressionism, vorticism, abstraction, suprematism, dadaism and more besides. Within just ten years artists were producing works, such as Malevich's *Black Square on White* and Duchamp's ready-mades, which would not previously have been regarded as art at all (and were not so regarded by the majority at the time), but which have subsequently achieved, at least within the art world, classic and iconic status. *Les Demoiselles* is a veritable revolution in paint—the art equivalent of the French Revolution, indeed of the Storming of the Bastille.

Another characteristic of traditional art, very closely bound up with its naturalism, was the high level of craft skills it involved and demanded. These skills, developed particularly in the 16th and 17th century, lay especially in the precise rendering of surfaces: lace, satin, velvet, sable, glass, silver, feathers, flesh tones, the folds in drapery or robes and so on.[3] This is reflected in the way people commonly talk about art—"Look at the detail!" or, "It makes you feel as if you can touch it"—and for many it was these skills that served as the surest guarantee of artistic quality, of the status of traditional paintings as "real" or "great" art. In retrospect it can be seen that the premium on these skills was waning from Claude Monet and impressionism onwards, but it was *Les Demoiselles* that was the decisive break. In 1907 it would have looked like not just a move away from the traditional skills, but a full-scale assault on them. This was the beginning of art which would

3: John Berger supplied the historical materialist explanation for this, linking it to the rise of capitalism and its fixation on property and commodities. See Berger, 1972a.

provoke the outraged cry, "My four year old can do better than that!"

For centuries, roughly from the Renaissance to the 19th century, "beauty" was a, perhaps the, dominant concept in aesthetic theory, the value, together with the closely related "harmonious form", to which it was held that art should aspire. Of course there was always art which could not reasonably be described as beautiful, for example the dark fantasies of Bosch or William Hogarth's satirical series (*Marriage à la Mode*, *The Rake's Progress*, etc), but such work was generally deemed of a lower order than that of artists such as Sandro Botticelli, Leonardo da Vinci and, especially, Raphael, where beauty and harmonious form were more clearly in evidence. The philosophers Edmund Burke and Immanuel Kant supplemented "beauty" with the concept of "the sublime" to accommodate works, such as Michelangelo's *Last Judgment,* which, if not beautiful, were manifestly awe inspiring. Above all, the concept of beauty ruled the genre of the female nude, where it had the added advantage of masking or providing an alibi for the issue of sexual desirability and lust. In the tradition of nude painting that stretches through Botticelli, Giorgione, Titian, Rubens, Velázquez, Goya, Ingres and Renoir the aim of the artists was always to present their female subjects as beautiful. (Rembrandt is, I think, the only significant exception prior to the 19th century.) Clear inroads into this tradition were made by Manet's *Olympia*, Paul Cézanne's *Bathers* series, and Toulouse Lautrec's brothel scenes, but again it is with *Les Demoiselles* that the sharpest confrontation takes place. Picasso not only does not attempt to make the women "beautiful" but, by the use of the African masks, positively insists on their ugliness (by the conventional standards of the day).

The enormously disturbing newness of *Les Demoiselles* is confirmed by the reaction, not of the public or the critics, but of Picasso's avant-garde artist friends when they first saw it in his studio. Both Henri Matisse and Georges Braque were at first repelled by it. Braque suggested that Picasso had been "drinking turpentine and spitting fire",[4] while André Derain is alleged to have claimed that "some day Picasso would hang himself behind his canvas".[5]

Les Demoiselles and theories of modernism

There have been, of course, a number of more rounded and theoretically sophisticated accounts of the emergence of modern art than the simple

4: Hughes, 1991, p24.

5: Warncke, 1997, p165. There is a significant difference between this and the outrage that greeted Manet and the impressionists in that the latter came from the public and the press, whereas this came from the artists in Picasso's immediate circle and resulted in the public not seeing the painting for nearly ten years.

distinctions discussed so far. Probably the most influential, at least within the art world, is that of the American art critic Clement Greenberg. Greenberg established himself by being the principal champion of abstract expressionism, and for 20 years or so (roughly the mid-1940s to the mid-1960s) was the leading art critic in America and, therefore, the world. His status in art criticism approximated to that of John Maynard Keynes in economics or F R Leavis in literature. Greenberg began in the late 1930s as at least a semi-Marxist in the Trotskyist influenced milieu around *Partisan Review*, but during and after the Second World War moved, like so many, towards a mainstream or right wing liberalism and in the process became a rigorous formalist in matters of art criticism and history, rejecting, more or less absolutely, any discussion of the content or social context of artworks.

For Greenberg, modernism was more than art and literature: it included "almost the whole of what is truly alive in our culture",[6] and its essence lay "in the use of the characteristic methods of a discipline to criticise the discipline itself—not in order to subvert it, but to entrench it more firmly in its area of competence".[7] Each art form had to demonstrate in practice that the kind of experience it provided was not to be obtained from any other activity. This meant each art form systematically shedding all conventions not essential to its survival as art, and focusing with increasing intensity on its unique and defining characteristics. In the case of painting this was the making of marks on a two-dimensional surface:

> The limitations that constitute the medium of painting—the flat surface, the shape of the support, the properties of pigment—were treated by the Old Masters as negative factors that could be acknowledged only implicitly or indirectly. Modernist painting has come to regard these same limitations as positive factors that are to be acknowledged openly. Manet's paintings became the first modernist ones by virtue of the frankness with which they declared the surfaces on which they were painted... It was the stressing, however, of the ineluctable flatness of the support that remained most fundamental in the processes by which pictorial art criticised and defined itself under modernism. Flatness alone was unique and exclusive to that art... and so modernist painting oriented itself to flatness as it did to nothing else.[8]

Greenberg's account cannot be accepted as adequate or satisfactory.

6: Greenberg, 1993, p754.
7: Greenberg, 1993, p755.
8: Greenberg, 1993, pp755-756. Neil Davidson has suggested that the position of the

First, it treats the development of art as almost completely (and quite implausibly) autonomous from society, history and politics (except in the very last analysis of the existence of "modern" society). Second, it operates by the sleight of hand of simply excluding from the canon of modernism all painting not participating in the project of flatness (for example surrealism, Diego Rivera and the Mexican muralists or Francis Bacon). Nevertheless, the history of European art from about 1850 to 1950 shows that Greenberg has identified a real and important tendency. From Manet, through impressionism, Gauguin, Cézanne, cubism, Kandinsky and Mondrian, to Pollock and abstract expressionism, one can clearly see the compression of the three-dimensional picture space, which had been opened up in the 14th and 15th centuries.[9] It is like watching a stage in which the backdrop moves ever closer to the apron until it has squeezed out, in Greenberg's words, "the kind of space that recognisable three-dimensional objects can inhabit".[10]

There is no single painting that so clearly illustrates and exemplifies Greenberg's argument as *Les Demoiselles*: the stripping away of inessential conventions, the replacement of sculptural modelling by flat planes, the extreme compression of space between background and foreground—all these undergo a qualitative intensification in this work.

If, however, we turn to more Marxist theorisations of modern art *Les Demoiselles* retains its pivotal role. John Berger does not fully discuss modernism as such, but he clearly regards cubism as the crucial modern movement and the revolutionary art of the 20th century.[11] For Berger, cubism synthesises the materialism of Gustave Courbet and the dialectics of Cézanne, and is a response to the scientific and technical breakthroughs of the period (Max Planck, Albert Einstein, electricity, the Eiffel Tower, the aeroplane, etc) and the positive economic promise of monopoly capitalism (the possibility of a world of material plenty and equality) before it was dashed by war and fascism. But for Berger it was by painting *Les Demoiselles* that "Picasso provoked cubism. It was the spontaneous and...primitive insurrection out of which, for good historical reasons, the revolution of cubism developed".[12]

---

younger Greenberg in his essay "Avant-Garde and Kitsch" is in some ways superior to the position cited here. I think that this is true, but space does not permit an account of the development of his views. Justice for Greenberg will have to wait.

9: What John Berger called "not so much a window on the world as a safe in the wall".

10: Greenberg, 1993, p756.

11: See Berger, 1972b, and Berger, 1965.

12: Berger, 1965, p75.

Perry Anderson's account of modernism in his article "Modernity and Revolution" has a similar point of departure to Berger, but is more systematic and is applied to the culture as a whole, not just painting:

> In my view, "modernism" can best be understood as a cultural field triangulated by three decisive coordinates. The first...was the codification of a highly formalised academicism in the visual and other arts, which itself was institutionalised within official regimes of states and society still massively pervaded, often dominated, by aristocratic or landowning classes... The second coordinate is...the still incipient, hence essentially novel, emergence within these societies of the key technologies or inventions of the second industrial revolution: telephone, radio, automobile, aircraft and so on... The third coordinate...was the imaginative proximity of social revolution.[13]

Les Demoiselles fits neatly into this schema. French art remained dominated by the aristocratic Academy with its annual salons more or less until the end of the 19th century, and Manet, the impressionists, and the post-impressionists (Seurat, Cézanne, Gauguin, Van Gogh) were all met with derision. The automobile is developed, essentially, in the 1890s in Germany and France, and the first mass production is undertaken in the US in 1902. The Wright Brothers made the first powered flights in December 1903 and in September 1906 Santos Dumont made a public flight in Paris. Guglielmo Marconi established the world's first radio station in 1897 on the Isle of Wight, and opened the first wireless factory in Chelmsford in 1898. Above all the attention of Europe was captured by the 1905 Revolution in Russia. Moreover, if we examine the chronology of the landmarks of the modernist revolution in the other art forms we find that *Les Demoiselles*, almost invariably, precedes them: in music, Igor Stravinsky's *Firebird* was composed in 1910, and *The Rite of Spring* between 1912 and 1913, while the Ballets Russes was formed 1909 and first performed *L'Après-midi d'un Faune* in 1912; in literature Marcel Proust's *A la Recherche du Temps Perdu* was begun in 1909, James Joyce's *Dubliners* appeared in 1914, Franz Kafka's *In the Penal Colony* in 1914 and his *Metamorphosis* in 1915.

Even from the standpoint of Georg Lukács, the principal Marxist opponent of modernism, I think it would be fair to say that *Les Demoiselles* exemplifies many of the tendencies—fragmentation, absence of perspective, abandonment of totality—which he held against modernism.

Of course one can push this too far. From a wider perspective,

13: Anderson, 1984.

such as that of Marshall Berman in his powerful work, *All That is Solid Melts into Air*, "modernism" is a cultural response to the whole experience of "modernity", ie modern capitalism, not the product of any individual work or artist—and this is surely right. Modern art and modernism would have happened in some form regardless of whether *Les Demoiselles* had been painted. Indeed in this wider view modernism long pre-dates Picasso, stretching back, perhaps, to Kant and Johann Wolfgang von Goethe or in painting to David and Goya, or Théodore Géricault and Courbet. Perhaps what we really need is the idea of two modernisms: one encompassing the progressive culture of the whole epoch inaugurated by the French and industrial revolutions and still continuing today; the other deriving from the specific conjuncture analysed by Anderson and Berger and lasting until the Second World War, which perhaps could be called High Modernism (on the model of the High Renaissance or High Stalinism). This would have the advantage of combining Berger's broad dynamic vision with Anderson's rigour, without the latter's numbing pessimism and the door it opens to postmodernism.[14]

Nevertheless this broad view does not negate the role played by *Les Demoiselles* at a crucial historical moment, or its exceptional influence on the tempo and form of modernism's development. Just as the knowledge that Lenin did not cause or create the Russian Revolution does not exclude the fact that his part in it was greater that of any other single individual, so understanding the wider historical determination of modernism is perfectly compatible with recognising the exceptional role of this particular work.

The Power of Les Demoiselles

I have so far discussed the impact of *Les Demoiselles* on the development of modern art in purely formal terms, and that was indeed the nature of its influence—it produced a flood of cubist paintings of men with guitars and cafe tables, not a flood of paintings of prostitutes. Nevertheless it would not and could not have had this massive formal influence if it had not been such an exceptionally powerful painting in its own right, that is if its formal innovations had not been seen by other artists (especially Braque) to work in practice. And the moment we consider or analyse the power of *Les Demoiselles* as an individual painting we have to deal with its subject matter, and see its formal qualities as a way of treating that subject matter. In other words we must view the painting as a totality, a particular fusion or unity of form and content.

14: Obviously such a periodisation requires a sustained argument of a depth and length that cannot be presented here.

This brings us to the simple and inescapable fact that *Les Demoiselles* is a picture of five prostitutes and is about prostitution. However, it is striking how many art historical and journalistic accounts do try to escape this fact or, at least, to avoid any serious discussion of it. *Guardian* art critic Jonathan Jones argues, "Most of all, this is a painting about looking...it's misguided to see [it] as a painting 'about' brothels, prostitutes or colonialism".[15] This is evasion. Yes, it is about looking, but precisely about looking at, and being looked at by, prostitutes. Everything in the picture's composition reinforces this. Many paintings position us when we look at them—Titian's *Venus d'Urbino* makes us the courtesan/Venus's lover or patron, Manet's *A Bar at the Folies Bergères* makes us a customer ordering a drink—but *Les Demoiselles* fixes us more definitively than any work I can think of: as the client of the brothel for whom the women are displaying themselves. The phallic bowl of fruit jutting upwards in the centre foreground becomes our phallus leading us into the brothel and towards the women. Thus the painting stages an "in our face" confrontation with the institution of prostitution.

But if Les Demoiselles is "about" prostitution, what exactly is it saying about prostitution?

There is, in the literature, a biographical story which purports to answer this question and thus to "explain" the meaning of the painting. Picasso had a friend who died of syphilis, having been infected by a prostitute, and, according to these accounts, *Les Demoiselles* is an expression of the fear and anger felt by Picasso as a result. But, regardless of the truth or otherwise of this story, it does not account, or accounts only very partially, for the nature and power of the finished work, which is making a more general statement.[16]

According to John Berger that general statement is "a raging, frontal attack, not against sexual 'immorality', but against life as Picasso found it—the waste, the disease, the ugliness, and the ruthlessness of it...instead of criticising modern life by comparing it, as much in sorrow as in anger, with a more primitive way of life, he now uses his sense of the primitive to violate and shock the civilised... He is not in the least concerned with formal problems. He is concerned with challenging civilisation. The dislocations in this picture are the result of aggression, not aesthetics".[17]

But, if the syphilis story is too narrow, Berger's "rage against

15: Jones, 2007.

16: The story relates better to some of the numerous preliminary studies for *Les Demoiselles*, which feature two male figures—a sailor, and a student carrying a skull, a possible "wages of sin" memento mori.

17: Berger, 1965, p72.

civilisation" is too broad. He is right about the element of rage in the painting, but insufficiently precise in identifying its target, again evading the issue of prostitution. Partly, I think, Berger is led astray by following the conventional view of the African heads on the women on the right as aggressive. My own view is that they are not intrinsically either frightening or savage and that they are present in the painting for two reasons: first because in African art, art from a pre-capitalist society, Picasso had found an important source for a new, non-naturalistic way of representing the world; second, in terms of the content of the painting, they occur precisely as masks, as blocking mechanisms behind which the real features of the women are concealed.[18]

A number of feminist art historians have seen the rage as directed primarily against women as such, and have viewed *Les Demoiselles* as a highly misogynistic painting. One of the most forceful of these, Carol Duncan, argues that the emergence of modern art coincided with women starting to claim equality (she cites the suffragist movement) and that a great deal of modern art expressed a defensive male sexist reaction to this:

> Indeed, as women's claims to full humanity grew, the more relentlessly would art rationalise their inferior status... In fact, the defence of male supremacy must be recognised as a central theme in modern art. Gauguin, Munch, Rodin, Matisse, Picasso and scores of other artists, consciously or unconsciously, identified some aspect of the sexist cause with all or part of their own artistic missions. Art celebrating sexist experience was accorded the greatest prestige, given the most pretentious aesthetic rationales, and identified with the highest and deepest of human aspirations. Nudes and whores—women with no identity beyond their existence as sex objects—were made to embody transcendent, "universally" significant statements...the image of the whore even came to stand for woman in her purest, most concentrated form.[19]

For Duncan *Les Demoiselles* is the epitome of this sexist trend:

> What is so remarkable about this work is the way it manifests the structural foundation underlying both the femme fatale and the new primitive woman. Picasso...dredged up from his psyche the terrifying and fascinating beast that gave birth to both of them. The *Desmoiselles* prismatically mirrors her

18: On the first point, see Molyneux, 2006.
19: Duncan, 1993, pp112-113.

> many opposing faces: whore and deity, decadent and savage, tempting and repelling, awesome and obscene, looming and crouching, masked and naked, threatening and powerless. In that jungle-brothel is womankind in all her present and past metamorphoses, concealing and revealing herself before the male... Picasso presents her in the form of a desecrated icon already slashed and torn to bits...no other work reveals more of the rock foundation of sexist anti-humanism or goes further and deeper to justify and celebrate the domination of woman by man.[20]

Duncan's comments on modern art in general have some truth in them, certainly more than is usually recognised in conventional art history. It is also true that Picasso's life, and some of his art, provides evidence of sexist attitudes. It is even the case that there is anger, misogynistic anger, in Picasso's depiction of the Avignon prostitutes. Nevertheless, I believe Duncan's judgment of *Les Demoiselles* is fundamentally mistaken and this brings us to heart of what the painting is about and the nature and cause of its power.

The central feature of *Les Demoiselles* is the confrontation between the artist/brothel client/viewer—at this moment they are one and the same—and the gaze of the central women (second and third from the left). Yes, he and we enter the brothel and look at the prostitutes with anger, but this look, and this anger, is returned in spades (if I may use the card playing metaphor) in the implacable gaze of the prostitutes, which functions as both an expression of their situation and feelings, and as a mirror reflecting back his/ours. Thus *Les Demoiselles*, far from being crudely sexist or simply misogynistic, is a uniquely intense and dramatic depiction of the mutual antagonism, estrangement and alienation involved in the institution of prostitution.

Bourgeois society oscillates between two attitudes to prostitution: on the one hand moral condemnation and legal persecution of the prostitute (largely the department of the church, the police and the courts); on the other hand, sometimes sentimental, sometimes risque, glamorisation, largely the province of the arts. In the latter, Hollywood has played its part but so has "high art" (Titian's *Venus d'Urbino*, Boucher's and Ingres's *Odalisques*). In both cases what is evaded is the economic deprivation and emotional trauma which lead women into prostitution, and the sexual deprivation and emotional alienation which lead men to prostitutes.

Once this is grasped it also becomes evident that the formal

20: Duncan, 1993, pp96-97.

innovations, which had such an impact on the course of art, all contribute to the intensity of the dramatic confrontation that is *Les Demoiselles*. Picasso needed the radical break with traditional forms of naturalistic representation, needed the assault on conventional standards of beauty, needed the African masks, to smash and eliminate any traces of sentimentality and glamorisation. Above all Picasso needed the flattening, the extreme foreshortening of space in the painting, to thrust the women into our faces, to stage this eyeball to eyeball confrontation between us and them, client and prostitute, and to cut through the ingrained habit of evasion of the reality of prostitution. And it is precisely the success of *Les Demoiselles* in achieving this that makes it so genuinely shocking, not just to Braque and Matisse a hundred years ago, but to us today, when its formal qualities have long become familiar. To look at *Les Demoiselles* is still to receive the visual equivalent of a sharp slap across the face.

The issue of prostitution is still very much with us, and in all its forms from the concentrated hatred of the Ipswich murders, and the extreme exploitation and alienation of the virtual slave trade in women from Eastern Europe and elsewhere, to the milder, but insidious, relegitimisation of sexism through lap dancing, lads' mags and raunch culture.

Moreover, there is more involved and more at stake here than just the critique of one particular social institution. Bourgeois society's mystification of prostitution and evasion of its realities (replicated in the art critics' evasion of the real content of *Les Demoiselles*) is habitual not just because of the hypocrisy of so many bourgeois politicians, priests and moralists, preaching "family values" in public while privately behaving quite otherwise, but because what the commodification of sex does to the human relations between the people involved is symptomatic of what alienation and commodification (ie capitalism) do to human relations as a whole. Marx explained this with great clarity:

> Prostitution is only a *specific* expression of the *general* prostitution of the *labourer*, and since it is a relationship in which not the prostitute alone, but also the one who prostitutes, fall—and the latter's abomination is still greater—the capitalist, etc, also comes under this head.[21]

Of course, it is not my argument that Picasso was intellectually conscious of all of this. We do not, and cannot, know exactly what passed through his mind as he worked on *Les Demoiselles*, and paintings are rarely

---

21: Marx, 1967, p93, Marx's emphasis.

visual illustrations of intellectual theses. My guess would be that Picasso worked part consciously, part intuitively, and was concerned more with the representation of feelings than of thought out ideas. But this is not really the point. What we have to work with and respond to is the painting itself, and this confronts us with the fact—surely a significant one—that the picture which revolutionised art was a hugely powerful statement of rage at the commodification of sex and life.

References

Anderson, Perry, 1984, "Modernity and Revolution", in *New Left Review 144* (March-April 1984).

Berger, John, 1965, *The Success and Failure of Picasso* (Harmondsworth).

Berger, John, 1972a, *Ways of Seeing* (Penguin).

Berger, John, 1972b, "The Moment of Cubism", in *Selected Essays and Articles: the Look of Things* (Harmondsworth).

Duncan, Carol, 1993, *The Aesthetics of Power* (Cambridge University).

Greenberg, Clement, 1993, "Modernist Painting", in Charles Harrison and Paul Wood (eds), *Art in Theory 1900-1990* (Blackwell).

Jones, Jonathan, 2007, "Pablo's Punks", the *Guardian*, 9 January 2007, http://arts.guardian.co.uk/critic/feature/0,,1985975,00.html

Lukács, Georg, 1948, Preface to *Studies in European Realism*, http://courses.essex.ac.uk/lt/lt204/lukacs_preface.htm

Marx, Karl, 1967, *Economic and Philosophic Manuscripts of 1844* (Progress), www.marxists.org/archive/marx/works/1844/manuscripts/preface.htm

Hughes, Robert, 1991, *The Shock of the New* (Thames and Hudson).

Molyneux, John, 2006, "Picasso, Modernism And The Non-European", *Socialist Worker*, 22 April 2006, www.socialistworker.co.uk/article.php?article_id=8678

Warncke, Carsten-Peter, 1997, *Picasso* (Taschen).

Wullschlager, Jackie, 2007, "The Day Modern Art Was Invented: Picasso's *Demoiselles*", the *Financial Times*, 4 January 2007.

The literature of a ravished continent

Ken Olende

During the late 1950s and early 1960s a wave of new literature emerged from a defiant Global South. Some of the best came from Africa, then caught up in a range of anti-colonial struggles and the promise of independence. The surge of hope that underpinned much of the writing turned to bitterness with the reality of independence. A flavour of the period can be gained by looking at novels by three of the leading writers of this period—*Things Fall Apart* by Chinua Achebe from Nigeria, *God's Bits of Wood* by Ousmane Sembène from Senegal and *Wizard of the Crow* by Ngugi wa Thiong'o from Kenya. These books are not necessarily representative, but they are among the best examples and show how the literature developed.

Each novel fits with one of three roughly chronological stages in this generation of sub-Saharan writing. The first and most clearly defined stage tends to concentrate on the social rupture caused by early contact with white people. It explores what life was like before the imperialists arrived, and dignifies indigenous African culture.[1] Novels from the second stage are more concerned with resistance to colonialism, often combined with the protagonist's alienation from more traditional society.[2] The third and most diverse stage grapples with disillusion at the experience of

1: As well as Achebe's *Things Fall Apart* and *Arrow of God*, examples from this period include Ngugi's *Weep Not Child*, Camara Laye's *The Dark Child* and Cyprian Ekwensi's *Burning Grass*.

2: Examples include Sembène's *God's Bits of Wood* and Ngugi's *The River Between*.

post-colonial society, often faced through satire.[3] In an interview last year Ngugi commented on the influence of the 1960s generation of authors:

> That literature created for the first time a genuine pan-African writing. Look at Wole Soyinka or Chinua Achebe. Those people are seen as our writers. People don't think of Achebe as a writer who comes from Nigeria, although he does. He is welcomed not as someone who comes from outside, but as one of our own. Whatever other roles they play, they have played a very important role in a very complex form it has created a pan-African awareness.[4]

While these writers can't be divorced from the anti-colonial movement, neither can they be reduced to it. Politically they are important because they look at Africa in a new and different way compared to European writers (even those sympathetic to the plight of Africa as a victim of imperialism). At the same time, though these writers are influenced by European traditions of writing or may draw on elements of native folklore, they transcend their sources.

First contact: Things Fall Apart

European capitalism's first assault on Africa, through the Atlantic slave trade, required remarkably little European presence in Africa itself. This situation changed with the growth of imperial empires. The Berlin conference of 1884-5 had divided Africa between the imperial powers, at the least inconvenience to those powers. This was followed by direct European intervention. In 1897 Sir Arthur Hardinge, the first British governor for what would become Kenya, said, "These people must learn submission by bullets—it's the only school; after that you may begin more modern and humane methods of education".[5]

However, in the literature of empire resentment by Africans was represented as irrational. One verse of Rudyard Kipling's notorious poem "The White Man's Burden"—written in 1899 to encourage the US to take a role in colonialism—concentrates on the ingratitude of the colonised for the benefits of empire:

3: Examples include Ngugi's *Devil on the Cross*, *Matigari* and *Wizard of the Crow*, Sembène's *Xala*, Achebe's *A Man of the People*, and Ayi Kwei Armah's *The Beautiful Ones Are Not Yet Born*.

4: Olende, 2006.

5: Berman and Lonsdale, 1992, p19.

Take up the White Man's burden—
The savage wars of peace—
Fill full the mouth of famine
And bid the sickness cease;
And when your goal is nearest
The end for others sought,
Watch sloth and heathen folly
Bring all your hopes to nought.

Though there were African responses in art to this kind of racist nonsense from the earliest days of colonialism, *Things Fall Apart* (1959) is often referred to as the first great African novel.[6] It was the first novel from Chinua Achebe, born in Ogidi, Nigeria, in 1930. The main character is Okonkwo, a successful man in an Ibo village. He has overcome the shame of a father who remained a poor singer rather than concentrating on his farm and making his family wealthy:

> Okonkwo ruled his household with a heavy hand. His wives, especially the youngest, lived in perpetual fear of his fiery temper, and so did his little children. Perhaps down in his heart Okonkwo was not a cruel man. But his whole life was dominated by fear, the fear of failure and weakness. It was deeper and more intimate than the fear of evil and capricious gods and of magic, the fear of the forest, and of the forces of nature, malevolent, red in tooth and claw.[7]

Okonkwo is renowned throughout the nine villages that make up his immediate society as a wrestler, a warrior and a farmer. Having earned high rank, he is chosen to be the guardian of a boy prisoner from a dispute with another village. The boy, Ikemefuna, ends up staying in Okonkwo's home, and comes to be treated as one of the family. He impresses Okonkwo as more "manly" than his own son, Nwoye. After three years, when it is eventually decided that the boy should be killed, Okonkwo is advised to have nothing to do with it, but ever determined to prove he is not soft like his father he joins in the murder. This act marks the start of a period of bad luck that eventually sees Okonkwo and his family exiled for seven years.

6: *Things Fall Apart* was far from the first African novel. Thomas Mofolo's *Chaka*, a novel telling the story of Chaka Zulu written in the Sesotho language, was published in South Africa in 1925. It had been written earlier, in 1909 or 1910.
7: Achebe, 1994, p13.

Achebe neither creates an idyllic past nor presents his characters as simply defined in relation to traditional society or colonialism. The moral certainty in the village that, for instance, twins must be left to die in the "bad forest" is shocking, and it is intended to be. However, Okonkwo's society is shown to make sense in its own terms. Okonkwo's knowledge of his society's norms allows him to advance through village life. He is unsettled by the run of bad luck—nothing seems to make sense any more. Later it is the behaviour of the whites that appears beyond understanding.

While Okonkwo's family is exiled in another village, white people arrive and society changes rapidly. Missionaries try to convert the villagers and the colonial government makes its first appearance. Partly in response to the treatment of Ikemefuna, Okonkwo's son Nwoye converts to the new religion. Okonkwo takes part in a violent attempt to restore traditional society and is imprisoned.

At the novel's end there is a dramatic shift in narrative voice. The viewpoint moves to the white district commissioner, who plans to write a book about the "primitive" Ibo. He is fascinated by Okonkwo's actions: "One could almost write a whole chapter on him—perhaps not a whole chapter, but a reasonable paragraph, at any rate. There was so much else to include, and one must be firm in cutting out details".[8]

Things Fall Apart was already a historical novel when it was written. At one level it was addressed to white settlers, insisting on a different way of looking at African society, but it also addressed contemporary Africans, saying that the customs described may have irreversibly vanished, but they deserve serious study and respect.

No Longer at Ease (1960) was written as a sequel showing the problems faced by those who "accepted" the white's ways. Obo Okonkwo tries to fit in with pre-independence Nigeria without being corrupt or abandoning his ideals. Obo is the grandson of the Okonkwo in *Things Fall Apart*—his tragedy partly develops as he tries to rebel against his father, Nwoye, who is still caught up in the consequences of rebelling against Okonkwo during the earlier novel. As with Okonkwo, Obo's life ceases to make sense in his own terms. As in Greek tragedy there is no avenue of escape for the protagonist.

Achebe's next novel *Arrow of God* (1964) was another tragedy of cultural misunderstanding, but the mood changes in *A Man of the People* (1966), a coruscating satire on post-colonial corruption. The measured, tragic tone is replaced with bleak, satirical comedy. The grotesque politician Mr Nanga

8: Achebe, 1994, p208.

shows the reality of the new political elite, as he corrupts the younger Odili, whose political outrage comes across as jealousy in contrast to Obo's fruitless quest for a moral way to reconcile the old and the new.

Resisting colonialism: God's Bits of Wood

At the end of the Second World War the colonial powers—especially Britain and France—sought to return to imperial business as normal. It is true that the British had started talking about colonial independence, but this was seen as lying in the future and, in Africa's case, a long way in the future. Two factors came together to frustrate these plans. On the one hand, there were changes in the world economy—the most important being that the US now demanded access to colonial markets. On the other hand, many Africans had seen a different side to Europeans during the war, both through the troops stationed in colonial countries and through direct experience of fighting. These people were not prepared to return to the pre-war situation.

The Second World War damaged the imperial economies, and often this meant that the level of oppression and exploitation faced by Africans was actually greater after the war. A series of resistance movements developed. They ranged from mass campaigning, including protests and strikes organised by Kwame Nkrumah's Convention People's Party on the Gold Coast—which would become independent as Ghana in 1957—to the Mau Mau uprising in Kenya. Kenya's radical trade union movement was suppressed after the Second World War. However, the Mau Mau rebellion was not simply a military struggle or a "tribal uprising" by the Kikuyu people, as is often suggested; much of its early leadership came out of the ethnically mixed trade union movement in the capital, Nairobi, and main port, Mombasa. The methods used in different areas did not simply reflect regional characteristics. Britain was more willing to accept the changing status of West African countries, such as Ghana or Nigeria, than countries in Eastern or Southern Africa, with their large settler populations.

In French colonial West Africa a tradition of strikes by Africans employed on the railways stretched back to the 19th century. Ousmane Sembène's novel *God's Bits of Wood* is based on the 1947 strike—the longest and most significant. More people were more involved than in any other strike, and the strikers' victory over the colonial administration boosted the movement for liberation with a strong dose of class struggle.

Sembène was born in Senegal in 1923, the son of a fisherman. He was conscripted and fought in the French army during the Second World War (this experience underlay his magnificent 1987 film, *Camp de Thiaroye*, which raised the issue of how returning soldiers were not prepared to accept the existing colonial situation). After the war he worked on the railways, and he himself took part in the epic rail strike that paralysed French West Africa in 1947 and 1948. Following the strike he moved to France, where he was an active trade unionist and member of the Communist Party. He worked in car plants and as a docker, an experience which inspired his first novel, *Black Docker* (1956). This novel follows an African who works on the docks in Marseille, while trying to establish himself as a writer. However, he is constantly on trial in a racist French society, eventually literally so, as he is accused of murder.

The magnificent *God's Bits of Wood* (1960) is Sembène's best known novel. It charts the great railway strike's development across three cities, showing how collective activity educated and matured the participants. As with much of his work it has the vividness of lived experience. Sembène himself is vague about how closely the novel mirrors his own experiences, preferring to place the strike itself in a wider context:

> The book is set in Africa, but look at the situation in Europe after the war. For us it was a period of awakening. War is always unfortunate. But for us in Africa the war was a real catalyst. Before the war we were colonised, we were on our knees. As youngsters we took part in the war and we saw that the colonisers we had idealised were as human as ourselves. They experienced fear. They had cowards and traitors. We went to war with a herd mentality like sheep, but we were transformed by the time we came back. As well as this, we had made contact with peasants and workers in the West. We learned a lot from that.[9]

Though he does not appear until the story is well under way, the central character is the charismatic union activist Bakayoko. The story unfolds through a large cast along the length of the railway, through Senegal and neighbouring Mali. Characters are both pro- and anti-strike from different classes and perspectives, both Africans and colonialists. As the strike develops and difficulties are faced, and on the whole overcome, the characters go through a process of collective development. The biggest shift takes place among the female characters, who grow as the strike continues, and they are forced to become breadwinners for their families. This development climaxes in a cross-country women's march, which is decisive in the strike's outcome:

9: Kimber and Olende, 2005.

> Ever since they left Thiès the women had not stopped singing. As soon as one group allowed the refrain to die, another picked it up, and new verses were born at the hazard of chance or inspiration, one word leading to another and each finding, in its turn, its rhythm and its place. No one was very sure any longer where the song began or if it had an ending. It rolled out over its own length, like the movement of a serpent. It was as long as life.[10]

It is the women who are prepared to physically fight with French forces. In the process they come to demand a place in decision making. The socialist nature of the novel at no point stops it being an "African" one. Most of the characters are from the Wolof people, and the background of colonial racist oppression is never far away. At several points the issue of language comes up. One of the women, N'Deye Touti, embarrasses a French constable by speaking French. He had assumed that, being black and female, she would not understand the language and is shamed after casually describing her to his companion in crude sexual terms.

The union activist Bakayoko puts the bosses in their place at one point during the negotiations when he says, "Since your ignorance of our language is a handicap for you, we will use French as a matter of courtesy." He clarifies this by adding that this courtesy is one "that will not last forever".[11] Forcing equality between the African and French languages is a step in making clear the equality between African and French humanity. Language, both in terms of what is spoken and what authors should write in is a continuing theme in African literature. A recurring issue for Sembène, as for other African writers, has been how to reach a wide audience, particularly an African audience, other than through the medium of written language.

Sembène has continued to write, but his main concern since the mid-1960s has been film-making, and he has become probably Africa's foremost film director. He has made films from his novels—*The Money Order* (1965) and *Xala* (1974)—and has produced an impressive body of films under difficult circumstances, including *Black Girl* (1966), *Mandabi* (1968), *Xala* (1975), *Camp de Thiaroye* (1987), *Faat Kiné* (2000), and *Moolaadé* (2004). These include urban and rural, modern and historical settings, realistic drama and satire. A few themes predominate—hatred for the brutal way in which capitalist and colonial society makes people behave, sympathy for the poor and dispossessed, and identification with and empowerment of women.

10: Ousmane, 1995, p192.
11: Ousmane, 1995, p180.

Independence and disillusion: Wizard of the Crow

From the independence of Ghana in 1957 through the 1960s there was a period of intense excitement about the potential of newly independent African countries. Leaders like Congo's Patrice Lumumba and Ghana's Kwame Nkrumah were seen as revolutionary icons on a par with Che Guevara. Through the 1970s this optimism turned to despair. Rather than pan-Africanist ideals spreading across the continent from vanguard states, the inertia and corruption that had dogged the more conservative countries became the norm. Activists and artists have been wrestling with the causes and solutions ever since.

There is not space here to go over the arguments, but the way states had been developed under colonialism was significant. Pan-African theorist Walter Rodney has argued, "It is typical of underdeveloped economies that they do not (or are not allowed to) concentrate on those sectors of the economy which in turn will generate growth and raise production to a new level altogether".[12]

Kenyan Ngugi wa Thiong'o is the novelist who has most consistently returned to this theme. Born in 1938, he published his first novel in 1964. At the time he was writing as James Ngugi. His later rejection of his "Christian" name was part of the deepening of his anti-imperialism. *Weep Not Child* follows a familiar pattern in recounting the early encounters between his own Kikuyu people and the white colonialists (as with *Things Fall Apart,* it takes its title from a poem by a Western poet, in this case Walt Whitman). As with his next novel, *The River Between* (1965), it tells of the impact of Western education, and the strengths and weaknesses this brings to the characters.

The protagonist in *Weep Not Child*, Njoroge, is shaped by both this education and the anti-colonial Mau Mau struggle, which his brothers participate in (as had Ngugi's elder brother). *The River Between* looks at the foundation of independent Kikuyu schools, as its main character Waiyaki becomes caught up in the struggle between the missionary schools and the locally set up independent schools. The fact that the issue that broke many Kikuyu from missionary education and established the anti-establishment schools was female circumcision is not ducked and is a central issue in the book.

Ngugi's third novel, *A Grain of Wheat* (1967), is transitional. It bridges the gap between discussing resistance to colonialism and the experience of independence. It tells the story of Mugo, a morally compromised

12: Rodney, 1973.

character, who has a reputation as a hero of the resistance. It is symbolically set on the eve of independence. Ngugi patterned the novel on Joseph Conrad's *Under Western Eyes* (1911), which is about revolutionaries in Russia, though Ngugi differs from Conrad in seeing a possibility of revolutionary success and redemption. Some critics have argued—wrongly in my opinion—that patterning the novel on Conrad's weakens it. To a Western audience this is certainly his most sophisticated, developed and satisfying book. However, Ngugi himself was becoming increasingly dissatisfied with his reception and his audience. He saw himself as a radical, who should be relating to the workers and peasants, developing a national culture in the way that Frantz Fanon had argued:

> We must work and fight with the same rhythm as the people to construct the future and to prepare the ground where vigorous shoots are already springing up. A national culture is not a folklore, nor an abstract populism that believes it can discover a people's true nature... A national culture is the whole body of efforts made by a people in the sphere of thought to describe, justify and praise the action through which a people has created itself and keeps itself in existence.[13]

However, his audience was largely Western; his novels were reviewed and well received in the Western press, and were starting to be put on university syllabuses, but they were not known by workers and peasants in Kenya. In his writing he shifted to a more straightforward didactic style for the play *The Trial of Dedan Kimathi* (1976), which he co-wrote with Micere Githae Mugo, recreating the 1956 trial of one of the leaders of the Mau Mau rebellion. The novel *Petals of Blood* (1977) concerns resistance to oppression in post-colonial Kenya. It is written in a simpler style, with less morally complex characters, though its scope is similar to earlier pieces. Both these works are implicitly opposed to the post-colonial Kenyan government.

What finally put Ngugi in trouble with the authorities was the play *Ngaahika Ndeenda*, co-written with Ngugi wa Mirii (which was translated as *I Will Marry When I Want*). The play was workshopped in Gikuyu—the Kikuyu language—with peasants and workers in Limuru. It was banned and Ngugi was detained for a year by the government. He has written a powerful memoir of this time, *Detained* (1981), and while imprisoned he also wrote his first novel in Gikuyu, *Devil on the Cross* (1981).

Devil on the Cross was very popular in Gikuyu, going into a second

13: Fanon, 1967, p188,

printing by popular demand.[14] It uses satire, combined with folkloric structures. Characters and plot are less complex (even *Petals of Blood*, by contrast, contained complex flashback sequences). A range of characters converge on the Devil's feast, where capitalists give presentations boasting of how they defraud and rob the poor and occasionally each other, leading to arguments and threats of violence.

The novel's method had precedents. Nigerian Amos Tutuola wrote *The Palm Wine Drinkard* (1952) and *My Life in the Bush of Ghosts* (1954) in a surreal folkloric style that foreshadowed later more sophisticated works like Ngugi's. Ngugi has said, "I think he is incredible. The way he could move from a modern technological image and somehow change it until it becomes part of the life beyond. Borrowing from the folkloric he managed to collapse the barriers of time and space".[15] A similar "dreamtime" from folklore has appeared in other books such as Ben Okri's *The Famished Road* (1991).

Further state repression forced Ngugi to leave Kenya. He went on to write another novel, *Matigari* (1986), using the same techniques. In this a semi-mythical guerrilla fighter returns from the forest and tries to find his family and justice in modern Kenya.

From this period on Ngugi has forcefully argued for writers to write in their mother tongue partly to fit themselves into existing artistic traditions, as he has with the folkloric, and partly as a liberation from imperialism.[16] This issue has been the subject of an ongoing dispute, with Chinua Achebe championing English as a tool that is available and, despite its origins, non-divisive: "If you take Nigeria as an example, the national literature, as I see it, is the literature written in English; and the ethnic literatures are in Hausa, Ibo, Yoruba, Efik, Edo, Ijaw, etc, etc".[17] The issue is not as divisive as may first appear. Ngugi has ensured that his novels also appear in English (translating his latest himself).

Though he has continued to write on both literature and politics, it was not until 2006 that another novel was published in English, the epic *Wizard of the Crow*. The book is a satire on neo-colonialism and the attitudes of the black ruling class. The Free Republic of Aburiria—a surrealistically exaggerated Kenya—is governed by a dictator known only as the Ruler. His three fawning ministers have each undergone plastic surgery to

14: Cook and Okenimkpe, 1983, p123.

15: Olende, 2006.

16: See in particular Ngugi, 1993.

17: Achebe, 1993, p429.

enlarge respectively their eyes, ears and tongue, the better to see, hear and denounce dissent. In a luxurious world separated from the suffering poor, the ministers compete to flatter the Ruler. To celebrate his birthday one suggests that they build a tower to heaven, so that the Ruler will be able to pop in on god.

Out in the city the impoverished Kamiti accidentally gains a reputation as a powerful sorcerer, the Wizard of the Crow. Along with the radical political activist and feminist Nyawira he uses his notoriety to help the poor and cure the rich of their various sicknesses with his "magic" mirror. The most debilitating of these illnesses is "whiteache", which incapacitates sufferers through a burning desire to be white, like their old colonial masters.

All through the book the Aburirian government try to get the Global Bank to fund Marching to Heaven, but are set back again and again by the activity of the poor, and particularly a group of militant women. Ngugi says of the book:

> I was very much influenced by the trickster tradition. The trickster character appears in tales all over the world. In West Africa it is Anansi the spider. Elsewhere it is Hare or Tortoise. The trickster is very interesting because he is always changing. He always questions the stability of a word or a narrative or an event. He is continually inventing and reinventing himself. He challenges the prevailing wisdom of who is strong and who is weak.[18]

The main characters Kamiti ("of the trees") and Nyawira ("she of work") are archetypal figures, and appear to represent a number of things, including the rural/urban division, and black pride versus class struggle. However, there is a price to pay for making the characters archetypes. One of the strengths of *God's Bits of Wood* is in the subtle complexity of the portrayal of the strike and its participants. In Ngugi's books *Devil on the Cross* and *Wizard of the Crow* most of the struggle takes place off stage.

In *Literature and Revolution* Leon Trotsky criticised some of Vladimir Mayakovsky's poetry, writing that Mayakovsky "speaks of the most intimate thing, such as love, as if he were speaking about the migration of nations".[19] The same could be said of some of Ngugi's passages, about both political organisation and love. This should not detract from the achievements of the novel and how his technique have been honed over time—and *Wizard of the Crow* is an advance on his earlier work, subtler and more assured.

18: Olende, 2006.
19: Trotsky, 1991, p180.

Conclusion

At the time *Things Fall Apart* was published another Nigerian, Cyprian Ekwensi, was already writing popular novels such as *People of the City* (1954) and *Jagua Nana* (1961) about the contradictions of colonial society. Similarly, another Kenyan writer, Meja Mwangi, has approached the problems of the post-colonial state from a different angle. His novels of modern Kenya also range from dealing with the Mau Mau in *Carcase for Hounds* (1974) to life in contemporary Nairobi in *Going Down River Road* (1976) or Aids in *The Last Plague* (2000). His thrillers reach a popular audience in Kenya. Such writers are relevant here, as the writers I have been discussing are consciously trying to relate to a popular audience themselves. Since the 1960s the amount and range of African writing available has increased—notably the number of women writers.

Still, the authors I have discussed fought for their alternative view to be seen and accepted. Achebe was one of the editors of the Heinemann African Writers series, which helped popularise African writers. There is an ongoing fight to defend resistance to empire against romanticisation of empire, whether in the Iraq war or Niall Ferguson's attempts to rehabilitate the British Empire. Writers such as Achebe, Sembène and Ngugi remind us that alternatives are possible, and give us an idea of what artistic masterpieces will emerge from the current anti-globalisation movement.

References

Achebe, Chinua, 1993, "The African Writer and the English Language", in Patrick Williams and Laura Chrisman (eds), *Colonial Discourse and Post-Colonial Theory: a Reader* (Longman).

Achebe, Chinua, 1994, *Things Fall Apart* (Anchor).

Cook, David, and Michael Okenimkpe, 1983, *Ngugi wa Thiong'o: an exploration of his writings* (Heinemann).

Berman, Bruce, and John Lonsdale, 1992, *Unhappy Valley: Conflict in Kenya and Africa books 1 and 2* (James Currey).

Fanon, Frantz, 1967, *Wretched of the Earth* (Harmondsworth).

Kimber, Charlie, and Ken Olende, 2005, interview with Ousmane Sembène, 1 June 2005. An edited version of this interview appeared as "Ousmane Sembène—Father Of African Film", *Socialist Worker*, 11 June 2005, www.socialistworker.co.uk/article.php?article_id=6654

Olende, Ken, 2006, interview with Ngugi wa Thiong'o, 10 August 2006. An edited version of this interview appeared as "Ngugi Wa Thiong'o Interviewed On His New Novel, Wizard Of The Crow", *Socialist Worker*, 4 November 2006, www.socialistworker.co.uk/article.php?article_id=10062

Ousmane, Sembène, 1995, *God's Bits of Wood* (Heinemann). Note that in some editions, including this one, Ousmane appears as the author's second name.

Ngugi wa Thiong'o, 1993, *Moving the Centre* (Heinemann).

Rodney, Walter, 1973, *How Europe Underdeveloped Africa* (Bogle-L'Ouverture), www.marxists.org/subject/africa/rodney-walter/how-europe/ch01.htm

Trotsky, Leon, 1991, *Literature and Revolution* (Redwords), www.marxists.org/archive/trotsky/1924/lit_revo/

Reviews

Snobs and snappers

Andy Jones

Steve Edwards, ***The Making of English Photography: Allegories*** *(Penn State University Press, 2006), £56.50*

The invention of photography was announced in 1839 and its commercial expansion began in earnest in the 1850s. By the time Karl Marx wrote *Capital* in the early 1860s, he would list photography as one of the small but significant new "fields of labour" created by developing capitalist industry in Britain (p1). Steve Edwards has written a fascinating Marxist account of 19th century debates generated by the growth of the photographic trade. In doing so, he explores ideas about art and work in capitalist society, and offers a rich exploration of the way in which the idea of "photography as art" upset some of the founding principles of bourgeois ideology.

Traditional histories of 19th century photography oscillate between, on the one hand, the description of technical advances and, on the other, the construction of a narrative of photography's struggle to be recognised as an art. Both approaches take the development of photography out of its historical context, and instead reduce it to the activities of particular individuals. Edwards challenges the assumptions of this kind of history and, in an initial chapter, reframes the invention of photography within a discussion of the mechanisation of work in 19th century industry.

The development of industry involved the replacement of artisan skills by the increasing use of machines. For capitalists, this provided a means of deskilling their workforce, introducing stricter discipline and removing the degree of control over the workplace that artisans retained. This was a major issue for bourgeois intellectuals such as Andrew Ure, who, in his *Philosophy of Manufactures,* used the example of a spinning machine to argue that when "capital enlists science in her service, the refractory hand of labour will always be taught docility" (p31).

The arrival of photography, Edwards argues, was one instance of this pattern of mechanisation: it meant that for the first time the manual skill necessary for the production of visual images could be wholly replaced by the operation of a machine. William Henry Fox Talbot, the inventor of photography, frequently talked of photographs as images that "make themselves". Fox Talbot was close to the "Cambridge network" of scientists, whose work was central to the development of a thorough division of labour within the field of science, and photography was initially championed, Edwards argues, by "men of science". For them the camera was infallible (unlike humans), and the photographs it produced were wholly reliable documents of reality. This promised a valuable rationalisation and standardisation of the making of scientific illustrations, and enabled a rigid separation of observation and theorisation.

But the book's focus is not the invention of photography in itself. Nor does

Edwards argue that the real history of photography is about science and industry rather than art. In this sense, his book provides an important critique of much of the writing on 19th century photography that emerged in the 1970s and 1980s. Heavily influenced by Michel Foucault's writings on "power/knowledge", those histories concentrated on photography's instrumental uses in state institutions such as prisons and asylums. In doing so, they challenged the complacency of most writing on photography, and shed light on a murky corner of the history of photographs. However, as Edwards points out, they tended to create a counter-history in which the idea of photography as art was ignored, and they thereby left that part of photography's history, as described in the conventional books on the subject, unchallenged.

Edwards argues that it was in the 1860s that professional photographers first demanded to be seen as artists, and he shows that the photographic journals of the time were obsessed with this question. But who were the people for whom this was so important? Until now this question has been ignored, but Edwards devotes a chapter to exploring what kind of people made up the growing business in photographic studios. Whereas conventional histories concentrate on one or two examples of grand studios operating on a large scale, he shows that the majority of studios at this time were in fact small affairs, and those running them were eking out a precarious existence. He argues, "The most direct comparison for this kind of economic activity is with those manufacturer-retailers who purveyed their commodities from a small outlet, such as tailors and shoemakers, butchers and bakers" (p100). Photographers were, for the most part, petty bourgeois producers. Edwards draws on recent historical studies, and Marxist (in particular, Trotsky's) accounts of this group, to provide a picture of petty bourgeois concerns at this time. "Caught between the rock of large capital and the hard place of labour" (p101), the petty bourgeoisie directed its resentment both at big business and—more particularly—the working class.

Through the rest of his book Edwards argues that "the fundamental conceptualisations of photography put into place during the 1860s were born of this anxiety and hostility" (p102). Art represented respectability, a central element of petty bourgeois ideology, but uncertainty over the status of the photographic image registered in the minds of photographers as a deep unease about their own precarious social position. And this social uncertainty fuelled the nervous debate about photographic art.

In claiming they were artists, photographers came up against a problem. Notions of art at the time drew heavily on ideas elaborated by Sir Joshua Reynolds, who had argued that art was an industry not "of the hands, but of the mind" (p139). Reynolds' argument was part of a wider discourse, rooted in the division of mental and manual labour. In Reynolds' view, art was based on the ability of "gentlemen" to generalise from immediate sensuous experience, and was opposed to mechanical work rooted in that experience. Mechanical workers remained, for Reynolds, in "a gross state of nature" (p140), compared to artists. Art was defined in opposition to manual work. For Reynolds the generalisation he sought in art was to be signalled by artists' refusal to merely "copy" nature—art was not about "details".

The problem for photographers was that photographs were precisely about copying nature, and the camera's ability to capture detail was a central part of the account of photography elaborated by "men of science". What's more, photographers had to contend with the fact that the camera was a machine, and the photograph was a mechanically produced image. It was commonly held that photography involved no skill or thought. As Lady Eastlake put it in 1857, "For all that requires mere manual correctness, and mere manual slavery, without any employment of artistic feeling, she [photography] is the proper and therefore the perfect medium" (p161).

Edwards carefully traces the development of the arguments photographers used to get round these problems. This takes him into some obscure, not to say ridiculous, arguments of the time—debates about whether photographs should be taken in focus, or slightly fuzzy (fuzzy was more "artistic"); disputes over the standard of studio backdrops, and so on. These debates were heavily loaded with connotations of social class (hence the "allegories" of the book's title).

One option open to photographers might have been to reject Reynolds' model of art. That would have meant rejecting the class prejudice on which it was based, placing themselves, symbolically, in a position of solidarity with manual workers. But by the 1860s the "radical alliance" that had once brought the petty bourgeoisie and the working class together had dispersed. Photographers wanted to put as much distance as possible between themselves and the working class. So photographers accepted Reynolds' model and then tried to shoehorn photography into it in order to protect themselves from what they saw as a slide down the social scale.

But the status of photography was not just a problem for photographers themselves. Through the debates of the 1860s, photography ended up as a problematic form that continued to trouble bourgeois ideas about art and work. Borrowing a term from chemistry, Edwards describes photography as an "allotropic" form of representation. Allotropic elements are those that appear simultaneously in different forms: carbon, for instance, can take the form of coal or diamond. Photography was increasingly put to many uses, both in science and industry and in art; therefore, Edwards argues, from the 1860s on, it would appear in the form of both "documents" (mechanical copies of nature) and "pictures" (artistic representations).

The values associated with the "document" were those of manual work (mindless reproduction), while the values of the "picture" were those of intellectual labour (mental abstraction). Bourgeois ideology depended on the separation of mental and manual labour, but photography seemed to mix these two categories up in disturbing ways.

For a brief moment photography appeared to expose the contradictions of bourgeois ideology. In an important chapter Edwards look at how, at the International Exhibition of 1861, photography upset the rigid classification system that separated "raw materials", "machinery", "manufactures" and "fine art". After a protracted argument over where photography should be placed, a compromise meant that it would appear in the "machinery" section, but a separate room in that section would be allocated to photographers' pictures.

Photographers were not happy, but the most revealing comments came from Lyon Playfair, the man who had designed the classification. Photography had caused, he said, "a gross philosophical error" to be brought into his system, one which would "disgrace the classification" (p196). By bringing art and machine work into close proximity, photography suggested that perhaps artists were not so different from workers after all. That, for Playfair and people like him, just would not do.

The Making of English Photography is not always an easy read. At times it feels that almost every paragraph is a retort to someone else's arguments. Nevertheless, it is a brilliant and original book and any readers of this journal with an interest in photography, or 19th century culture in general, will be excited to read a study that combines extensive primary research and a rigorous application of Marxist theoretical concepts to illuminate a subject on which there is so much other bad writing.

An abstract view of the past

Matt Perry

David Laibman, ***Deep History: A Study in Social Evolution and Human Potential*** *(SUNY, 2006), £42*

A strange title and ugly cover design would probably put off most casual readers interested in the Marxist view of history, so there is probably little point in me warning all but the most determined about this book. It is a complex text addressing some of most intricate debates within academic Marxism. Judged in its own terms, it is an interesting but ultimately flawed contribution to the debates.

It does address some very important issues and is (over-) ambitious in its scope. This, by the way, makes reviewing the book necessarily selective. Fundamentally, *Deep History* seeks to outline the laws governing different categories of society (what Laibman calls "abstract social totalities") over the entire scope of human development. He goes through slave, feudal, capitalist and "socialist" societies identifying what he believes to be the essential moving parts of these societies, and thereby allowing an understanding of how these societies developed and how one form of society is superseded by the next.

In the face of the pervasive influence of postmodernism, he makes a defence of a scientific approach to an understanding of history. In some respects, this is very useful. He makes the very telling point that those who reject this scientific understanding on the grounds that the diversity of cultures defies the quest for universal characteristics in human history overlook the universality of systems of symbolic representation (like the use of language, signs, etc). This culture of symbolic systems defines our humanity, our distinctiveness from other animals. Other species may have instincts, or may be able to learn by trial and error, but they are incapable of abstract conceptual thought. This is what makes the architect different from the bee. This is, of course, crucially what makes human labour and production possible. The aspiration to write a history of the whole of human history, or at least to put the different parts of history in the context of the rest of history, is necessary and unfashionable.

The book is in three parts. In the first Laibman outlines his method. He seeks to explain history rather than simply assemble facts and describe it. In order to do this, he defends Marx's use of the concepts of the productive forces and the productive relations, and this ties into the debate about the transition from feudalism to capitalism as well as the standard mainstream criticism that Marx was a "productive force determinist".

In the second part he seeks to define the logic and stages of development of capitalism. He makes a strong case for viewing capitalism as going through a series of stages. He argues that markets cannot be simply equated with capitalism, and points out that inequality seems to be fair under capitalism because of widespread private property, which is presented as natural and eternal (as well as the "lottery effect"—the slender possibility that exists for the poor to become rich). He makes a worthwhile critique of so-called analytical Marxism, which shares the assumptions of free market economics.

His focus on the question of the extensive development or diffusion of capitalism is also interesting. But one of the problems with the stages that he offers is that they are abstract, highly disputable and, given that they are stripped of the necessity of empirical verification, arbitrary. He also attempts to establish a complex model of capitalist crisis. This encompasses different elements of the process of capitalist accumulation, demonstrating the crisis riddled nature of the system.

In the third part, Laibman looks at a world beyond capitalism, that of socialism and communism. Having established the crisis prone character of capitalism, he considers the possibilities of a socialist society based on democratic and non-bureaucratic planning operating through coordination at both the central and local level. He puts a strong case that central economic coordination, a term he prefers to as planning, is not inimical to democracy. Such processes could be conducted through forms of direct democratic control.

He addresses key issues such as the combination of moral and material, individual and collective, incentives in a situation where inequalities are being reduced; the planned core of economy and an informal sector of small producers; the transformation of the price mechanism beyond competitive markets; the potentiality that the internet offers for economic democracy. The discussion of the experience of the Soviet Union and the other "socialist" states is evasive and problematic. The contribution of great revolts from below against regimes to their collapse are denied (p183). This is not the place to rehearse the analysis of Tony Cliff and the theory of state capitalism here. However, given that understanding capitalism as a series of phases of development is fundamental to Laibman's approach, this might have pushed him in the direction of conceiving of these states as conforming to wider trends within the development of world capitalism from the First World War onwards—trends which gave the state a much greater role. Instead he looks to Soviet scholars of the 1960s for inspiration on the question of planning and their reforms, which were never implemented, as a model for what can be achieved.

The major problem with this text is that in attempting to explain history, to establish the underlying patterns or structures of development, his answer at every turn is to escalate the level of abstraction. Marx, by contrast, deployed abstraction in order to return to historical realities and events with greater clarity of thought and explanatory force. Laibman's method diminishes his ability to revitalise Marxism and to make it robust in the face of contemporary onslaughts.

An ideal version of historical epochs functions like clockwork, represented with flow diagrams and "conceptual geometry". There is a strong tendency in work of this kind for Marxists to end up talking to themselves. For example, the question of the role of the military in the transition from feudalism to capitalism (the military revolution debate), which has become influential in academia, is entirely overlooked. Also his defence of a scientific approach overlooks the insights of chaos and complexity theories and their points of similarity with Marxism. Marx always sought to engage critically with trends within bourgeois thought and science.

The defence of Marxism does depend on the defence of a scientific explanatory account of human history, but it cannot deal exclusively in abstractions and it must find the proper place for human action to bring about the goal of social change. As graffiti on a blackboard in France during the student rebellion and general strike of 1968 put it, "Structures do not protest in streets."

Stalin's Irish victims

Paul O'Brien

Barry McLoughlin, ***Left to the Wolves: Irish Victims of Stalinist Terror*** *(Irish Academic Press, 2007), £20*

Since the collapse of the Soviet Union access to the Soviet archives has allowed historians to reconstruct the political and personal history of many of those who perished during Joseph Stalin's purges in the 1930s and 1940s. As the Russian Revolution degenerated, Stalin and his supporters waged a relentless internal war against anyone who showed the slightest sign of disloyalty.

Up until Stalin's death in 1953 the Soviet secret police sentenced over four million people for political crimes against the state. Over 800,000 were shot and millions died in the slave camps of the gulag system. Stalin reputedly remarked to Winston Churchill, "One victim is a tragedy; a million are a statistic." The enormity of the terror is difficult to comprehend: individuals were reduced to statistics, their political and personal history apparently lost forever.

Left to the Wolves is based on painstaking research in the Moscow archives. Part history, part biography, it reads in places like a John le Carré spy novel. Barry McLoughlin reconstructs the story of three Irish socialists, detailing their formative years in the Irish and British socialist movement through to their deaths in Stalin's gulag, and interweaves the drama of their lives with the drama of this unfolding maelstrom. Their lives and political activity crisscrossed Europe and touched on many of the major events of the century. McLoughlin wonderfully evokes the texture of the social and cultural relations of the period and provides a fascinating insight into the world of international revolutionaries, Comintern agents, and the expatriate community in the Soviet Union in the 1930s. By personalising the narrative, McLoughlin makes it more understandable. He has provided a micro-history not only of the important events in Soviet and Irish history, but also of the political history of Europe in the 20th century.

Pat Breslin was one of 20 Irish delegates, sent as students to the International Lenin School (ILS) in Moscow in 1928. The primary function of the ILS was transforming revolutionaries into party functionaries, who on their return home would implement the "Soviet line". Breslin's experience of surveillance and denunciation during his time at the ILS quickly turned to disillusionment with Stalin's Russia. He was expelled from the ILS, but asked to stay in Moscow to be with his pregnant wife. He worked as a journalist on the *Moscow Daily News*, which catered mainly for foreign residents in the Soviet Union. But by 1937 foreigners were seen as prospective fifth columnists and the need for newspapers to cater for their interests belonged to the past. Foreigners were pressurised to abandon their native citizenship for the scarlet passport of the

USSR, and when Breslin surrendered his Irish citizenship and applied for a Soviet passport in 1936 his chances of returning to Ireland were severely diminished.

Breslin was arrested in 1940 and charged with having a "hostile attitude" to Soviet power. Confession became everything—a legal justification for the mass arrests and a popular justification for the terror in the USSR as well as in the West. But to sign a confession was in effect a death warrant. Breslin was interrogated over a seven month period and sentenced to eight years imprisonment. He lasted less than a month in the gulag before dying as a result of the torture and deprivation. McLoughlin's account of his interrogation, including a list of questions and answers from his extensive file, makes grim and compulsive reading.

Brian Goold-Verschoyle came from an upper class Anglo-Irish family and, in the tradition of the Cambridge spies, joined the Communist Party in the 1920s. He was recruited by the Soviet intelligence agency, trained as a radio operator in Moscow and returned to Britain. There he became active in one of the many Soviet spy rings. He was sent to Spain following the outbreak of the civil war and worked as a radio technician in Barcelona.

Goold-Verschoyle quickly realised the Stalinists had no real interest in a mass revolutionary movement that was potentially independent of Moscow. His letters home reveal a growing sympathy for the Socialist Party and the Trotskyist-influenced Poum. In April 1937 he was asked to report to Barcelona harbour to repair a ship's radio. When he embarked he was escorted to the radio cabin and the door was locked behind him. He had in effect been kidnapped and when the ship arrived in Russia he was immediately transferred to the Lubianka prison in Moscow. He was sentenced to eight years for counter-revolutionary Trotskyist activities and died in confinement in 1942.

Sean McAteer worked as a docker in Dublin and was a member of James Connolly's Irish Citizen Army. He emigrated to America and became an activist with the Industrial Workers of the World. On his return to Ireland he joined the Communist Party and in January 1922, along with writer Liam O'Flaherty, he was part of a group that occupied the Rotunda in Dublin and declared a "Soviet Republic". The soviet, which lasted only a matter of days, was one of many factory occupations in the period immediately after Irish independence, inspired by the Russian Revolution, that hoisted the red flag. Fearing arrest during the Irish Civil War he went to Liverpool and during a raid on a post office to raise funds for the Republican movement a man was shot.

Once more McAteer was forced to flee, and with the assistance of Elena Stasova, Lenin's former secretary, who in December 1922 had set up the International Red Help organisation to assist revolutionaries all over the world, he made his way to Russia. He worked as a propagandist, recruiting foreign sailors in the Seamen's Club in Odessa. In 1927 he was sent to China as an agent of the Comintern and after the collapse of the Chinese revolution he returned to his old job in Odessa. The murder of Kirov in December 1934 unleashed a purge of foreign Communists. McAteer was arrested and shot as a spy in 1937. The Soviet Red Cross later informed Jim Larkin's son that he had disappeared during the Nazi occupation of Odessa.

Left to the Wolves is a fascinating read that takes us inside the terror with a cast of revolutionaries, spies and informers, which straddled the international movement. McLoughlin is good at describing the process of the terror—the numbers, the organisation, the minute details of the interrogation and the confessions extracted from the men. But he has no political explanation as to why it happened. He is forced to rely on irrational explanations: Stalin was paranoid, the Bolsheviks were "hard men", or the party functionaries failed to carry out the plan. McLoughlin throws up a mass of information but the analysis fails to identify the key issues in Soviet history. He has no sense of the degeneration of the revolution, the counter-revolutionary nature of Stalinism and the theory of "socialism in one country". There is no sense of a new class society emerging.

There were real threats to Stalin's power in the mid-1930s; the old Bolsheviks who had led the revolution in 1917 were increasingly dissatisfied with Stalin's leadership, and sections of the army who had served with Trotsky during the Civil War in the early 1920s posed a real challenge. Foreign revolutionaries who had sought sanctuary in the USSR were particularly vulnerable, as the regime feared that they might have been influenced by Trotskyist ideas. All of these elements had to be liquidated if the new social order was to consolidate its position.

The three men McLoughlin describes deserved more. They were not friends or acquaintances; all they shared was their Irish nationality and their belief in the Soviet Union as a haven from prosecution and their belief that it was the heartland of world revolution. They were minor figures in the Communist movement, but McLoughlin has forensically pieced together their involvement in the movement and their confidence in the future. They found a new class society emerging from the destruction of the revolution. Their disillusionment with the USSR led to their arrest, transportation and death.

The making of an agitator

Chris Bambery

Bryan D Palmer, ***James P Cannon and the Origins of the American Revolutionary Left 1890-1928*** *(University of Illinois, 2007), £29*

For me the decisive moment in James P Cannon's life was when he gave up his swivel chair.

In 1928 Cannon turned his back on a career as a Communist Party leader in the United States, facing inevitable expulsion by coming out in support of Leon Trotsky and the left opposition to Stalinism. As Joseph Stalin began to exert complete control over both Russia and the Communist International, Cannon must have been a prime candidate to be installed as leader of the US party. Stalin liked his general secretaries to be staunchly proletarian and devotedly loyal. Maurice Thorez in France, Ernest Thalmann in Germany and, on a smaller stage, Harry Pollitt in Britain all fitted that mould.

Cannon was a "native" radical, born and brought up in harsh industrial conditions in Kansas and with a track record as a frontline organiser for the Industrial Workers of the World (known as the Wobblies) and a key figure in the creation of the US Communist Party. By 1928 Stalin was moving to axe Jay Lovestone as general secretary because he was aligned with the Russian leader's rival Nikolai Bukharin. Stalin was also distrustful of another contender for the post, the trade union leader William Z Foster.

Looking back Cannon explained why he chose to surrender the relative comfort of party office—a decision made all the more honourable because he knew he was heading into obscurity (though he could not possibly be aware just how isolated he would be over the following six years):

"The footloose Wobbly rebel that I used to be had imperceptibly begun to fit comfortably into a swivel chair, protecting himself in his seat by small manoeuvres and evasions, and even permitting himself a certain conceit about his adroit accommodation to this shabby game. I saw myself for the first time then as another person, as a revolutionist who was on the road to becoming a bureaucrat. The image was hideous, and I turned away from it in disgust.

"I never deceived myself for a moment about the most probable consequences of my decision to support Trotsky in the summer of 1928. I knew it was going to cost me my head and also my swivel chair, but I thought: What the hell—better men than I have risked their heads and their swivel chairs for truth and justice."

This does not quite do justice to his growing unease with the degeneration of the Russian Revolution and the Communist International. That probably dates from Moscow's directive to British Communists to uncritically tail the trade union leaders during the 1926 general strike.

At the sixth congress of the Communist International, held in 1928, Cannon went to Moscow representing the faction he led within the US party. As the lesser force to Lovestone and Foster's groupings he was sidelined by being sent to the commission considering a new programme to be adopted by the International.

Cannon was unexpectedly handed an English translation of *The Draft Programme of the Communist International: A Criticism of Fundamentals* (now available as *The Third International After Lenin*), by the Bolshevik leader Leon Trotsky, who had been expelled from the Soviet Communist Party and was in exile in Alma Ata. The document was a searing attack on Stalin's notion of "socialism in one country" and an appeal for the International's policy to be based on the primacy of international revolution over Soviet diplomatic interests. Trotsky's document was smuggled out, apparently stuffed into a teddy bear belonging to an offspring of one of Cannon's pals.

On his return to the US Cannon won over his partner, Rose Krasner, his young factional supporters, Max Shachtman and Martin Abern in New York City, Albert Glotzer and Arne Swabeck in Chicago, and then a group of worker militants in Minneapolis. They formed the nucleus of the most stable international grouping that rallied to Trotsky.

Cannon and his allies spun out the disciplinary proceedings against them, increasing their audience, before dramatically declaring their support for Trotsky. Within 24 hours of their expulsion, copies of their declaration were circulating in the party. Within a week they had launched a new paper, *The Militant*, its first edition headlined: "For The Russian Revolution".

Bryan D Palmer's book pays tribute to Cannon's courage, but it does much more than that. It is a serious study of the US left in the decade before and after the First World War.

James Patrick Cannon was born in 1890 to parents of Irish origin who had immigrated to the US and pitched up in Rosedale, Kansas, just as the town's good times ended. By the age of 12 he was working in a meat packing plant, having been denied a secondary education. When a high school was opened in Rosedale he went back to secure an education.

Cannon's political involvement began at the age of 14 when he got involved in the defence of Big Bill Haywood, who was being framed on murder charges for his role in a miners' strike. At 18 Cannon joined the Socialist Party, attracted by its presidential candidate, Eugene Debs. The party had 100,000 members and Debs polled just short of a million votes in 1912. But Debs refused to get involved in inner party matters, allowing cautious reformists to dominate the party. Cannon reacted to this by joining the Industrial Workers of the World in 1910. Palmer's account of this period is the most gripping part of the book.

Starting in Kansas City, Cannon and his comrades would go into working class areas, particularly where itinerant workers, "hoboes", teemed. Competing against Christians, the sellers of fake medicinal cures and so on, the Wobblies had to draw a crowd and hold them. Cannon was a great soapbox agitator. Later he recalled, "You are either a soapboxer or you are not. You are tested by whether you hold the crowd, by the literature sold, and the money given to the collection."

At the 1912 congress of the Wobblies, Cannon caught the eye of the union's general secretary, Vincent St John. In February 1913 "The Saint" pitched Cannon into a labour uprising in Akron, Ohio, where 23,000 workers were employed in the tyre industry.

A strike at the Firestone plant sparked a walkout across the city's plants. The Wobblies threw every organiser and agitator at the uprising. Eclipsed by the silk weavers' uprising in Paterson, New Jersey—which attracted the help of John Reed, Elizabeth Gurley Flynn and Big Bill Haywood—Akron was a dispute uniting American and foreign born workers, men and women. In a sense it was more representative of the US proletariat at the time.

The Wobblies held meetings and issued leaflets in English, Serbian, German, Slovak, Italian and Hungarian, holding mass pickets, parades, street corner meetings and strike rallies. At the beginning the dispute had a carnival atmosphere, but this was not to last. Armed police and specially recruited "deputies"—in reality anti-strike vigilantes—were unleashed on strikers. Street fighting lasted a week but the forces of "order" emerged on top. The official American Federation of Labour (AFL) chipped in, denouncing the strike. The numbers attending strike mobilisations fell away and a drift back to work began before the AFL brokered a return to work. The Wobblies had little permanent organisation on the ground. Their itinerant organisers and agitators were brilliant when a strike was on the up, but found it difficult to hold the line when things went into reverse, and far more so to build anything from defeat.

By the time the First World War broke out in Europe, Cannon was back in Kansas City, married with two children and attempting to earn a living. But in 1917 two events brought him back into the struggle—US entry into the war and the Russian Revolution. Reading John Reed's *The Liberator* and other pro-Bolshevik journals, Cannon was won to the idea of a new combat party, firm on principles but rooted in the class.

Like Reed he rallied to the pro-Bolshevik left wing of the Socialist Party, travelling to that party's 1919 congress in New York City. The events there are portrayed well in Warren Beatty's film *Reds*. The leadership used every procedural trick to defeat the left, eventually calling the police to evict them. In the process the left split, with one grouping based on the foreign language sections of the party leaving to proclaim itself the Communist Party, while Reed's supporters wanted to fight to the last in the Socialist Party to try to secure the largest possible support. Eventually two Communist Parties formed.

A post-war strike wave and the fear of revolution led to a ferocious witch-hunt with strikes suppressed, mass arrests and deportation of leftists. The revolutionary left was forced underground (and the Wobblies were effectively destroyed).

The largely foreign language Communist Party argued that clandestine organisation was a matter of Bolshevik principle. Cannon, by contrast, realised revolutionaries had to seize any opportunity for open, legal work in order to get mass support.

From 1920-3 Cannon campaigned for Communist unity and for open work. The matter was settled at the Communist International's fourth congress where the Russians Gregory Zinoviev and Nikolai Bukharin supported those championing clandestinity. In Moscow Cannon secured an interview with Trotsky who, together with Lenin, ridiculed the "champions of the underground".

On paper Cannon should have become party leader. He cheered Zinoviev's campaign to "Bolshevise" the Communist Parties, though this amounted to greater bureaucratic control from Moscow. Then disaster struck when a Comintern emissary Joseph Pepper succeeded in installing himself as effective party leader, promoting Jay Lovestone within the party leadership.

Whatever his doubts about the growing demonisation of Trotsky, Cannon was formally a loyal supporter of the Communist International until his final trip to Moscow, agreeing to suppress references to Trotsky and Zinoviev (after he became an opponent of Stalin) in the party press. This is important because some on the left, echoing Max Shachtman after his break with Cannon, have tried to rubbish him as a bureaucrat, while others have tried to paint him as an immaculate Trotskyist.

The former charge does not stand up to Cannon's commitment to revolution, which lasted until his death in 1974. The latter charge ignores the fact that Trotsky made tactical mistakes in his fight with Stalin in the 1920s, and few in the international movement were in a position to understand the importance of that fight.

Palmer ends this volume with Cannon's expulsion and the creation of the grouping that would subsequently become the Communist League of America and then the US Socialist Workers Party. A further volume is planned on Cannon's subsequent role in the Trotskyist movement. On the basis of this volume's conclusion I somehow feel this will not be as satisfactory.

For a generation of Trotskyists Cannon's book detailing the 1939-40 faction fight with Shachtman, Abern, Glotzer and James Burnham, *The Struggle for the Proletarian Party*, became a sort of manual on how to conduct an internal faction fight. Unfortunately, it was a fairly disastrous manual. The dispute centred on matters of deep substance such as the class nature of Stalin's Russia and Burnham's rejection of historical materialism. But factional quarrels had been almost continuous throughout the 1930s, meaning that from start to finish the fight was between two camps rigid in their loyalties.

Trotsky urged Cannon on, but was also critical of his refusal to try to generalise the discussion. By taking the discussion to a higher plane, educating all concerned and creating space for a change of views, Cannon could have avoided the retreat into two armed camps.

The other problem with *The Struggle for*

the Proletarian Party was that it labelled the Shachtman-Abern faction a "petty bourgeois opposition". Cannon would subsequently portray all faction fights within the party as a clash between a proletarian centre and alien class forces. That implies matters can only be resolved by a split.

Cannon's problems were compounded after the Second World War. Trotsky had predicted that the Soviet Union, which he still saw as a degenerated workers' state, would not survive the war, which would end with recession and revolution. Cannon clung to this perspective even as Western capitalism entered its greatest ever economic boom, and Stalinism expanded into Eastern Europe and China. Arguing that the Eastern European regimes were somehow workers' states led to the notion that capitalism could be overthrown by Russian tanks, rather than the self-emancipation of the working class

On the domestic front Cannon and his allies tended to retreat into a more propagandist approach following the Second World War, stressing the centrality of "the programme" in an increasingly sterile and lifeless manner. He finally ceased to direct the day to day running of the US Socialist Workers Party in 1953, at the height of the McCarthyite witch-hunts.

But whatever criticisms are made of Cannon, he remained a link to the glory days of the US left—the days of John Reed, Vincent St John, Big Bill Haywood, Elizabeth Gurley Flynn, Eugene Debs and the Wobblies. He represented an authentic, "native" leftism—the idea, which goes against the grain of much of the left, that US workers can be won to socialism and revolution. This book is a fitting tribute to Cannon—soapboxer, Wobbly and American Bolshevik.

The search for theory

Ian Birchall

Duncan Thompson, ***Pessimism of the Intellect? A History of*** **New Left Review** *(Merlin), £16.95*

To produce uninterruptedly, every two to three months, a socialist theoretical journal with a consistently high standard of analysis and commentary from 1960 to the present is no small achievement. Only two journals in Britain fit the description—*International Socialism* and *New Left Review* (*NLR*). Though in some sense rivals, the two journals have been complementary, and on occasion—the Revolutionary Socialist Students' Federation and the Balkans war—have cooperated. Anyone who (like myself) has a complete set of *NLR* since 1960 possesses a rich collection of contributions to socialist thought. The left as a whole would have been poorer without *NLR*; any negative comments in this review should not be seen as detracting from that.

So those interested in the history of the British left should welcome Duncan Thompson's history of *NLR*. Written from a point of view of general support for the left, it makes some sharp and fundamental criticisms of *NLR*, but never in a hostile or sectarian manner.

NLR emerged from the aftermath of the events of 1956. In 1962 the original editorial team around the historian Edward Thompson was replaced by a group headed by Perry Anderson. Anderson proposed to make *NLR* the British equivalent of *Les Temps Modernes*, the French journal founded by Jean-Paul Sartre in 1945. He never came remotely close. In its heroic years during the Algerian War *Les Temps Modernes* formed a focus for the opponents of the war; it published denunciations of torture and testimonies by French soldiers about the brutalities of the war. It was seized four times by the authorities in Algeria in 1957. It is hard to imagine the police bothering to confiscate *NLR*.

Duncan Thompson gives a careful account of *NLR*'s political evolution, aptly described as "skittish"—a series of sharp political turns made without justification or self-criticism. In its first few years *NLR* had more than its share of illusions in the modernising potential of Harold Wilson's Labour government. But the emergence of the student movement in 1968 produced a sharp swing to the ultra-left. *NLR* argued (rightly) that ideology was of great importance and (wrongly) that ideology was primarily the product of intellectuals. Hence the working class could not be approached directly; instead the student movement would produce a Marxist intelligentsia who would bring "theory" to the working class which was so sadly deprived of it.

The *NLR* of these years was a peculiar mixture of student ultra-leftism (one article urged students to "behave as provocatively as necessary and to effectively sanction the university to the extent that they need to use force, probably the police"—the author was "Baron" Triesman, now foreign office minister) and esoteric theory, notably discussion of the work of Louis Althusser who attempted a pathetic rearguard defence of Stalinism by dressing it up in pretentious academic jargon.

After a brief flirtation with Maoism, *NLR* turned to "Trotskyism", though it was a Trotskyism filtered through the work of Isaac Deutscher and Ernest Mandel. But the journal became ever more remote from the actual course of political events—neither the massive industrial struggles of the 1970s nor the rise of racism made any impression on it. (I suspect Trotsky himself would have judged *NLR* in the same way as he did *Partisan Review*: a "small cultural monastery, guarding itself from the outside world by scepticism, agnosticism and respectability".)

Although *NLR* defended dissident currents in the Eastern bloc, it continued to regard Russia and its satellites as representing a higher form of society. So the "collapse of Communism" in 1989 induced a considerable pessimism, and a shift towards a far more defensive position with the advocacy of constitutional reform, tactical voting and on occasion "market socialism". When *NLR* was relaunched in 2000 Anderson announced that "for the first time since the Reformation, there are no longer any significant oppositions...within the thought-world of the West".

The root of *NLR*'s failure lay in a progressive distancing from the working class movement. In its first years *NLR* made at least two positive contributions. One was the production of a very useful Penguin compilation, edited by Robin Blackburn and Alexander Cockburn, called *The Incompatibles* (1967)—a set of essays on British trade unionism (the pick of the bunch was Paul Foot on the 1966 seafarers' strike). The other was a series in *NLR* entitled "Work", overseen by Ronald Fraser. This gave first-person accounts of the alienation experienced in everyday employment by those in a wide variety of jobs. It pioneered later work in the field of "oral history".

But with the euphoria of 1968 this attempt at concrete engagement with the working class disappeared, never to be seen again. From now on if the working class appeared in the pages of *NLR* it was as a concept in Marxist theory, never as the women and men in the factory down the road whom you might join on a picket line—except in the important case of an interview it ran with Arthur Scargill on the mass pickets of the 1972 miners' strike.

NLR was never the journal of an organisation. That was its strength—as Blackburn put it, *NLR* was not "a journal for recycling an already established truth"—but also its weakness. *NLR* frequently wrote about "strategy", but it was never clear who would implement that strategy. Hence it was never tested against reality. Lessons can be learned from a failed strategy, but an untested hypothesis can only be eternally debated.

"Left clubs" founded by the first editorial team in the early 1960s soon evaporated. Although some members of the later editorial committee were for a time members of the International Marxist Group (IMG), there was never any close connection between *NLR* and IMG activity. In the 1980s there was an attempt to expand the editorial committee by adding a group of leading feminist writers. One of the conditions they proposed was the establishment of "readers' groups". This was promptly vetoed by the existing committee.

Duncan Thompson has no startling revelations about the somewhat secretive internal workings of *NLR*. He has worked on the basis of printed material, without interviewing the main protagonists. He has, however, had access to some illuminating "internal documents".

"Democratic centralism" is much maligned. Yet it has some merits compared to what was described as the "common-law variety of democratic centralism" as practised by *NLR*. *NLR* was produced by a small team—for years numbering no more than seven or eight—accountable to nobody. The dominating figure was undoubtedly Anderson, described here as "overbearing". He is without question a man of enormous erudition, but one who often uses his knowledge to intimidate his readers rather than enlighten them. The situation was further complicated by the fact that Anderson was also the paymaster—his private income bailed out *NLR* in its financial crisis in 1962. There is no indication that Anderson actually threatened to take his bat home if his editorial will was denied, but it must have been a factor in the minds of those concerned.

Anderson is a somewhat reclusive individual (as one who has been active on the left for over 45 years, I have seen Anderson in the flesh just once). In this he contrasts sharply with his closest ally, Blackburn. Whatever criticisms one might make of Blackburn, he has been an activist. At the height of the student movement of the late 1960s, he put his head on the line and lost his job at the London School of Economics. In the early 1980s, when *NLR* helped to launch a "Socialist Society", it was Blackburn who was the entrepreneurial driving force. Anderson made only a token appearance at the founding conference.

Though small, the *NLR* team was never homogeneous: there were major differences within it. But apart from periodic resignations, these were never made clear. Preserving the cohesion of the team was regarded as more important than political clarity.

The striking example is the question of Ireland. There were deep disagreements within the committee. Some favoured the slogan "Victory to the IRA", while others, to put it mildly, were less enthusiastic. This might have been a matter for debate and, at worst, for a split. Instead, from 1970 to 1994, there was "by common consent" silence about Ireland: this throughout a time when bombs were exploding in the streets of Britain, and theoretical clarity—on terrorism, on the violence of the oppressed, on national liberation—was urgently needed.

In 1964 another of Anderson's collaborators, Tom Nairn, declared that the English working class "needed theory". He was right. Sadly *NLR*, despite its real achievements, has rarely delivered.

The merchant and the Middle Ages

Chris Harman

*Eric H Mielants, **The Origins of Capitalism and the "Rise of the West"** (Temple University Press, 2007), £30*

Over the past 30 years two views have dominated debates on the rise of capitalism in Europe. "World systems theory", associated with Immanuel Wallerstein, sees the crucial move to capitalism as originating in the colonisation of the Americas and, in particular, the flow of precious metals from Peru to Spain and from there, through various routes, to purchase merchandise in Asia. By contrast the view associated with Robert Brenner argues capitalism came about with the exploitation of free labour on the land in England after failure of either the lords or the peasants to achieve a decisive victory in the class struggles of the 14th century.

Mielants sets out to challenge both views. He says they both ignore the key role played by the development of merchant capital in medieval Europe—Wallerstein because he locates capitalism's development as too late historically, Brenner because he ignores the merchants completely (or at least until the English Revolution of the 1640s).

Most of Mielants' fire is directed against Brenner and those who accept his main arguments, such as Ellen Meiksins Wood. Their mistake, he claims, is not to see that the merchant capitalism of the Middle Ages was a form of capitalism and, as such, prepared the ground for other forms.

This book brings together a mass of material from a vast number of sources showing the impact merchants and money lenders had on the society around them—financing kings and emperors, dominating city states, stretching out to exploit the peasantry in the countryside around the cities. Mielants performs a useful service in showing that it is not possible, as Brenner and Wood do, to look at what happens in the countryside without seeing the interconnections with the towns. He also shows that the trading networks of the merchants were not just concerned with luxury goods, as is often argued, but also included staple products, especially those that could be carried by sea.

Merchant capital, he argues, as an economic factor alongside feudal production, began to exercise political influence, creating state forms that the made industrial and agrarian capitalist development possible in Europe.

The second part of the book tries to show why this did not happen elsewhere. His argument is that merchant capitalism did also develop China, the Indian subcontinent, the East Indies and Africa, but never achieved the political importance it had in Europe, and therefore could not lay the groundwork for further capitalist development. But on this his arguments are not convincing.

That merchant capitalism had an impact on the societies in which it developed should not be contentious, even it is often ignored by those belonging to the Brenner and Wood schools. Everywhere the merchants managed, to a greater or lesser degree, to find ways of gathering wealth in their hands on a basis different to those of the pre-capitalist landowners. They established towns (or built up influence within certain sections of towns still controlled by the old ruling classes) where relations of exploitation were different to those in the countryside and where new patterns of life developed. This was as true of northern China or the Maghreb as it was of Florence or Bruges.

Attempts to explain the emergence of productive capitalism which ignore the impact merchants could have—and the limits of that impact in many situations—end up with the tautological argument that productive capitalism (usually in its agrarian form) developed because it developed. Such attempts ignore something that Karl Marx pointed out—that the selling of products as commodities to outsiders by groups that produce under pre-capitalist conditions acts like an acid eating into the relations between people in those groups. To get capitalist relations of exploitation a step must then be taken—moving from buying and selling material goods to buying and selling labour power—but it is not necessarily such an enormous step.

There is, however, a central weakness with Mielants' argument. He does not explain how it was that merchants gained political influence in some places and not in others. His case essentially is that in most of Asia the state was too strong for the merchants to develop independent bases of power in towns; an argument which, although he denies it, is in itself little different from the old "Asiatic mode of production" or "Oriental despotism" argument. By contrast, he argues that in Africa the state was too weak to protect the merchants. It seems capitalism only developed in the end because of a version of the Goldilocks effect—the states were neither too strong nor too weak. It does not explain why capitalism was strong enough to influence and even revolutionise the old state in some places and not others.

The failure comes from ignoring the same thing that is ignored by the Brenner and Wood schools—the way the development of the forces of production impinges on people, encouraging new social relations that eventually clash with the superstructures of ruling class power. Mielants criticises what he calls a "Marxist" and a "Neo-Marxist" approach, but never confronts the elements of the account to be found by Marx himself in *The Communist Manifesto* and the *Preface to the Critique of Political Economy*.

The merchants emerged as a class within pre-capitalist agrarian societies. By buying in one place and selling in another they prospered in so far as they provided a service to the classes of those societies—including the agrarian ruling classes. It was this that allowed them to accumulate wealth, and so to control the internal life of towns, influence the preaching of churches, temples and mosques, and, if necessary, buy arms to assert their political autonomy. But insofar as they did not develop forces of production of their own (or ally with craftsmen or peasants who were doing so), they remained prisoners of the old society, never able to be more than relatively autonomous.

Mielants shows how they often did get control of productive processes. But the examples he gives are usually of when they took over from the agrarian rulers the pre-capitalist exploitation of the peasants. He writes of how the towns established "dominance" or "uneven exchange" over the neighbouring countryside. But establishing this relationship involves pre-capitalist exploitation based on force, not capitalist relations based on exchange. And in so far as they were involved in pre-capitalist exploitation, the city merchants only turned themselves into one extra fragment of the pre-capitalist landed class.

This is most graphic in the case of Italian city-states such as Florence. Mielants repeatedly refers to them as cases where merchants began the development of capitalism. He forgets that what might have begun came to an abrupt stop in the early 16th century. Italy's Renaissance cities did not develop smoothly to modern capitalism, but regressed into just another part of the country's feudal patchwork, with Florence's most important merchant family, the Medicis, merging into the old ruling class. The case was no different with many of the other European towns he refers to. The further advance to capitalism did not take place in pioneering late medieval cities like Bruges, Strasburg, Prague, Lisbon or Milan. To this extent, things were not that much different in Europe to Asia and Africa. To pose the issue in terms of "Europe" versus "Asia" and "Africa", or, as the Brenner school does, in terms of England versus France, misses an essential point. There were places where the old order began to be challenged everywhere—and everywhere the old order could strike back.

It was only where production began to take new forms, as some people began to shape new social relations of exploitation around more advanced ways of producing, that the old society was truly undermined from within. Even then it required successful revolutionary struggle for the decisive breakthroughs to occur.

One of the things missing from Mielants' account is any sense of the battles that were waged, and usually lost, before the superstructures of the old order finally fell to the advanced guard of the new. In his account of the Islamic cities there is little mention of the integration of local religious notables, with their role in interpreting civil law, into the merchant elite. Nor is there any recognition of the tensions in Sung China as economic advance produced challenges to the old elite and its conservative neo-Confucian ideology. He mentions the "pirate" merchants of south east China who resisted control from the Ming emperor in the 16th century, but does not see that their attitude had something in common with those who cut off the king of England's head a century later.

Once you understand that the forces of production were developing in similar ways and creating groups with new ways of looking at the world right across Europe, Asia and Africa, the fact that the breakthrough to sustained capitalist development took place first in Holland and England does not seem any greater an issue than the fact that under the pounding of spring tides a sea wall crumbles at one point before another.

The very backwardness of north western Europe in the early medieval period meant there were weaker political superstructures than elsewhere and fewer obstacles to the new ways associated with new productive methods that spread right across Eurasia and northern Africa. A momentum developed causing parts of Europe to leapfrog over the world's previously more economically advanced regions. Yet there were places elsewhere in the world which had to the potential to break through to capitalism, had Britain and Holland not forestalled—and then often conquered—them.

Mielants has pulled together a vast mass of material and challenges hypotheses that have been in danger of being repeated as unquestionable dogmas in some circles. But he ultimately fails to provide a coherent alternative view.

Professor Jekyll and Comrade Hyde

Viren Swami

Andrew Brown, ***J D Bernal: The Sage of Science*** *(Oxford University Press, 2007), £12.99*

As a young reader of psychology, I was made to believe, through constant cajoling and the occasional threat of lost marks, that the consummate scientist was one who sought the truth in an objective and disinterested manner. Within this paradigm, science is pursued for the knowledge that it brings, and any emotion, political conviction or social belief serves only to sully the pristine waters of truth seeking. Of course, science and scientists are very rarely entirely disinterested in their work; nor has this penchant for objectivity always been held in such high regard. Following the First World War a movement emerged within British academia that stressed the social responsibility of scientists: science was pursued not merely for the knowledge it offered, but also for the uses to which that knowledge could be put for the betterment of society.

Most notable among this group were J D Bernal, J B S Haldane, Hyman Levy, Joseph Needham, and Lancelot Hogben. Through their academic work and political conviction—all were Marxists—they became known as leading intellectuals, and were conferred the highest accolades by the British scientific establishment. There has been much discussion of the contribution of this group to academia and society, most notably in Gary Werskey's *The Visible College: A Collective Biography of British Scientists and Socialists of the 1930s*, but evaluating and understanding the legacy of its individual members has proved difficult. In 1980, for instance, Maurice Goldsmith published *Sage: A Life of J D Bernal*, but the short biography met with resistance from Bernal himself.

Fortunately, Goldsmith's biography has now been supplanted by Andrew Brown's *J D Bernal: The Sage of Science*, which is both an outstanding example of a scientific biography and a valuable work of scholarship in itself. Brown benefited not just from better cooperation from Bernal's family and associates, but also from extensive use of the Bernal archives in Cambridge. His biography of Bernal is an elegant, comprehensive and thoroughly knowledgeable account of the scientific, political and personal aspects of Bernal's life, and heaves with interviews with the scientist's children, associates (a collection of individuals who range from Nobel laureates to lab technicians) and many, many lovers.

This interest in Bernal is not misplaced: he was one of the most extraordinary figures of 20th century British science, an inventive scientist whose intellectual energy and polymathic ability earned him the sobriquet "Sage" while he was still an undergraduate at Cambridge University. By all accounts, Bernal reached the heights of academe, particularly through his work on X-ray crystallography in the 1920s and 1930s, for which he narrowly missed receiving the Nobel Prize. Perhaps the most evident example of Bernal's achievements was his influence on others: Francis Crick, for instance, described Bernal as his "scientific grandfather" and students of Bernal have gone on to become Nobel Prize laureates.

Where opinion often divides, however, is in relation to Bernal's political convictions. While still at Cambridge, Bernal became a Marxist and in the late 1920s he signed up to the Communist Party with his wife, Eileen Sprague. He was one of a number of British scientists impressed by the unity, scientific vitality and social purpose of a Russian delegation, led by Nikolai Bukharin, to the 1931 International Congress of the History of Science in London. Bernal himself went on to develop an important Marxist analysis of past and present science, culminating in his influential monograph *The Social Function of Science*.

Bernal's radical critique of traditional structures of power within academia, his analysis of science and society, his political activism and, most importantly, his Marxism are sometimes a source of bemusement for contemporary commentators. Just as some writers sought to divorce Stephen J Gould's early political engagement with Marxism from his academic achievements, so some commentators have striven to explain away Bernal's commitment to Marxism. In his review of Brown's biography in *Nature*, for instance, Kenneth Holmes writes, "In the 1930s, Bernal became committed to Marxism. How a man with such a marvellous analytical mind could come to terms with dialectical materialism is still a subject of discussion—it seems to have been an act of faith, a substitute for Catholicism."

Brown, in his biography of the Sage, is likewise condescending towards Bernal's philosophy and politics. Certainly, Bernal's steadfast support for the Soviet Union and Soviet science—particularly his defence of Trofim Lysenko, whose ideas on genetics were completely at odds with mainstream work—served to alienate him from many of his erstwhile colleagues, marginalising him within British science and politics in the 1950s and 1960s.

But to malign Bernal's politics as somehow peculiar or irreverent is to forget that he came to Marxism consciously, intelligently and resolutely. In Marxism, Bernal found a philosophical framework that enabled his academic work, opening him up to new ideas, allowing him to combine academic life with political involvement. The suggestion, implicit in Brown's biography, that Bernal's Marxism served to constrict his intellectual capability is unfortunate.

Bernal considered his Marxist philosophy, particularly the tradition of dialectical materialism (which, incidentally, made possible his break with Catholicism, and which followed directly in the tradition of Frederick Engels), to be the most suitable philosophy for scientific endeavour. Marxist philosophy, Bernal believed, provided the basis not only for a revolutionary transformation of society, but also for the development of science. Bernal's Marxism was no dogma, no scientific credo to hang on to come what may, but was rather a scientific method of "doing" science, a method that had itself been developed through scientific knowledge.

It was Bernal's view (based on a detailed grasp of the history of science—a science of science) expounded in *The Social Function of Science* and later in *Science in History*, that science could only arrive at its full potential under socialism. The goals of capitalism, he believed, were not compatible with those of science, and thus generated a distrust of science and academia that, if left unattended, resulted in a rebellion against scientific rationality itself. Only socialism could harness the intellectual and practical prowess necessary to fulfil the promise of science. And in doing so, socialism would ensure that scientists took a keen interest in social responsibility, using knowledge and learning to benefit not an elite (whether in academia, politics or wider society) but rather the working class.

In short, then, Brown's insistence that Bernal's true legacy lies in his academic achievements, and that his Marxism was at best a distraction, ensures that his biography fails to paint a complete picture of Bernal's life. Of course, Brown's book is much more than a biography—it attempts a social history of the first half of 20th century science, in which Bernal played a constituent part. But Brown's failure to understand that Bernal's political and philosophical convictions were an integral part of his scholarly work means that Bernal's true legacy is not captured in this biography.

Science has come a long way since Bernal died in 1971, but in many ways his belief that capitalism would stunt the growth of science has since become all the more evident. As a researcher, I typically spend my days engaging in micro-debates with other researchers, picking at scraps of information, hoping that others believe I am as disinterested and objective as they believe they are, and in doing so, singularly failing to look at the way in which science affects wider society. Nor am I alone in this. Under capitalism, science has become reclusive, narrow and shallow, driven by market demand; universities are forced to operate as profit seekers; commercial need has outstripped any interest in searching for truths that can shape public interest.

There is, however, an antidote. Bernal's Marxism, which he shared with other Marxist scientists of the first half of the 20th century, and which laid the basis for a later generation of scientists in the Marxist tradition (Richard Lewontin, Stephen J Gould, Richard Levins, Steven Rose, to name but a few), remains relevant for our times. The qualities that Bernal strived to incorporate in his life and work, the totality of his thinking and his socialist commitments, are exactly the qualities that contemporary science lacks.

Persian proletariat

Naz Massoumi

Andreas Malm and Shora Esmailian, ***Iran on the Brink: Rising Workers and Threats of War*** *(Pluto, 2007), £17.99*

There are two predominant images of Iran in the West. One is a racist depiction of Iran as a backward country of religious fanaticism. The other sees the principles of Western liberal democracy lying underneath the confines of a religious government. This image is often used by those urging war against Iran, but also by some who want to counter the one-dimensional view of a Muslim country. But it would remain a complete distortion of the truth to use this element as the sole representation, despite the admiration of Western culture that exists.

The first half of *Iran on the Brink* aims to paint a different image, drawn "from the point of view of the poor and workers". The principal argument of this book—that a new labour movement in Iran is being suffocated by Western interference and threats of war—is more than welcome. However, the analysis has shortcomings (not surprising, given that the authors are journalists from *Arbetaren*, an Swedish anarcho-syndicalist newspaper) and fails to fully take into account the processes that have changed Iranian society over the past three decades.

Iran possesses a rich history of struggle from below, from the protests against the British monopoly over Iranian tobacco in the 1890s through to the creation of anjumans (local councils) during the Constitutional Revolution of 1906. The power of the Iranian working class was first realised during the mass strikes and unionisation of the 1940s. The most profound working class intervention was in 1978, when mass strikes, particularly by oil workers, brought about the revolution that overthrew the Shah's military dictatorship. Committees were set up to coordinate the strikes, and these led to the creation of new democratic forms—factory councils known as shoras.

The book quite rightly highlights the negative impact the Iranian left had on this process during the revolution. The powerful legacy of Stalinist Russia was particularly damaging. A dominant theory was that of "dependent" capitalism, which regarded Iran as purely an agent of foreign capital.

There's no doubt that the Shah, as the US's policeman in the Gulf, gave foreign (and particularly US) capital an easy ride. But this was less significant than the domestic sector. The state remained the principal driving force of industrial growth and it was this process, begun by the Shah's father at the start of the century, which had brought about the uneven development of Iranian capitalism. The Shah was not simply an agent of imperialism—the indigenous bourgeoisie had their own interests in maintaining Iranian capital. The theory of "dependent" capitalism meant seeing the "national bourgeoisie" as somehow more progressive than the "reactionary" agents of imperialism. Such a model also placed the Iranian working class in a secondary role, and the majority of the revolutionary left, looking to other forces, ended up with minimal roots inside the working class. Yet while the authors recognise such errors, they rely on the same theory and categorise the Shah's ruling classes as "compradors".

The left's failures meant the shoras never managed to develop into workers' councils able to act as a pole of attraction to other sections of society such as the urban poor. A space opened up for other forces. Khomeini, who had led an effective movement with anti-imperialist slogans against the Shah, entered this void. A shrewd political operator, he played secular nationalists and the left (religious and secular) off against one another before crushing them brutally and, with the start of the Iran-Iraq War, the shoras too. The process is charted in Phil Marshall's book, *Revolution and Counter-revolution in Iran*.

The prospect of a cleric leading a revolution confused most analysts at first. But Khomeini was a nationalist, albeit a religious one. As Dilip Hiro's recent book, *Iran Today*, points out, the social character of the clerical leadership was not very different from the military officers who led the nationalist revolutions of Egypt and Iraq. It's important to recognise this to appreciate the contradictions that lie at the heart of the Islamic Republic. The authors of *Iran on the Brink* rightly quote Iranian historian Ervand Abrahamian's definition of populism: "a middle class movement that mobilises the masses with radical-sounding rhetoric against the external powers and entrenched classes. But in attacking the establishment, it is careful to respect private property and avoid concrete proposals that would undermine the petty bourgeoisie."

This explains the political factions that immediately surfaced during the 1980s. There were the "leftists", who favoured a strong centralised state with welfare and social programmes for the poorer sections of society; and the "right", who represented the bazaari (mercantile capitalists). Their divisions were held together under the intense nationalism of the eight-year war with Iraq and by Khomeini's tactical support for each faction. But with the end of the war and the death of Khomeini, Iranian capitalism came under increasing pressure to move away from an economy of self-sufficiency and adapt to global capitalism. A group of conservatives known as the "pragmatists" under Rafsanjani (as president) and Khamenei (as supreme leader) emerged to take that process forward. The reformist Khatami took up their programme of economic liberalisation—privisatisation, deregulation and the influx of foreign capital—after his election in 1997.

While there was high inflation and unemployment in the 1980s, the government had provided health and education to the majority, dismantled shanty towns and redistributed the Shah's property to some of the poorest sections of society. By the late 1990s inflation, unemployment and inequality had grown, while some of those welfare institutions had turned into large capitalist organisations. One consequence was disaffection and the rise of working class struggle, which is well documented in this book. The bloody repression of strikes and sit-ins after the sacking of 250 construction workers at a copper smelting plant in the village of Khatoonabad in January 2004 led to labour unrest across the country. There were strikes by teachers for higher wages, textile workers against unfair dismissals and workers at Iran-Khodro (the largest automobile manufacturer in the Middle East). Most notable was the bus workers' strike for union recognition and collective bargaining in December 2005.

Another consequence was electoral. The election of Ahmadinejad in 2005, with his promise to redistribute oil wealth to the poor, was regarded as a return to the Khomeiniism of the 1980s and a rejection of the economic policies of the 1990s.

However, the most interesting development, the Second Khordad Movement, later also known as the reform movement—came earlier. It was a result of a number of factors. The participation of religious women in civil society and the labour force during the 1980s raised gender consciousness, challenged the sexist ideology of the state and precipitated demands for social and political equality. There was an expansion of the education system (where over 60 percent of students are now women). Finally, many participants in the revolution returned to the question of its ideals with the end of the suffocating conditions of war with Iraq. A movement led by women and students, many from within an Islamic framework, demanded change.

Unfortunately, the authors make no attempt to understand this movement, even if they recognise the significance of what came along with it—the relaxation of press censorship, the growing strength of civil society, and increasing political and social freedoms. But they point to the conservative backlash as proof that the project was always doomed to fail and that the regime could never be reformed.

This is far too simplistic. Whatever their shortcomings, Khatami and the reformists made some progressive changes. At the height of the student movement the conservatives were on the back foot, so there is nothing to suggest that the success of the conservative backlash was inevitable had Khatami not held the movement back.

More importantly, the authors fail to recognise how the political fractures from which the likes of Khatami emerged were a product of social processes which would not have happened without the intervention of a courageous movement led by women and students. The day of Khatami's election was comparable to the anti-war demonstrations that shook the British ruling class on 15 February 2003, but harnessing even greater hope and expectations.

It is likely that the embryonic labour struggles drew inspiration from these movements. For example, the teachers' strikes cannot be seen in isolation from the student and women's movement when 80 percent of Iran's teachers are women.

Although suffering setbacks and splits, the movement has certainly matured and radicalised. The question of neoliberalism is the most important test. Having failed to deliver on his promises to create jobs, reduce inflation and redistribute wealth, Ahmadinejad is now facing opposition even within his traditional constituency of support. Under pressure from an alliance of moderate conservatives and reformists, he has gone as far as vowing to follow through the process of privatisation that he once promised to reverse.

With the reformist leaders hell bent on privatisation, an effective grassroots opposition to neoliberalism is needed that unites the fight for women's equality, and social and political freedoms, with the economic demands and struggle for better workers' rights and conditions of the labour movement.

Over the past few months hardliners have attempted to quell a new wave of social unrest. The arrest of 32 women activists on 8 March failed to prevent International Women's Day celebrations. In the same month teachers staged a number of protests demanding higher wages (nearly 90 percent are paid below the official poverty line). More recently May Day celebrations organised by the official government union Khane Kargar (Workers' House) saw slogans against the government and privatisation. Some, including union representatives, were detained.

The crackdowns come on the back of intensified threats from the US, the subject of the last chapter of this book. Here the authors point to Iran's geopolitical position, and its huge oil and gas reserves, rather than its nuclear programme, as the main reasons behind Washington's hostile rhetoric. The detailed US plans for an attack and its funding for dissident groups give Iran's hardliners a favourable climate in which to quell dissent.

Iran on the Brink is an accessible guide to Iran's recent history and the questions that this history has thrown up. But while it recognises the important emergence of a new radical economic struggle, it ignores the significance of a political movement which could potentially take that struggle forward.

A handbook for activism

Katherine Connelly

*David McNally, **Another World is Possible** (Merlin, 2007), £12.95*

There is a war being waged over corporate globalisation. The leaders of the G8 countries tell us we must trust capitalism to solve the problems of war, poverty and climate change, while the gap between rich and poor reaches historically unprecedented proportions across the globe. As David McNally points out in this newly updated edition of his book, three billionaires now have assets worth more than the gross national product of countries with a combined population of 600 million.

McNally's book is a kaleidoscopic reflection of resistance from below. He attempts nothing less than an understanding of capitalism, what it has done to the world and the revolts against it. He traces the emergence of capitalist ideology back to the Putney Debates of the English Revolution, where Henry Ireton, a general in Oliver Cromwell's New Model Army, declared his "eye for property"; McNally, by contrast, has an eye for humanity. Neoliberalism in rural India is condemned for having impoverished farmers, and then McNally reveals the heartache: up to 3,000 farmers have committed suicide over six years in the state of Andhra Pradesh.

He expresses the distortion of humanity using Karl Marx's writings on alienation, which he effectively sums up through "the familiar expression, 'Thank God It's Friday'...a depressing acknowledgment that work is, for the majority, oppressive, alienating, boring and dehumanising". Marx's view is vindicated through frightening examples of how much of ourselves capitalism has managed to sell—20 percent of the human genome "is now privately owned".

However, for all the book's dynamism and scope, the reader is left with the feeling that McNally is energetically depressed about half of the world. He sees the "Global North" as a graveyard of activism. The demise of resistance in the North can, according to McNally, be traced back to 9/11, which "came as a godsend for the ruling classes". The global anti-war movement, which brought about the world's largest international demonstration, is almost entirely ignored throughout the book because it "has been unable to stop the US war machine".

There is no discussion of the US neo-conservatives' project and how much its sinister idea that "American leadership is good both for America and for the world" has been challenged and stalled by resistance in the heart of the empire and in the Middle East. Nor is there a sharp analysis of the rise of Islamophobia. In fact, McNally concludes that the current wave of prejudice merely "taps into powerful racist associations of Muslims with evil" because "fear of Muslims has been central to the Euro-American identity since the Middle Ages". It would be difficult to prove that any American in the Middle Ages even knew about Islam.

However much George Bush might see himself as a "crusader", what we see today in the Middle East is an attack driven by capitalism to wrench open markets and assert US dominance. The resistance to this "project" forced Western ruling classes to demonise Muslims as international conspirators, in a pattern not dissimilar to attacks on Jews and Communists in the 20th century.

To renew the movement McNally calls for "Marxists" and "anarchists" to unite around "common goals"; he calls for "revolutionary pluralism, an ethos that, rather than trying to force adherence to a single revolutionary outlook, welcomes a plurality of radical perspectives, each of which brings different strengths and weaknesses to the common anti-capitalist project". However, this fails to explain at what point activists should reject pluralism and insist on principle.

McNally tends to avoid any discussion about the relationship between movement activists and the working class. He sees the division in today's movements as existing between "the cautious approaches of NGOs and labour leaders in the North and the more confrontational tactics of generally younger 'direct action' militants and activists from the South, who organise street protests at trade meetings". While there is often more dynamism in the labour movements in the South, McNally's analysis is based purely on geography, rather than a discussion about the legacy of social democracy and reformism.

Despite these criticisms, the detailed research in this book makes it a useful handbook for activists who want to counter the lies we are told.

Revamping old formulas

Iain Ferguson

Gregor Gall (ed), ***Is there a Scottish Road to Socialism?*** *(Scottish Left Review, 2007), £9.99*

Growing up in the West of Scotland in the 1960s and 1970s, I commonly heard people remark at election time that if you stood a monkey on a Labour Party ticket, the monkey would be elected. To the best of my knowledge, the theory was never put to the test and, in fact, support for Labour was probably never quite as automatic or unthinking as this suggests. What the saying did identify, however, was the profound loyalty that a majority of working class people in Scotland felt towards the Labour Party over several decades in the post-war period. In many communities support for Labour was, as one journalist recently put it, part of the emotional wallpaper. In a very real sense, Labour was "the party of the working class".

The elections for the Scottish Parliament of 4 May 2007 show the extent to which that has ceased to be the case. For the first time in more than 50 years Labour is no longer the majority party in Scotland. That mantle is now worn, at least temporarily, by the Scottish National Party (SNP) which, under its leader Alex Salmond, won 47 seats to New Labour's 46 in the new parliament. It is true that the defeat for New Labour was less devastating than widely predicted (it lost four seats). It is also true that the election itself was a travesty of democracy, with complicated voting forms and problems with "e-counting" of votes resulting in 100,000 "spoiled" ballot papers and comparisons with Jeb Bush's Florida elections of 2000.

The SNP's victory was, nevertheless, a historic one, and more than a flash in the pan. The fact that only a month previously the general council of the Scottish Trades Union Congress had agreed by a majority of just one vote to support New Labour in the election campaign provides, if anything, even more convincing evidence of just how much New Labour's grip on the working class movement in Scotland has slipped in recent years.

In this context, a book which took a fresh and critical look at how socialists and campaigners against war, Trident missiles and neoliberalism could engage with the challenges and opportunities of the new political terrain would be both timely and welcome.

Unfortunately, a fresh and critical look is precisely what Gregor Gall's edited collection fails to provide. For the most part, the book feels rather old and tired. One reason for this is the choice of contributors. At least a third of those included adhere to one or another of the offshoots of the defunct British Communist Party, and at times there is an uncanny sense of being transported back to the Communist Party's internal debates of the 1970s.

Thus David Purdy is given space to restate his view that greedy workers were responsible for the rise of Thatcherism,

John Foster extols the politics of the popular front, and, in a real gem of unreconstructed Stalinism, Eric Canning suggests that the examples of "Cuba, Vietnam, Mongolia, China and North Korea" prove that "socialism can obviously develop in relative isolation and within a single country". By contrast, there are no contributions from those who led the huge protests against the G8 summit at Edinburgh and Gleneagles in 2005, despite the fact that several chapters acknowledge the profound importance of these events for the development of the left in Scotland.

More generally, many of the 14 chapters rehash the lazy and erroneous assumptions that make up the ideological furniture of much of the Scottish left. Chief among these are the notions that Scotland is an oppressed nation, that Scottish workers are more militant than their brothers and sisters south of the border, that an independent Scotland would inevitably be left wing and that independence would provoke a crisis for the British ruling class. All of these arguments are expertly refuted by Neil Davidson in what is by far the best chapter in the book (see also his contribution to the previous issue of this journal).

In fact, the SNP's success in the Scottish elections in May owed little to its policy of support for an independence referendum, which its leader consistently downplayed during the campaign and from which he has continued to backtrack since. Instead it was due to the fact that it presented itself at every opportunity as the anti-war, anti-Trident party, committed to essentially social democratic policies. As its billboard posters proclaimed, "More hospitals and schools, not Trident missiles." It offered the voters, in other words, an Old Labour programme much more in tune with their values and aspirations than the pro-market, pro-war policies of New Labour. The result is that the level of expectation in an SNP-led government is likely to be very high indeed. At the same time, to its wealthy business supporters, the SNP presents a very different face, as a party fully committed to neoliberal policies whose model is the Irish "Celtic Tiger". If the left in Scotland can engage with that contradiction and insist that an SNP-led government lives up to its anti-militarist pretensions—for example, by ending all army recruitment in schools and colleges—as opposed to debating tired and irrelevant old formulas about independence, the prospects for the coming period could be very good indeed.

Transformation made easy

Joseph Choonara

Andrew Kliman, ***Reclaiming Marx's "Capital": A Refutation of the Myth of Inconsistency*** *(Lexington, 2007), £17.99*

Since the publication of the third volume of *Capital* in 1894 Karl Marx's analysis has suffered at the hands not simply of those who openly oppose Marxism, but also of those who claim to stand in his tradition. Two key planks of Marx's work have been challenged. The first is the "law of the tendency of the rate of profit to fall". The second is Marx's solution to what has become known as the "transformation problem"—the shift from the analysis of "values" in the first volume of *Capital* to the analysis of "prices" in the third.

Andrew Kliman's book answers Marx's critics new and old. Setting aside the question of whether Marx's ideas are right or wrong, Kliman argues that *Capital* can, and should, be interpreted in such a way as to render it "internally consistent". Only by following this method can a sensible interpretation be constructed and tested against reality. Kliman's book sets out one such interpretation of *Capital*, which satisfies this criterion. All this is done with admirable clarity, in stark contrast to most of the literature on "value theory".

Kliman responds to the attacks on Marx's law of the tendency of the rate of profit to fall in a chapter that parallels the article by Chris Harman in this issue of *International Socialism*. But it is the second challenge to Marx, the so-called "transformation problem", that forms the most interesting section of this book. The problem has often been posed using complicated mathematical formulations, making it seem like the preserve of *Capital* geeks, but the basic issues are relatively easy to grasp.

For Marx the value of a commodity reflects the amount of "living labour" expended by workers in its creation, plus the amount of "dead labour"—past labour crystallised in the instruments of production, raw materials, etc—used up in its production. The value can be measured as a sum of money reflecting the "socially necessary labour time" required to produce the commodity. Here "socially necessary" refers to the labour time required under normal conditions with the average prevalent skill and intensity.

The capitalist has to purchase the dead labour, and makes no profit from this. The living labour, on the other hand, has a double value. The capitalist receives a day's labour, but only has to pay enough, in the form of a day's wages, for the reproduction of the labour power. Because the wage merely reflects the amount of value needed to get the worker back to work, and raise the next generation of workers, it will tend to be less than the new value the worker creates. The remaining hours create "surplus value" for the capitalist, and this is the basis of profit. The rate of profit is the ratio of surplus value to the total capital advanced in wages and inputs of dead labour.

Marx provides this basic account in the first volume of *Capital*. Here he is considering "capital in general". He abstracts from the effect of competition between different capitals or the coexistence of different sectors of the economy. This allows him to locate the origin of surplus value in the exploitation at the heart of the capitalist production process. In the third volume of *Capital* he goes beyond the concept of capital in general and considers capitalism as a concrete system where there are "many capitals"; to do this he must integrate the sphere of "production" with the sphere of "exchange".

On the basis of the analysis of value in the first volume of *Capital* each industry would have a different "rate of profit", because each uses a different ratio of living and dead labour (different "organic compositions of capital", as Marx put it). But in capitalism as it actually exists, profit rates tend to equalise across economies. Marx argues that capital flows between sectors, from those with low rates of profit to those with high ones, as capitalists seek to maximise their profitability. Those goods in sectors with a high rate of profit will be produced in greater quantities, lowering their prices, while those in sectors with a low rate of profit will become scarce and their prices will rise. Over time these changes in price will tend to equalise profit rates between sectors. This process is the "transformation" of values into what Marx called "prices of production".

According to this analysis, prices of production are a more complicated expression of value. The surplus value created across the whole economy is reallocated to different capitalists in such a way as to form a "general rate of profit". Marx showed that, from the point of view of the capitalists, this process seems to happen the other way round. In calculating the price of their goods, capitalists look at their input costs (their "costs of production") and then mark up the price according to the general rate of profit multiplied by the capital invested. It appears as if the capitalist simply receives from society a share of total profit reflecting their investment.

Because prices of production are, in Marx's analysis, simply a complex form assumed by value, a number of "aggregate equalities" must hold. The total price of the outputs of an economy must equal the total value of the outputs, and total profit must equal the total surplus value produced.

Marx's account has proved remarkably controversial. In particular, papers by Ladislaus Bortkiewicz from 1906-7, and similar accounts that have followed, sought to prove that "Marx's account produces a difference between input and output prices, and that this difference leads to 'internal contradiction'—specifically, to a spurious disruption of the production process" as inputs and outputs fail to match up. Having taken this step, "Borkiewicz 'corrected' Marx's account" with a solution that "severed values and prices into two discordant systems" (p46).

Kliman shows that there are two fundamental problems with approaches such as Borkiewicz's.

First, like most interpretations of *Capital*, Borkiewicz's is what Kliman calls a "dual-system interpretation". In chapter nine of the third volume of *Capital* Marx gives numeric examples to illustrate his transformation. But in these examples he does not appear to apply this transformation to the cost of the inputs into production that the capitalist purchases.

In the same chapter Marx comments, "We had originally assumed that the cost price of a commodity equalled the *value* of the commodities consumed in its production. But for the buyer the price of production of a specific commodity is its cost price, and may thus pass as cost price into the prices of other commodities. Since the price of production may differ from the value of a commodity, it follows that the cost price of a commodity containing this price of production of another commodity may also stand above or below that portion of its total value derived from the value of the means of production consumed by it." Dual-system interpreters conclude from this passage that the values of inputs must also be transformed into prices to complete the transformation process, leading to two separate systems.

One influential version of this is the "New Interpretation", which emerged in the 1980s. This account attempts to reconnect the value and price systems through wages—which are held to be equal in the two systems. Both the traditional dual-system accounts and the New Interpretation are flawed according to Kliman because "cost prices and capital advances differ across value and price systems. There are consequently two distinct and unequal general rates of profit as well, and the remaining aggregate equalities cannot hold true, contrary to what Marx concluded" (p33).

Kliman argues for a single-system interpretation. Such interpretations also emerged in the 1980s. They offer an alternative solution to the problems posed by Marx's shift from value to price in *Capital*. The inputs into production (wages, raw materials, machinery, and so on) are always values, rather than prices. But they are not the values required to produce these things, they are the values the capitalist must advance to purchase them. And, "to acquire the needed means of production...the firm needs to buy them at their actual *price*—not at their value" (p34). So the value advanced to purchase an input is its "price of production". Kliman provides textual evidence to show that this is a possible interpretation of Marx's writings. However, the evidence is hardly decisive either way. Kliman's case rests heavily on whether his interpretation allows a consistent account of *Capital*.

There is a second problem with Borkiewicz and most of those who have followed him. Borkiewicz assumes that the values of commodities when they are treated as inputs into a cycle of production are the same as their values when they leave the same cycle as outputs. Kliman refers to this as "simultaneous valuation", and he rejects it in favour of "temporal valuation". Kliman's point is simple: you can't produce anything using inputs that have not yet been produced! The value that must be advanced to obtain the inputs in a given period depends on the output price in the *previous* period.

Kliman gives a number of powerful examples to justify this claim. One of the most straightforward is to consider the entire economy as being based on the production of corn, which is itself grown from corn seed (corn is both the input and output). Kliman shows through a simple calculation that if a drought means that ten bushels of corn were planted but only nine were harvested, the living labour put in by the farmers must, by the simultaneous interpretation, be negative (equal to minus one bushel worth of labour). Ridiculous results such as this are avoided if it is assumed that prices of outputs and inputs do not have to match in a given cycle. In the example cited, the price of corn rises after the drought.

Kliman also shows that simultaneous valuation leads directly to what he calls "physicalism". If inputs and outputs have the same value for a given commodity, then, whatever the intention of the author (and many claim to reject physicalism), the physical quantities of outputs, rather than the labour embodied within the outputs, are all that matters.

Kliman's shift to temporal valuation immediately undermines Bortkiewicz's argument. Borkiewicz bases his critique on a "simple reproduction" model, in which the same physical quantities of goods are produced in each cycle of production. Here the input and output values can be made to match up, so, for example, there is always sufficient demand for wage goods to match the output of the sector producing wage goods. Once values are transformed to prices, supply and demand no longer match and reproduction cannot continue. But Kliman can simply construct a second cycle such that the supply in the first cycle matches demand in the second cycle.

Once this is combined with the idea that prices of production of outputs are the values advanced to purchase inputs (the single-system approach) it can be shown that Marx's aggregate equalities still hold—price is seen to be complex expression of value, and total profit equals total surplus value. The dual-system interpretations that Kliman surveys do not maintain these equalities.

Kliman's solution will look counter-intuitive to anyone more familiar with dual-system interpretations—the total value of inputs and outputs changes between cycles (and this is not simply a question of quantities of money; the amounts equally represent labour time), even though the physical output and production methods are identical in each cycle. But counter-intuitive solutions are not always wrong, and Kliman's case is powerfully stated.

This book is the clearest exposition of what has become known as the temporal single-system interpretation (TSSI), an approach shared with authors such as Guglielmo Carchedi and Alan Freeman.

Unfortunately, the most convincing recent rival interpretation—provided by Alfredo Saad Filho in his book *The Value of Marx*—is dismissed by Kliman in a single footnote. Saad Filho's account builds on Ben Fine and Laurence Harris's 1979 work *Rereading Capital* and John Weeks's 1981 work *Capital and Exploitation*. This body of work does seem to lead to two separate systems. As Fine and Saad Filho write in their most accessible account of Marx's theory, *Reading Capital*, "commodities have values as well as prices...two distinct account systems (not necessarily equally significant either in theory or practice) are possible". However, whatever one thinks of this, their work presents persuasive evidence that Marx's transformation is not primarily a theory of prices, and the various attempts to "solve" the "transformation problem" are therefore missing the point.

This body of work has also sought to capture some of the temporal nature of capitalist accumulation by highlighting the distinction drawn by Marx between the organic and value compositions of capital. Both are value measures of the technical composition of capital (the physical ratio of dead labour to living labour). The organic composition abstracts from the sphere of exchange, ignoring the continual changes to the value of inputs due to technical change in other sectors; the value composition integrates the two spheres of exchange and production and takes into account these changes.

Saad Filho claims that Marx sets out his "transformation" using the organic composition of capital, not the value composition, proving that Marx was not concerned with developing a price theory at this point. The role of Marx's transformation is merely to show how prices are formed in the sphere of production as surplus is reallocated. Only then is a "second stage" possible in which, Saad Filho argues, the value composition must be used and inputs transformed to prices. A more direct engagement with this account would both challenge this body of work and strengthen Kliman's analysis.

Finally, no attention is given to the possibility of developing temporal dual-system interpretations. There is an important, but little known, article, first published in English in *International Socialism 5* (1979), by Miguel Angel Garcia. Garcia, in one of the earliest temporalist critiques of the "transformation problem", writes, "Since von Borkiewicz it has frequently been assumed that Marx's solution to the 'transformation problem' is faulty. In this article we shall try to show: (a) that Marx's solution was correct; (b) that it leads to no inconsistencies in his theory of value."

The system Garcia presents is similar to that of Kliman: it preserves the aggregate equalities of Marx and it explicitly rejects the use of simultaneous equations. Garcia writes that even if the inputs needed to be transformed, "this transformation could not be the same as that involving the commodities that they create. When they were acquired these products did not yet exist... To determine cost prices of commodities by their sales prices is a 'solution' which recalls that of Baron Munchausen, who descended from the moon several times tying one end of a rope to another, and in order to do this he had to untie them first of all."

However, Garcia's critique differs from Kliman's in two respects. First, it is a system of prices, not values, although "prices remain linked to values". Second, Garcia maintains that "simple reproduction" makes no sense in this context (and it can be shown that Garcia's solution does not work in simple reproduction models). Once the analysis shifts to many capitals and away from capital in general (which Garcia wrongly associates with pre-capitalist commodity production), he argues that "equalisation of the rate of profit...is a consequence of the way in which commodities appear, not now as simple values, but as means for the realisation of the capitals that produce them. This implies expanded accumulation and not simple accumulation."

If Garcia is right, there may still be space to develop a "temporal dual-system interpretation" of *Capital*. Kliman himself seems less than decisive in dismissing this possibility: "Direct textual evidence suggests that Marx was a single-system theorist. A good deal of evidence clearly favours this interpretation. Evidence adduced on behalf of the dual-system interpretation is equally compatible with the single-system interpretation."

Nonetheless, the interpretation developed by Kliman and others must certainly have a strong case to be considered the most compelling and consistent interpretation of *Capital*. This book deserves to be read and debated by all those interested in getting to grips with Marx's theory.

Pick of the quarter

The rapid growth of the Chinese economy is gaining admiration not just from the columnists of the *Financial Times*, but also from sections of the left internationally. So the Left Front government in West Bengal in India (see Aditya Sarkar in this journal) is consciously adopting an economic model based on the Chinese experience, with the Communist Party of India (Marxist) quite willing to see the Chinese ruling party as fellow Communists. There is also a section of the Cuban leadership that sees the Chinese model as one it would adopt if it could, and it recently welcomed a delegation from the Chinese Communist Party. But is China today really a model for the left? Martin Hart-Lindbergh and Paul Burkett provide an excellent analysis of China's economy in the May 2007 issue of *Monthly Review*.

They argue there are limits to Chinese growth that most observers do not take account of—particularly that most of its exports are based on the assembly of imported components from elsewhere in East Asia and are part of international production networks controlled by foreign multinationals. They also bring out the degree to which capitalist development does not mean a rise in secure employment and rising living standards for the mass of people. Their figures show that casual employment in the informal sector—the spreading blight in the burgeoning cities of Latin America, South Asia and Africa—is also the picture in China.

The authors would not agree with some of the analyses of the development of Chinese society during the Mao era we have made in this journal. But their article is a very useful complement to the articles by Charlie Hore in issue 103 and Chris Harman in issue 109.

New left Review 44 (March-April) is worth getting hold of for five articles. Two are pieces on Putin's Russia. Vladimir Popov provides an overview of economic and social changes (http://newleftreview.org/?page=article&view=2658). He shows that the economy has revived somewhat in recent years, based on the devaluation of the currency nine years ago and the booming oil prices of the past five years. This comes after a slow deterioration of the economy in the final years of the Soviet Union, which escalated massively under the restructuring of the 1990s. Tony Wood (http://newleftreview.org/?page=article&view=2659) accepts most of Popov's empirical material, but is critical of his tendency to see the Putin regime as producing "stability". Particularly interesting is Wood's account of the merging on the industrial and state elites, and of the degree of continuity with the pre-1991 set up.

Forrest Hylton (http://newleftreview.org/?page=article&view=2660) writes on the Colombian city of Medellín, showing how old antagonisms between its traditional elite and the drug gangs were overcome as they united to physically smash the left. And there is a fascinating piece by Stephen Graham on how the US is training its troops for warfare by building imitation Middle Eastern towns.

But the high point of the issue is

an account of the interaction of economics and politics in Turkey by Cihan Tugal (http://newleftreview.org/?page=article&view=2657). It shows how the ruling Justice and Development Party, whose origins were in Islamist politics, has found no difficulty in imposing neoliberal policies—and retained some of its popular support while doing so.

Turkey also features in an important article in April's *Science and Society* by Fuat Ercan and Sebnem Oguz. They argue strongly against the dominant notion on the country's left that it can fight the neoliberal strategy of the government by uniting with some nationalist section of the bourgeoisie. This is to fail to see that it is Turkey's place in global capitalism that leads its capitalists to attack the conditions of the mass of people and to link up with multinational capital. But, as the authors point out, implementing such policies does not rule out local capitalists themselves using nationalist agitation to try to improve the terms on which they are accepted as partners by multinational capital.

In *New Politics* (volume XI, number 2) John Giblet describes how a teachers' strike in the Mexican city of Oaxaca turned into a peaceful rising against the national government—with the creation of "popular power" locally. This issue, available from www.wpunj.edu/newpol/ also contains an interesting article by Michael Löwy on the relation of Max Weber to Karl Marx. Löwy provides a rather more favourable view of Weber than does Kieran Allen's excellent book *Max Weber*, which we reviewed a couple of years ago.

Readers interested in following up some of the things Kim Moody refers to in this journal should look at Paul J Wyden's account in March's *Monthly Review* of the rank and file rebellion of America's miners in the 1960s and 1970s: www.monthlyreview.org/0307nyden.htm

Over the past decade the lives of teachers in British universities has been increasingly dominated by the Research Assessment Exercise, which makes appointment and promotion dependent upon getting articles published in specialist "peer reviewed" journals. This brings its own version of the assembly line into higher education. But a fascinating piece of research by Frederic Lee in the *Cambridge Journal of Economics* shows it has another effect—of encouraging ideological conformity. He shows how the system works in economics to promote mainstream, neoclassical economics at the expense of "heterodox" economics, which challenges the neoclassical and neoliberal assumptions.

He shows that, as a result, "72 percent of economic students inhabit an educational environment in which heterodox economic ideas are very weak if not non-existent". "The RAE," he argues, "is essentially driven by the pro-market ideologies of the Thatcher, Major and Blair administrations" and has resulted in economics in Britain being no more than "an unintellectual, settled doctrine that supports the government's pro-market agenda".

Illusions in the United Nations as an impartial force for peace still befog the minds of many people on the left. Perry Anderson has written a review of two recent biographies of former UN secretary general Kofi Annan which provide a very different picture. This appeared in the 10 May edition of the *London Review of Books*, but unfortunately is not available on their website. So if you can get hold of a copy, read it, photocopy it and show it to those who still, as an editorial in this journal put it 40 years ago, "confuse the thieves' kitchen in New York with the soup kitchen in Geneva".

CH

Back issues

Issues of 107 to 114 of *International Socialism* are still available. Each costs £6 for UK customers, £7.50 for Europe or £9 for the rest of world (including p&p). To order or enquire about earlier back issues phone +44 (0) 20 7819 1177, e-mail isj@swp.org.uk or write to ISJ, PO Box 42184, London SW8 2WD. Cheques should be made payable to 'ISJ'.

To browse the content of these back issues, visit our website www.isj.org.uk

International Socialism online
www.isj.org.uk

Read all of our recent articles in full
Extra articles, replies and audio recordings
Translations of selected articles in Spanish, Arabic, Urdu and French
Selections from our archives

Recent additions include

- •Giles Ji Ungpakorn's book, *A Coup For the Rich: Thailand's Political Crisis,* available to download.
- •Colin Barker's critique of Nicos Poulantzas from 1979.
- •Replies to articles on the origins of capitalism from John Game and Neil Davidson.
- •Audio recording of Ernest Mandel in debate with Mike Kidron on State Capitalism (1969).